PELICAN
AN
BEFORE PHILOSOPHY

BEFORE PHILOSOPHY

THE INTELLECTUAL ADVENTURE
OF ANCIENT MAN

AN ESSAY ON SPECULATIVE THOUGHT

IN THE ANCIENT NEAR EAST

BY

H. AND H. A. FRANKFORT · JOHN A. WILSON

THORKILD JACOBSEN

PENGUIN BOOKS

Penguin Books Ltd, Harmondsworth, Middlesex
U.S.A.: Penguin Books Inc., 3300 Clipper Mill Road, Baltimore 11, Md
AUSTRALIA: Penguin Books Pty Ltd, 726 Whitehorse Road,
Mitcham, Victoria

—

AN ORIENTAL INSTITUTE ESSAY

Original Edition
The Intellectual Adventure of Ancient Man
first published by
The University of Chicago Press, Chicago, 1946
Published in Pelican Books March 1949
Reprinted 1951, 1954, 1959

Made and printed in Great Britain
by Hazell Watson & Viney Ltd
Aylesbury and Slough

CONTENTS

PREFACE

THIS book is an attempt to understand the view which the ancient peoples of Egypt and Mesopotamia took of the world in which they lived. They were the most civilized people of their time; and they have left us a rich and varied literature which has been deciphered to a large extent during the last hundred years. But the modern reader, confronted with the translations, will in most cases feel that the deeper meaning eludes him. This is true even of many texts dealing with the norms of human behaviour – the so-called 'wisdom literature' of which the books of *Proverbs* and *Ecclesiastes* in the *Old Testament* are familiar examples. It is certainly true of the great official inscriptions in which rulers define their task or record their achievements. And it is most conspicuously true of those writings which claim to elucidate the nature of the universe. For these assume throughout the form of myths, and the medley of tales about gods seem to lack a common viewpoint altogether.

Yet nothing is more misleading (though nothing is more common) than a piecemeal interpretation of myths, based on the tacit assumption that the Ancients were preoccupied with problems very similar to ours, and that their myths represent a charming but immature way of answering them. We have tried to show in our first chapter that such an assumption simply ignores the gulf which separates our habits of thought, our modes of experience, from those remote civilizations, even in cases where man faced perennial problems: the problem of man in nature, the problem of fate, the problem of death. We have attempted to penetrate into this alien world of 'mytho-poeic' – myth-making – thought and to analyse its peculiar logic, its imaginative and its emotional character. The reader may find this first chapter the most difficult to follow and he may prefer to read it after the main sections of the book, in which the myths and beliefs of Egyptians and Mesopotamians are concretely described.

In the last chapter we have described how the Hebrews reduced the mythical element in their religion to a minimum,
and how the Greeks evolved critical from mythopoeic thought.
This chapter has given rise, among some reviewers of our
American edition, to the misconception that we sing the praise
of rationalism or equate religion with superstition. We may
state, then, emphatically that we are fully aware of the creative
function of myth as a living cultural force, and one which sus-
tains in greater or lesser degree all religious or metaphysical
thought. In any case it should be clear that we have conceived
of myth throughout as a matter of high seriousness.

At the end of each chapter appear *Notes* referring professional readers to our sources, and *Selected Readings* for those
unfamiliar with our subject. The translations of ancient texts
in each chapter are made by the respective authors except
where their source is indicated in the notes; but Mrs H. A.
Groenewegen Frankfort is responsible for the poetical render-
ings of the translations from Sumerian and Akkadian in
Chapters V–VII.

INTRODUCTION

H. and H. A. Frankfort

CHAPTER I

Myth and Reality

IF WE look for 'speculative thought' in the documents of the ancients, we shall be forced to admit that there is very little indeed in our written records which deserves the name of 'thought' in the strict sense of that term. There are very few passages which show the discipline, the cogency of reasoning, which we associate with thinking. The thought of the ancient Near East appears wrapped in imagination. We consider it tainted with fantasy. But the ancients would not have admitted that anything could be abstracted from the concrete imaginative forms which they left us.

We should remember that even for us speculative thought is less rigidly disciplined than any other form. Speculation – as the etymology of the word shows – is an intuitive, an almost visionary, mode of apprehension. This does not mean, of course, that it is mere irresponsible meandering of the mind, which ignores reality or seeks to escape from its problems. Speculative thought transcends experience, but only because it attempts to explain, to unify, to order experience. It achieves this end by means of hypotheses. If we use the word in its original sense, then we may say that speculative thought attempts to *underpin* the chaos of experience so that it may reveal the features of a structure – order, coherence, and meaning.

Speculative thought is therefore distinct from mere idle speculation in that it never breaks entirely away from experience. It may be 'once removed' from the problems of experience, but it is connected with them in that it tries to explain them.

In our own time speculative thought finds its scope more severely limited than it has been at any other period. For we possess in science another instrument for the interpretation of experience, one that has achieved marvels and retains its full fascination. We do not allow speculative thought, under any circumstances, to encroach upon the sacred precincts of science. It must not trespass on the realm of verifiable fact; and it must never pretend to a dignity higher than that of working hypotheses, even in the fields in which it is permitted some scope.

Where, then, is speculative thought allowed to range today? Its main concern is with man – his nature and his problems, his values and his destiny. For man does not quite succeed in becoming a scientific object to himself. His need of transcending chaotic experience and conflicting facts leads him to seek a metaphysical hypothesis that may clarify his urgent problems. On the subject of his 'self' man will, most obstinately, speculate – even today.

*

When we turn to the ancient Near East in search of similar efforts, two correlated facts become apparent. In the first place, we find that speculation found unlimited possibilities for development; it was not restricted by a scientific (that is, a disciplined) search for truth. In the second place, we notice that the realm of nature and the realm of man were not distinguished.

The ancients, like the modern savages, saw man always as part of society, and society as imbedded in nature and dependent upon cosmic forces. For them nature and man did not stand in opposition and did not, therefore, have to be apprehended by different modes of cognition. We shall see, in fact, in the course of this book, that natural phenomena were regularly conceived in terms of human experience and that human experience was conceived in terms of cosmic events. We touch here upon a distinction between the ancients and us which is of the utmost significance for our inquiry.

The fundamental difference between the attitudes of modern and ancient man as regards the surrounding world is this: for modern, scientific man the phenomenal world is primarily an 'It'; for ancient – and also for primitive – man it is a 'Thou'.

This formulation goes far beyond the usual 'animistic' or 'personalistic' interpretations. It shows up, in fact, the inadequacies of these commonly accepted theories. For a relation between 'I' and 'Thou' is absolutely *sui generis*. We can best explain its unique quality by comparing it with two other modes of cognition: the relation between subject and object and the relation that exists when I 'understand' another living being.

The correlation 'subject-object' is, of course, the basis of all scientific thinking; it alone makes scientific knowledge possible. The second mode of cognition is the curiously direct knowledge which we gain when we 'understand' a creature confronting us – its fear, let us say, or its anger. This, by the way, is a form of knowledge which we have the honour of sharing with the animals.

The differences between an I-and-Thou relationship and these two other relationships are as follows: In determining the identity of an object, a person is active. In 'understanding' a fellow-creature, on the other hand, a man or an animal is essentially passive, whatever his subsequent action may turn out to be. For at first he receives an impression. This type of knowledge is therefore direct, emotional, and inarticulate. Intellectual knowledge, on the contrary, is emotionally indifferent and articulate.

Now the knowledge which 'I' has of 'Thou' hovers between the active judgment and the passive 'undergoing of an impression'; between the intellectual and the emotional, the articulate and the inarticulate. 'Thou' may be problematic, yet 'Thou' is somewhat transparent. 'Thou' is a live presence, whose qualities and potentialities can be made somewhat articulate – not as a result of active inquiry but because 'Thou', as a presence, reveals itself.

There is yet another important difference. An object, an 'It', can always be scientifically related to other objects and appear as part of a group or a series. In this manner science insists on seeing 'It'; hence, science is able to comprehend objects and events as ruled by universal laws which make their behaviour under given circumstances predictable. 'Thou', on the other hand, is unique. 'Thou' has the unprecedented, unparalleled, and unpredictable character of an individual, a presence known only in so far as it reveals itself. 'Thou', moreover, is not merely contemplated or understood but is experienced emotionally in a dynamic reciprocal relationship. For these reasons there is justification for the aphorism of Crawley: 'Primitive man has only one mode of thought, one mode of expression, one part of speech – the personal.' This does not mean (as is so often thought) that primitive man, in order to explain natural phenomena, imparts human characteristics to an inanimate world. Primitive man simply does not know an inanimate world. For this very reason he does not 'personify' inanimate phenomena nor does he fill an empty world with the ghosts of the dead, as 'animism' would have us believe.

The world appears to primitive man neither inanimate nor empty but redundant with life; and life has individuality, in man and beast and plant, and in every phenomenon which confronts man – the thunderclap, the sudden shadow, the eerie and unknown clearing in the wood, the stone which suddenly hurts him when he stumbles while on a hunting trip. Any phenomenon may at any time face him, not as 'It', but as 'Thou'. In this confrontation, 'Thou' reveals its individuality, its qualities, its will. 'Thou' is not contemplated with intellectual detachment; it is experienced as life confronting life, involving every faculty of man in a reciprocal relationship. Thoughts, no less than acts and feelings, are subordinated to this experience.

*

We are here concerned particularly with thought. It is likely that the ancients recognized certain intellectual problems and asked for the 'why' and 'how', the 'where from' and 'where to.' Even so, we cannot expect in the ancient Near Eastern documents to find speculation in the predominantly intellectual form with which we are familiar and which presupposes strictly logical procedure even while attempting to transcend it. We have seen that in the ancient Near East, as in present-day primitive society, thought does not operate autonomously. The whole man confronts a living 'Thou' in nature; and the whole man – emotional and imaginative as well as intellectual – gives expression to the experience. All experience of 'Thou' is highly individual; and early man does, in fact, view happenings as individual events. An account of such events and also their explanation can be conceived only as action and necessarily take the form of a story. In other words, the ancients told myths instead of presenting an analysis or conclusions. We would explain, for instance, that certain atmospheric changes broke a drought and brought about rain. The Babylonians observed the same facts but experienced them as the intervention of the gigantic bird Imdugud which came to their rescue. It covered the sky with the black storm clouds of its wings and devoured the Bull of Heaven, whose hot breath had scorched the crops.

In telling such a myth, the ancients did not intend to provide entertainment. Neither did they seek, in a detached way and without ulterior motives, for intelligible explanations of the natural phenomena. They were recounting events in which they were involved to the extent of their very existence. They experienced, directly, a conflict of powers, one hostile to the harvest upon which they depended, the other frightening but beneficial: the thunderstorm reprieved them in the nick of time by defeating and utterly destroying the drought. The images had already become traditional at the time when we meet them in art and literature, but originally they must have been seen in the revelation which the experience entailed. They are products of imagination, but they are not mere fantasy. It is essential that true myth be distinguished from legend, saga, fable, and fairy tale. All these may retain elements of the myth. And it may also happen that a baroque or frivolous imagination elaborates myths until they become mere stories. But true myth presents its images and its imaginary actors, not with the playfulness of fantasy, but with a compelling authority. It perpetuates the revelation of a 'Thou'.

The imagery of myth is therefore by no means allegory. It is nothing less than a carefully chosen cloak for abstract thought. The imagery is inseparable from the thought. It represents the form in which the experience has become conscious.

Myth, then, is to be taken seriously, because it reveals a

significant, if unverifiable, truth – we might say a metaphysical truth. But myth has not the universality and the lucidity of theoretical statement. It is concrete, though it claims to be in-assailable in its validity. It claims recognition by the faithful; it does not pretend to justification before the critical.

The irrational aspect of myth becomes especially clear when we remember that the ancients were not content merely to recount their myths as stories conveying information. They dramatized them, acknowledging in them a special virtue which could be activated by recital.

Of the dramatization of myth, Holy Communion is a well-known example. Another example is found in Babylonia. During each New Year's festival the Babylonians re-enacted the victory which Marduk had won over the powers of chaos on the first New Year's Day, when the world was created. At the annual festival the Epic of Creation was recited. It is clear that the Babylonians did not regard their story of creation as we might accept the theory of Laplace, for instance, as an intellectually satisfying account of how the world came to be as it is. Ancient man had not thought out an answer; an answer had been revealed to him in a reciprocal relationship with nature. If a question had been answered, man shared that answer with the 'Thou' which had revealed itself. Hence, it seemed wise that man, each year, at the critical turn of the sea-sons, should proclaim the knowledge which he shared with the powers, in order to involve them once more in its potent truth.

We may, then, summarize the complex character of myth in the following words: Myth is a form of poetry which tran-scends poetry in that it proclaims a truth; a form of reasoning which transcends reasoning in that it wants to bring about the truth it proclaims; a form of action, of ritual behaviour, which does not find its fulfilment in the act but must proclaim and elaborate a poetic form of truth.

*

It will now be clear why we said at the beginning of this chapter that our search for speculative thought in the ancient Near East might lead to negative results. The detachment of intellectual inquiry is wanting throughout. And yet, within the framework of mythopoeic thought, speculation may set in. Even early man, entangled in the immediacy of his perceptions, recognized the existence of certain problems which transcend the phenomena. He recognized the problem of origin and the problem of *telos*, of the aim and purpose of being. He recognized the invisible order of justice maintained by his customs, mores, institutions; and he connected this invisible order with the visible order, with its succession of days and nights, seasons and years, obviously maintained by the sun. Early man even pondered the hierarchy of the different powers which he recognized in nature. In the Memphite Theology, which will be discussed in chapter ii, the Egyptians, at one point, reduced the multiplicity of the divine to a truly monotheistic conception and spiritualized the concept of creation. Nevertheless, they spoke the language of myth. The teachings of such documents can be termed 'speculative' in recognition of their intention, if not of their performance.

To give an example, let us anticipate our colleagues and consider various possible answers to the question of how the world came into being. Some modern primitives, the Shilluk, in many respects related to the ancient Egyptians, give the following answer to this question: 'In the beginning was Ju-ok the Great Creator, and he created a great white cow who came up out of the Nile and was called Deung Adok. The white cow gave birth to a man-child whom she nursed and named Kola.'[1] Of such a story (and there are many of this type) we can say that apparently any form which relates the coming into being as a concretely imagined event satisfies the inquirer. There is no shadow of speculative thought here. Instead there is immediacy of vision – concrete, unquestioned, inconsequential.

We move one step farther if the creation is imagined, not in a purely fantastic manner, but by analogy with human conditions. Creation is then conceived as birth; and the simplest form is the postulate of a primeval couple as the parents of all that exists. It seems that for the Egyptians, as for the Greeks and the Maoris, Earth and Sky were the primeval pair.

The next step, this time one which leads in the direction of speculative thought, is taken when creation is conceived as the action of one of the parents. It may be conceived of as birth by a Great Mother, either a goddess, as in Greece, or a demon, as in Babylonia. Alternatively it is possible to conceive creation as the act of a male. In Egypt, for instance, the god Atum arose unaided from the primeval waters and started the creation of cosmos out of chaos by begetting on himself the first pair of gods.

In all these creation stories we remain in the realm of myth, even though an element of speculation can be discerned. But we move into the sphere of speculative thought – albeit mythopoeic speculative thought – when it is said that Atum was the Creator; that his eldest children were Shū and Tefnūt, Air and Moisture; that their children were Geb and Nūt, Earth and Sky; and their children, again, the four gods of the Osiris cycle through whom (since Osiris was the dead king as well as god) society is related to the cosmic powers. In this story of creation we find a definite cosmological system as the outcome of speculation.

Nor does this remain an isolated instance in Egypt. Even chaos itself became a subject of speculation. It was said that the primeval waters were inhabited by eight weird creatures, four frogs and four snakes, male and female, who brought forth Atum the sun-god and creator. This group of eight, this Ogdoad, was part, not of the created order, but of chaos itself, as the names show. The first pair was Nūn and Naunet, primeval, formless Ocean and primeval Matter; the second pair was Hūh and Hauhet, the Illimitable and the Boundless. Then came Kūk and Kauket, Darkness and Obscurity; and, finally, Amon and Amaunet, the Hidden and Concealed ones – probably the wind. For the wind 'bloweth where it listeth and thou hearest the sound thereof but canst not tell whence it cometh and whither it goeth' (John iii : 8). Here, surely, is speculative thought in mythological guise.

We also find speculative thought in Babylonia, where chaos is conceived, not as a friendly and co-operative Ogdoad which brings forth the creator, Sun, but as the enemy of life and order. After Ti²amat, the Great Mother, had given birth to countless beings, including the gods, the latter, under the guidance of Marduk, fought a critical battle in which she was overcome and destroyed. And out of her the existing universe was constructed. The Babylonian placed that conflict at the basis of existence.

Throughout the ancient Near East, then, we find speculative thought in the form of myth. We have seen how the attitude of early man toward the phenomena explains his mythopoeic form of thought. But, in order to understand its peculiarities more fully, we should consider the form it takes in somewhat greater detail.

THE LOGIC OF MYTHOPOEIC THOUGHT

We have hitherto been at pains to show that for primitive man thoughts are not autonomous, that they remain involved in the curious attitude toward the phenomenal world which we have called a confrontation of life with life. Indeed, we shall find that our categories of intellectual judgment often do not apply to the complexes of cerebration and volition which constitute mythopoeic thought. And yet the word 'logic' as used above is justified. The ancients expressed their 'emotional thought' (as we might call it) in terms of cause and effect; they explained phenomena in terms of time and space and number. The form of their reasoning is far less alien to ours than is often believed. They could reason logically; but they did not often care to do it. For the detachment which a purely intellectual attitude implies is hardly compatible with their most significant experience of reality. Scholars who have proved at length that primitive man has a 'prelogical' mode of thinking are likely to refer to magic or religious practice, thus forgetting that they apply the Kantian categories, not to pure reasoning, but to highly emotional acts.

We shall find that if we attempt to define the structure of mythopoeic thought and compare it with that of modern (that is, scientific) thought, the differences will prove to be due rather to emotional attitude and intention than to a so-called prelogical mentality. The basic distinction of modern thought is that between *subjective* and *objective*. On this distinction scientific thought has based a critical and analytical procedure by which it progressively reduces the individual phenomena to typical events subject to universal laws. Thus it creates an increasingly wide gulf between our perception of the phenomena and the conceptions by which we make them comprehensible. We see the sun rise and set, but we think of the earth as moving round the sun. We see colours, but we describe them as wave-lengths. We dream of a dead relative, but we think of that distinct vision as a product of our own subconscious minds. Even if we individually are unable to prove these almost unbelievable scientific views to be true, we accept them, because we know that they can be proved to possess a greater degree of objectivity than our sense-impressions. In the immediacy of primitive experience, however, there is no room for such a critical resolution of perceptions. Primitive man cannot withdraw from the presence of the phenomena because they reveal themselves to him in the manner we have described. Hence the distinction between subjective and objective knowledge is meaningless to him.

Meaningless, also, is our contrast between reality and appearance. Whatever is capable of affecting mind, feeling, or will has thereby established its undoubted reality. There is, for instance, no reason why dreams should be considered less real than impressions received while one is awake. On the contrary, dreams often affect one so much more than the humdrum events of daily life that they appear to be more, and not less, significant than the usual perceptions. The Babylonians, like the Greeks, sought divine guidance by passing the night in a sacred place hoping for a revelation in dreams. And pharaohs, too, have recorded that dreams induced them to undertake certain works. Hallucinations, too, are real. We find in the official annals of Assarhaddon of Assyria[2] a record of fabulous monsters – two-headed serpents and green, winged creatures – which the exhausted troops had seen in the most trying section of their march, the arid Sinai Desert. We may recall that the Greeks saw the Spirit of the Plain of Marathon arisen in the fateful battle against the Persians. As to monsters, the Egyptians of the Middle Kingdom, as much horrified by the desert as are their modern descendants, depicted dragons, griffins, and chimeras among gazelles, foxes, and other desert game, on a footing of perfect equality.

Just as there was no sharp distinction among dreams, hallucinations, and ordinary vision, there was no sharp separation between the living and the dead. The survival of the dead and their continued relationship with man were assumed as a matter of course, for the dead were involved in the indubitable reality of man's own anguish, expectation, or resentment. 'To be effective' to the mythopœic mind means the same as 'to be.'

Symbols are treated in the same way. The primitive uses symbols as much as we do; but he can no more conceive them as signifying, yet separate from, the gods or powers than he can consider a relationship established in his mind – such as resemblance – as connecting, and yet separate from, the objects compared. Hence there is coalescence of the symbol and what it signifies, as there is coalescence of two objects compared so that one may stand for the other.

In a similar manner we can explain the curious figure of thought *pars pro toto*, 'a part can stand for the whole'; a name, a lock of hair, or a shadow can stand for the man because at any moment the lock of hair or shadow may be felt by the primitive to be pregnant with the full significance of the man. It may confront him with a 'Thou' which bears the physiognomy of its owner.

An example of the coalescence of a symbol and the thing it stands for is the treating of a person's name as an essential part of him – as if it were, in a way, identical with him. We have a number of pottery bowls which Egyptian kings of the Middle Kingdom had inscribed with the names of hostile tribes in Palestine, Libya, and Nubia; the names of their rulers; and the names of certain rebellious Egyptians. These bowls were solemnly smashed at a ritual, possibly at the funeral of the king's predecessor; and the object of this ritual was explicitly stated. It was that all these enemies, obviously out of the pharaoh's reach, should die. But if we call the ritual act of the breaking of the bowls symbolical, we miss the point.

The Egyptians felt that *real* harm was done to the enemies by the destruction of their names. The occasion was even used to cast a propitious spell of wider scope. After the names of the hostile men, who were enumerated 'that they should die', were added such phrases as: 'all detrimental thought, all detrimental talk, all detrimental dreams, all detrimental plans, all detrimental strife', etc. Mentioning these things on the bowls to be smashed diminished their actual power to hurt the king or lessen his authority.

For us there is an essential difference between an act and a ritual or symbolical performance. But this distinction was meaningless to the ancients. Gudea, a Mesopotamian ruler, describing the founding of a temple, mentions in one breath that he moulded a brick in clay, purified the site with fire, and consecrated the platform with oil. When the Egyptians claim that Osiris, and the Babylonians that Oannes, gave them the elements of their culture, they include among those elements the crafts and agriculture as well as ritual usages. These two groups of activities possess the same degree of reality. It would be meaningless to ask a Babylonian whether the success of the harvest depended on the skill of the farmers or on the correct performance of the New Year's festival. Both were essential to success.

Just as the imaginary is acknowledged as existing in reality, so concepts are likely to be substantialized. A man who has courage or eloquence possesses these qualities almost as substances of which he can be robbed or which he can share with others. The concept of 'justice' or 'equity' is in Egypt called *ma*^c*at*. The king's mouth is the temple of *ma*^c*at*. *Ma*^c*at* is personified as a goddess; but at the same time it is said that the gods 'live by *ma*^c*at*.' This concept is represented quite concretely: in the daily ritual the gods are offered a figure of the goddess, together with the other material offerings, food and drink, for their sustenance. Here we meet the paradox of mythopoeic thought. Though it does not know dead matter and confronts a world animated from end to end, it is unable to leave the scope of the concrete and renders its own concepts as realities existing per se.

An excellent example of this tendency toward concreteness is the primitive conception of death. Death is not, as for us, an event – the act or fact of dying, as Webster has it. It is somehow a substantial reality. Thus we read in the Egyptian Pyramid Texts a description of the beginning of things which runs as follows:

> When heaven had not yet come into existence,
> When men had not yet come into existence,
> When gods had not yet been born,
> When death had not yet come into existence. ...[3]

In exactly the same terms the cupbearer Siduri pities Gilgamesh in the Epic:

> Gilgamesh, whither are you wandering?
> Life, which you look for, you will never find.
> For when the gods created man, they let
> death be his share, and life
> withheld in their own hands.

Note, in the first place, that life is opposed to death, thus accentuating the fact that life in itself is considered endless. Only the intervention of another phenomenon, death, makes an end to it. In the second place, we should note the concrete character attributed to life in the statement that the gods withheld life in their hands. In case one is inclined to see in this phrase a figure of speech, it is well to remember that Gilgamesh and, in another myth, Adapa are given a chance to gain eternal life simply by eating life as a substance. Gilgamesh is shown the 'plant of life', but a serpent robs him of it. Adapa is offered bread and water of life when he enters heaven, but he refuses it on the instruction of the wily god Enki. In both cases the assimilation of a concrete substance would have made the difference between death and immortality.

*

We are touching here on the category of *causality*, which is as important for modern thought as the distinction between the subjective and the objective. If science, as we have said before, reduces the chaos of perceptions to an order in which

typical events take place according to universal laws, the instrument of this conversion from chaos to order is the postulate of causality. Primitive thought naturally recognized the
relationship of cause and effect, but it cannot recognize our
view of an impersonal, mechanical, and lawlike functioning of
causality. For we have moved far from the world of immediate
experience in our search for true causes, that is, causes which
will always produce the same effect under the same conditions.
We must remember that Newton discovered the concept of
gravitation and also its laws by taking into account three
groups of phenomena which are entirely unrelated to the
merely perceptive observer: freely falling objects, the movements of the planets, and the alternation of the tides. Now the
primitive mind cannot withdraw to that extent from percep-
tual reality. Moreover, it would not be satisfied by our ideas.
It looks, not for the 'how', but for the 'who', when it looks
for a cause. Since the phenomenal world is a 'Thou' confronting early man, he does not expect to find an impersonal law
regulating a process. He looks for a purposeful will commit-
ting an act. If the rivers refuse to rise, it is not suggested that
the lack of rainfall on distant mountains adequately explains
the calamity. When the river does not rise, it has *refused* to rise.
The river, or the gods, must be angry with the people who
depend on the inundation. At best the river or the gods intend
to convey something to the people. Some action, then, is
called for. We know that, when the Tigris did not rise, Gudea
the king went to sleep in the temple in order to be instructed
in a dream as to the meaning of the drought. In Egypt, where
annual records of the heights of the Nile flood were kept from
the earliest historical times, the pharaoh nevertheless made
gifts to the Nile every year about the time when it was due to
rise. To these sacrifices, which were thrown into the river,
a document was added. It stated, in the form of either an order
or a contract, the Nile's obligations.

Our view of causality, then, would not satisfy primitive man
because of the impersonal character of its explanations. It
would not satisfy him, moreover, because of its generality. We
understand phenomena, not by what makes them peculiar, but

by what makes them manifestations of general laws. But a general law cannot do justice to the individual character of each event. And the individual character of the event is precisely what early man experiences most strongly. We may explain that certain physiological processes cause a man's death. Primitive man asks: Why should *this* man die *thus* at *this* moment? We can only say that, given these conditions, death will always occur. He wants to find a cause as specific and individual as the event which it must explain. The event is not analysed intellectually; it is experienced in its complexity and individuality, and these are matched by equally individual causes. Death is *willed*. The question, then, turns once more from the 'why' to the 'who', not to the 'how'.

This explanation of death as willed differs from that given a moment ago, when it was viewed as almost substantialized and especially created. We meet here for the first time in these chapters a curious multiplicity of approaches to problems which is characteristic for the mythopoeic mind. In the Gilgamesh Epic death was specific and concrete; it was allotted to mankind. Its antidote, eternal life, was equally substantial: it could be assimilated by means of the plant of life. Now we have found the view that death is caused by volition. The two interpretations are not mutually exclusive, but they are nevertheless not so consistent with each other as we would desire. Primitive man, however, would not consider our objections valid. Since he does not isolate an event from its attending circumstances, he does not look for one single explanation which must hold good under all conditions. Death, considered with some detachment as a state of being, is viewed as a substance inherent in all who are dead or about to die. But death considered emotionally is the act of hostile will.

The same dualism occurs in the interpretation of illness or sin. When the scapegoat is driven into the desert, laden with the sins of the community, it is evident that these sins are conceived as having substance. Early medical texts explain a fever as due to 'hot' matters having entered a man's body. Mythopoeic thought substantializes a quality and posits some of its occurrences as causes, others as effects. But the heat that caused the fever may also have been 'willed' upon the man by hostile magic or may have entered his body as an evil spirit.

Evil spirits are often no more than the evil itself conceived as substantial and equipped with will-power. In a vague way they may be specified a little further as 'spirits of the dead', but often this explanation appears as a gratuitous elaboration of the original view, which is no more than the incipient personification of the evil. This process of personification may, of course, be carried much further when the evil in question becomes a focus of attention and stimulates the imagination. Then we get demons with pronounced individuality like Lamashtu in Babylonia. The gods also come into being in this manner.

We may even go further and say that the gods as personifications of power among other things fulfil early man's need for causes to explain the phenomenal world. Sometimes this aspect of their origin can still be recognized in the complex deities of later times. There is, for instance, excellent evidence that the great goddess Isis was, originally, the deified throne. We know that among modern Africans closely related to the ancient Egyptians the enthroning of the new ruler is the central act of the ritual of the succession. The throne is a fetish charged with the mysterious power of kingship. The prince who takes his seat upon it arises a king. Hence the throne is called the 'mother' of the king. Here personification found a starting-point; a channel for emotions was prepared which, in its turn, led to an elaboration of myth. In this way Isis 'the throne which made the king' became 'the Great Mother', devoted to her son Horus, faithful through all suffering to her husband Osiris – a figure with a powerful appeal to men even outside Egypt and, after Egypt's decline, throughout the Roman Empire.

The process of personification, however, only affects man's attitude to a limited extent. Like Isis, the sky-goddess Nūt was considered to be a loving mother-goddess; but the Egyptians of the New Kingdom arranged for their ascent to heaven without reference to her will or acts. They painted a life-sized figure of the goddess inside their coffins; the dead body was laid in her arms; and the dead man's ascent to heaven was assured. For resemblance was a sharing of essentials, and Nūt's image coalesced with its prototype. The dead man in his coffin rested already in heaven.

In every case where we would see no more than associations of thought, the mythopoeic mind finds a causal connection. Every resemblance, every contact in space or time, establishes a connection between two objects or events which makes it possible to see in the one the cause of changes observed in the other. We must remember that mythopoeic thought does not require its explanation to represent a continuous process. It accepts an initial situation and a final situation connected by no more than the conviction that the one came forth from the other. So we find, for instance, that the ancient Egyptians as well as the modern Maoris explain the present relation between heaven and earth in the following manner. Heaven was originally lying upon earth; but the two were separated, and the sky was lifted up to its present position. In New Zealand this was done by their son; in Egypt it was done by the god of the air, Shū, who is now between earth and sky. And heaven is depicted as a woman bending over the earth with outstretched arms while the good Shū supports her.

Changes can be explained very simply as two different states, one of which is said to come forth from the other without any insistence on an intelligible process – in other words, as a transformation, a metamorphosis. We find that, time and again, this device is used to account for changes and that no further explanation is then required. One myth explains why the sun, which counted as the first king of Egypt, should now be in the sky. It recounts that the sun-god Rē became tired of humanity, so he seated himself upon the sky-goddess Nūt, who changed herself into a huge cow standing four square over the earth. Since then the sun has been in the sky.

The charming inconsequentiality of this story hardly allows us to take it seriously. But we are altogether inclined to take explanations more seriously than the facts they explain. Not so primitive man. He knew that the sun-god once ruled Egypt; he also knew that the sun was now in the sky. In the first account of the relation between sky and earth he explained how Shū, the air, came to be between sky and earth; in the last account he explained how the sun got to the sky and, moreover, introduced the well-known concept of the sky as a cow. All this gave him the satisfaction of feeling that images and known facts fell into place. That, after all, is what an explanation should achieve (cf. p. 25).

The image of Rē seated on the cow of heaven, besides illustrating a non-speculative type of causal explanation which satisfies the mythopoeic mind, illustrates a tendency of the ancients which we have discussed before. We have seen that they are likely to present various descriptions of identical phenomena side by side even though they are mutually exclusive. We have seen how Shū lifted the sky-goddess Nūt from the earth. In a second story Nūt rises by herself in the shape of a cow. This image of the sky-goddess is very common, especially when the accent lies on her aspect as mother-goddess. She is the mother of Osiris and, hence, of all the dead; but she is also the mother who gives birth each evening to the stars, each morning to the sun. When ancient Egyptian thought turned to procreation, it expressed itself in images derived from cattle. In the myth of sun and sky the image of the sky-cow does not appear with its original connotation; the image of Nūt as a cow evoked the picture of the huge animal rising and lifting the sun to heaven. When the bearing of the sun by Nūt was the centre of attention, the sun was called the 'calf of gold' or 'the bull'. But it was, of course, possible to consider the sky, not predominantly in its relation to heavenly bodies or to the dead who are reborn there, but as a self-contained cosmic phenomenon. In that case Nūt was described as a descendant of the creator Atum through his children, Shū and Tefnūt, Air and Moisture. And she was, furthermore, wedded to the earth. If viewed in this manner, Nūt was imagined in human form.

We see, again, that the ancients' conception of a phenomenon differed according to their approach to it. Modern scholars have reproached the Egyptians for their apparent inconsistencies and have doubted their ability to think clearly.

Such an attitude is sheer presumption. Once one recognizes the processes of ancient thought, their justification is apparent. After all, religious values are not reducible to rationalistic formulas. Natural phenomena, whether or not they were personified and became gods, confronted ancient man with a living presence, a significant 'Thou', which, again, exceeded the scope of conceptual definition. In such cases our flexible thought and language qualify and modify certain concepts so thoroughly as to make them suitable to carry our burden of expression and significance. The mythopoeic mind, tending toward the concrete, expressed the irrational, not in our manner, but by admitting the validity of several avenues of approach at one and the same time. The Babylonians, for instance, worshipped the generative force in nature in several forms: its manifestation in the beneficial rains and thunderstorms was visualized as a lion-headed bird. Seen in the fertility of the earth, it became a snake. Yet in statues, prayers, and cult acts it was represented as a god in human shape. The Egyptians in the earliest times recognized Horus, a god of heaven, as their main deity. He was imagined as a gigantic falcon hovering over the earth with outstretched wings, the coloured clouds of sunset and sunrise being his speckled breast and the sun and moon his eyes. Yet this god could also be viewed as a sun-god, since the sun, the most powerful thing in the sky, was naturally considered a manifestation of the god and thus confronted man with the same divine presence which he adored in the falcon spreading its wings over the earth. We should not doubt that mythopoeic thought fully recognizes the unity of each phenomenon which it conceives under so many different guises; the many-sidedness of its images serves to do justice to the complexity of the phenomena. But the procedure of the mythopoeic mind in expressing a phenomenon by manifold images corresponding to unconnected avenues of approach clearly leads away from, rather than toward, our postulate of causality which seeks to discover identical causes for identical effects throughout the phenomenal world.

*

We observe a similar contrast when we turn from the category of *causality* to that of *space*. Just as modern thought seeks to establish causes as abstract functional relations between phenomena, so it views space as a mere system of relations and functions. Space is postulated by us to be infinite, continuous, and homogeneous – attributes which mere sensual perception does not reveal. But primitive thought cannot abstract a concept 'space' from its experience of space. And this experience consists in what we would call qualifying associations. The spatial concepts of the primitive are concrete orientations; they refer to localities which have an emotional colour; they may be familiar or alien, hostile or friendly. Beyond the scope of mere individual experience the community is aware of certain cosmic events which invest regions of space with a particular significance. Day and night give to east and west a correlation with life and death. Speculative thought may easily develop in connection with such regions as are outside direct experiences, for instance, the heavens or the nether world. Mesopotamian astrology evolved a very extensive system of correlations between heavenly bodies and events in the sky and earthly localities. Thus mythopoeic thought may succeed no less than modern thought in establishing a co-ordinated spatial system; but the system is determined, not by objective measurements, but by an emotional recognition of values. The extent to which this procedure determines the primitive view of space can best be illustrated by an example which will be met again in subsequent chapters as a remarkable instance of ancient speculation.

In Egypt the creator was said to have emerged from the waters of chaos and to have made a mound of dry land upon which he could stand. This primeval hill, from which the creation took its beginning, was traditionally located in the sun temple at Heliopolis, the sun-god being in Egypt most commonly viewed as the creator. However, the Holy of Holies of each temple was equally sacred; each deity was – by the very fact that he was recognized as divine – a source of creative power. Hence each Holy of Holies throughout the land could be identified with the primeval hill. Thus it is said of the temple of Philae, which was founded in the fourth century

B.C.: 'This (temple) came into being when nothing at all had yet come into being and the earth was still lying in darkness and obscurity.' The same claim was made for other temples. The names of the great shrines at Memphis, Thebes, and Hermonthis explicitly stated that they were the 'divine emerging primeval island' or used similar expressions. Each sanctuary possessed the essential quality of original holiness; for, when a new temple was founded, it was assumed that the potential sacredness of the site became manifest. The equation with the primeval hill received architectural expression also. One mounted a few steps or followed a ramp at every entrance from court or hall to the Holy of Holies, which was thus situated at a level noticeably higher than the entrance.

But this coalescence of temples with the primeval hill does not give us the full measure of the significance which the sacred locality had assumed for the ancient Egyptians. The royal tombs were also made to coincide with it. The dead, and, above all, the king, were reborn in the hereafter. No place was more propitious, no site promised greater chances for a victorious passage through the crisis of death, than the primeval hill, the centre of creative forces where the ordered life of the universe had begun. Hence the royal tomb was given the shape of a pyramid which is the Heliopolitan stylization of the primeval hill.

To us this view is entirely unacceptable. In our continuous, homogeneous space the place of each locality is unambiguously fixed. We would insist that there must have been one single place where the first mound of dry land actually emerged from the chaotic waters. But the Egyptian would have considered such objections mere quibbles. Since the temples and the royal tombs were as sacred as the primeval hill and showed architectural forms which resembled the hill, they shared essentials. And it would be fatuous to argue whether one of these monuments could be called the primeval hill with more justification than the others.

Similarly, the waters of chaos from which all life emerged were considered to be present in several places, sometimes playing their part in the economy of the country, sometimes

necessary to round out the Egyptian image of the universe.
The waters of chaos were supposed to subsist in the form of
the ocean surrounding the earth, which had emerged from
them and now floated upon them. Hence these waters were
also present in the subsoil water. In the cenotaph of Seti I at
Abydos the coffin was placed upon an island with a double
stair imitating the hieroglyph for the primeval hill; this island
was surrounded by a channel filled always with subsoil water.
Thus the dead king was buried and thought to rise again in
the locality of creation. But the waters of chaos, the Nūn, were
also the waters of the nether world, which the sun and the
dead have to cross. On the other hand, the primeval waters
had once contained all the potentialities of life; and they were,
therefore, also the waters of the annual inundation of the Nile
which renews and revives the fertility of the fields.

*

The mythopoeic conception of *time* is, like that of space,
qualitative and concrete, not quantitative and abstract. Mythopoeic thought does not know time as a uniform duration or as
a succession of qualitatively indifferent moments. The concept
of time as it is used in our mathematics and physics is as unknown to early man as that which forms the framework of our
history. Early man does not abstract a concept of time from
the experience of time.

It has been pointed out, for example, by Cassirer, that the
time experience is both rich and subtle, even for quite primitive people. Time is experienced in the periodicity and rhythm
of man's own life as well as in the life of nature. Each phase
of man's life – childhood, adolescence, maturity, old age – is
a time with peculiar qualities. The transition from one phase
to another is a crisis in which man is assisted by the community's uniting in the rituals appropriate to birth, puberty,
marriage, or death. Cassirer has called the peculiar view of
time as a sequence of essentially different phases of life 'bio-
logical time'. And the manifestation of time in nature, the
succession of the seasons, and the movements of the heavenly
bodies were conceived quite early as the signs of a life-process
similar, and related, to that of man. Even so, they are not

viewed as 'natural' processes in our sense. When there is change, there is a cause; and a cause, as we have seen, is a will. In Genesis, for instance, we read that God made a covenant with the living creatures, promising not only that the flood would not recur but also that 'while the earth remaineth, seed-time and harvest, cold and heat, summer and winter, day and night shall not cease' (Gen. viii, 22). The order of time and the order of the life of nature (which are one) are freely granted by the God of the Old Testament in the fulness of his power; and when considered in their totality, as an established order, they are elsewhere, too, thought to be founded upon the willed order of creation.

But another approach is also possible, an approach not toward the sequence of phases as a whole but toward the actual transition from one phase to another – the actual succession of phases. The varying length of the night, the ever-changing spectacles of sunrise and sunset, and the equinoctial storms do not suggest an automatic smooth alternation between the 'elements' of mythopoeic time. They suggest a conflict, and this suggestion is strengthened by the anxiety of man himself, who is wholly dependent upon weather and seasonal changes. Wensinck has called this the 'dramatic conception of nature'. Each morning the sun defeats darkness and chaos, as he did on the day of creation and does, every year, on New Year's Day. These three moments coalesce; they are felt to be essentially the same. Each sunrise, and each New Year's Day, repeats the first sunrise on the day of creation; and for the mythopoeic mind each repetition coalesces with – is practically identical with – the original event.

We have here, in the category of time, a parallel to the phenomenon which we recognized in the category of space when we learned that certain archetypal localities, like the primeval hill, were thought to exist on several sites throughout the land because these sites shared with their prototype some of its overwhelmingly important aspects. This phenomenon we called coalescence in space. An example of coalescence in time is an Egyptian verse which curses the enemies of the pharaoh. It must be remembered that the sun-god Rē had been the first ruler of Egypt and that the pharaoh was, to the extent that he ruled, an image of Rē. The verse says of the enemies of the king: 'They shall be like the snake Apophis on New Year's morning.'[4] The snake Apophis is the hostile darkness which the sun defeats every night on his journey through the nether world from the place of sunset in the west to the place of sunrise in the east. But why should the enemies be like Apophis on New Year's morning? Because the notions of creation, daily sunrise, and the beginning of the new annual cycle coalesce and culminate in the festivities of the New Year. Hence the New Year is invoked, that is, conjured up, to intensify the curse.

Now this 'dramatic conception of nature which sees everywhere a strife between divine and demoniac, cosmic and chaotic powers' (Wensinck), does not leave man a mere spectator. He is too much involved in, his welfare depends too completely upon, the victory of the beneficial powers for him not to feel the need to participate on their side. Thus we find, in Egypt and Babylonia, that man – that is, man in society – accompanies the principal changes in nature with appropriate rituals. Both in Egypt and in Babylonia the New Year, for instance, was an occasion of elaborate celebrations in which the battles of the gods were mimed or in which mock-battles were fought.

We must remember again that such rituals are not merely symbolical; they are part and parcel of the cosmic events; they are man's share in these events. In Babylonia, from the third millennium down to Hellenistic times, we find a New Year's festival which lasted several days. During the celebration the story of creation was recited and a mock-battle was fought in which the king impersonated the victorious god. In Egypt we know mock-battles in several festivals which are concerned with the defeat of death and rebirth or resurrection: one took place at Abydos, during the annual Great Procession of Osiris; one took place on New Year's Eve, at the erection of the Djed pillar; one was fought, at least in the time of Herodotus, at Papremis in the Delta. In these festivals man participated in the life of nature.

Man also arranged his own life, or at least the life of the society to which he belonged, in such a manner that a harmony with nature, a co-ordination of natural and social forces, gave added impetus to his undertakings and increased his chances for success. The whole 'science' of omens aims, of course, at this result. But there are also definite instances which illustrate the need of early man to act in unison with nature. In both Egypt and Babylon a king's coronation was postponed until a new beginning in the cycle of nature provided a propitious starting-point for the new reign. In Egypt the time might be in the early summer, when the Nile began to rise, or in the autumn, when the inundation receded and the fertilized fields were ready to receive the seed. In Babylonia the king began his reign on New Year's Day; and the inauguration of a new temple was celebrated only at that time.

This deliberate co-ordination of cosmic and social events shows most clearly that time to early man did not mean a neutral and abstract frame of reference but rather a succession of recurring phases, each charged with a peculiar value and significance. Again, as in dealing with space, we find that there are certain 'regions' of time which are withdrawn from direct experience and greatly stimulate speculative thought. They are the distant past and the future. Either of these may become normative and absolute; each then falls beyond the range of time altogether. The absolute past does not recede, nor do we approach the absolute future gradually. The 'Kingdom of God' may at any time break into our present. For the Jews the future is normative. For the Egyptians, on the other hand, the past was normative; and no pharaoh could hope to achieve more than the establishment of the conditions 'as they were in the time of Rē, in the beginning.'

But here we are touching on material which will be discussed in subsequent chapters. We have attempted to demonstrate how the 'logic', the peculiar structure, of mythopoeic thought can be derived from the fact that the intellect does not operate autonomously because it can never do justice to the basic experience of early man, that of confrontation with a significant 'Thou'. Hence when early man is faced by an intellectual problem within the many-sided complexities of life, emotional and volitional factors are never debarred; and the conclusions reached are not critical judgments but complex images.

Nor can the spheres which these images refer to be neatly kept apart. We have intended in this book to deal successively with speculative thought concerning (1) the nature of the universe; (2) the function of the state; and (3) the values of life. But the reader will have grasped that this, our mild attempt to distinguish the spheres of metaphysics, politics, and ethics, is doomed to remain a convenience without any deep significance. For the life of man and the function of the state are for mythopoeic thought imbedded in nature, and the natural processes are affected by the acts of man no less than man's life depends on his harmonious integration with nature. The experiencing of this unity with the utmost intensity was the greatest good ancient oriental religion could bestow. To conceive this integration in the form of intuitive imagery was the aim of the speculative thought of the ancient Near East.

NOTES

1. Seligmann, in *Fourth Report of the Wellcome Tropical Research Laboratories a the Gordon Memorial College, Khartoum* (London, 1911), Vol. B: *General Science*, p. 219.

2. D. D. Luckenbill, *Ancient Records of Assyria and Babylonia*, Vol. II, par. 558.

3. Sethe, *Die altägyptischen Pyramidentexte nach den Papierabdrücken und Photographien des Berliner Museums* (Leipzig, 1908), par. 1466.

4. Adolph Erman, *Ägypten und ägyptisches Leben im Altertum*, ed. Hermann Ranke (Tübingen, 1923), p. 170.

SUGGESTED READINGS

CASSIRER, ERNST. *Philosophie der symbolischen Formen II: Das mythische Denken.* Berlin, 1925.

LEEUW, G. VAN DER. *Religion in Essence and Manifestation: A Study in Phenomenology.* New York, 1938.

LEVY-BRÜHL, L. *How Natives Think.* New York, 1926.

OTTO, RUDOLF. *The Idea of the Holy: An Inquiry into the Non-rational Factor in the Idea of the Divine and Its Relation to the Rational.* London, 1943.

RADIN, PAUL. *Primitive Man as Philosopher.* New York, 1927.

H. FRANKFORT, *Kingship and the Gods: A Study of Ancient Near Eastern Religion as the Integration of Society and Nature.* Chicago, 1948. (London, Cambridge University Press, 1948).

EGYPT

John A. Wilson

CHAPTER II

Egypt: The Nature of the Universe

GEOGRAPHIC CONSIDERATIONS

THE SEPARATION of these chapters into the fields of Egypt and Mesopotamia is a necessary separation, because the two cultures exhibited their general uniformity in individual terms and with distinctly different developments. As the case was presented in the introductory chapter, the common attitude of mind toward the phenomena of the universe was governing for each of the two separate treatments. It is no thesis in our material that the Egyptian phenomena were unique, even though our exclusive pre-occupation with Egypt may seem to ignore the many elements common to Egypt and her neighbours. The common ground is the important consideration for those who wish to know something about the developing human mind rather than the mind of the Egyptian alone. We consider, then, that our documentary material illustrates the early and pre-classical mind with examples from one of the two cultures.

Within that uniformity of viewpoint the cultures were different, as British culture differs from that of continental Europe or from that of the United States. Geography is not the sole determinant in matters of cultural differentiation, but geographic features are subject to description which is practically incontrovertible, so that a consideration of the geographic uniqueness of Egypt will suggest easily some of the factors of differentiation. Throughout the Near East there is a contrast between the desert and the sown land; Egypt had and still has a concentration of that contrast.

The essential part of Egypt is a green gash of teeming life cutting across brown desert wastes. The line of demarcation between life and non-life is startlingly clear: one may stand at the edge of the cultivation with one foot on the irrigated black soil and one foot on the desert sands. The country is essentially rainless; only the waters of the Nile make life possible where otherwise there would be endless wastes of sand and rock.

But what a life the Nile makes possible! The little agricultural villages contract themselves within smallest compass, in order not to encroach upon the fertile fields of rice, cotton, wheat, or sugar cane. When properly cared for, the land can yield two crops a year. Normally Egypt has a very comfortable surplus of agricultural produce for export.

This richness is confined to the green Nile Valley. Only 3.5 per cent. of the modern state of Egypt is cultivable and habitable. The remaining 96.5 per cent. is barren and uninhabitable desert. Today perhaps 99.5 per cent. of the population lives on the 3.5 per cent. of the land which will support population. That means an even greater contrast between the desert and the sown, and it means that on the cultivable land there is a concentration of people close to the saturation point. Today *habitable* Egypt has over 1,200 persons to the square mile. The figures for Belgium, the most densely populated country of Europe, are about 700 to the square mile; for Java, about 900 to the square mile. The density of population in modern Egypt is therefore so great that the concentration approaches that of an industrial and urban country rather than that of an agricultural and rustic country. Yet Egypt, with her fertile soil, is always essentially agricultural.

No figures are available for ancient Egypt, of course, and the population could not have been as great as today; but the main features were surely the same as at the present: a hermetically sealed tube containing a concentration of life close to the saturation point. The two features of isolation and semi-urban population combine to make Egypt different from her neighbours. At the present day the Arabs of Palestine and of Iraq concede the general cultural leadership of Egypt, as being the most sophisticated of the Arab countries; and yet they do not feel that the Egyptians are truly Arabs. The Egyptians are not subject to the great conservative control of the Arabian Desert. The deserts adjacent to Palestine and Iraq are potential breeding-grounds for fierce and puritanical elements in the populations of those countries. Egypt, with her agricultural wealth and with her people lying cheek by jowl, developed an early sophistication, which expressed itself intellectually in tendencies toward catholicity and syncretism. Within Egypt the most divergent concepts were tolerantly accepted and woven together into what we moderns might regard as a clashing philosophical lack of system, but which to the ancient was inclusive. The way of the Semite, who held a contact with the desert, was to cling fiercely to tradition and to resist innovations, which changed the purity and simplicity of life. The way of the Egyptian was to accept innovations and to incorporate them into his thought, without discarding the old and outmoded. This means that it is impossible to find in ancient Egypt a system in our sense, orderly and consistent. Old and new lie blandly together like some surrealist picture of youth and age on a single face.

However, if the ancient Egyptian was tolerant of divergent concepts, it does not necessarily follow that he was tolerant of other peoples. He was semi-urban and sophisticated of mind and felt foreigners to be rustic and uninitiated. He was cut off from his neighbours by sea and desert and felt that he could afford a superior isolationism. He made a distinction between 'men', on the one hand, and Libyans or Asiatics or Africans, on the other.[1] The word 'men' in that sense meant Egyptians: otherwise it meant 'humans' in distinction to the gods, or 'humans' in distinction to animals. In other words, the Egyptians were 'people'; foreigners were not. At a time of national distress, when the stable, old order had broken down and social conditions were upside-down, there was a complaint that 'strangers from outside have come into Egypt. . . . Foreigners have become people everywhere.'[2] The concept that only our group is 'folks', that outsiders lack something of humanity, is not confined to the modern world.

However, the Egyptian isolationist or nationalist feeling was a matter of geography and of manners rather than of racial theory and dogmatic xenophobia. 'The people' were those who lived in Egypt, without distinction of race or colour. Once a foreigner came to reside in Egypt, learned to speak Egyptian, and adopted Egyptian dress, he might finally be accepted as one of 'the people' and was no longer the object of superior ridicule. Asiatics or Libyans or Negroes might be accepted Egyptians of high position when they had become acclimatized – might, indeed, rise to the highest position of all, that of the god-king who possessed the nation. The same Egyptian word means the 'land' of Egypt and the 'earth'. It is correct to say that, when any element was within this land, it merited full and tolerant acceptance.

The ancient Egyptian's sense that his land was the one land that really mattered was fostered by a knowledge that those other countries with which he had immediate contact were not so fully developed in culture as his own. Babylonia and the Hittite region were too distant for proper comparison, but the near-by lands of the Libyans, the Nubians, and the Asiatic Bedouins were clearly inferior in cultural development. Palestine and Syria were sometimes colonized by Egypt, or were sometimes under Egyptian cultural and commercial leadership. Until the Assyrians and Persians and Greeks finally came in conquering domination, it was possible for the Egyptian to feel a comforting sense that his civilization was superior to all others. An Egyptian story puts into the mouth of a Syrian prince this sweeping statement to an envoy who had come to him from the land of the Nile: 'For (the imperial god) Amon founded all lands. He founded them, but first he founded the land of Egypt, from which thou hast come. For skilled work came forth from it to reach this place where I am, and teaching came from it to reach this place where I am.'[3] Because the source is Egyptian, we cannot be sure that a prince of Syria actually did say such words, acknowledging Egyptian leadership in learning and craftsmanship, but this story from Egypt carries the assurance that it was a comforting doctrine to those who believed themselves to live at the centre of the world.

Thus it may be claimed that the physical isolation of Egypt from other lands produced a self-centred feeling of separateness, within which Egypt had an intellectual development of diverse elements in admixture. It is our part to try to resolve some of these seeming incongruities into a semblance of order which the reader will be able to grasp. To be sure, it is unjust to leave an impression that there was anarchical chaos; no people could maintain a way of life for 2,000 visible years without established foundations. We shall find foundation stones and a sensible structure rising from those stones; but it is sometimes puzzling to a visitor to find a front door on each of four sides of a building.

Let us return again to the geography of Egypt. We have the picture of the green gash of life cutting through the brown stretches of non-life. Let us examine the mechanics of the Egyptian scene. The Nile cuts north out of Africa, surmounts five rocky cataracts, and finally empties into the Mediterranean. These cataracts form the barriers of Egypt against the Hamitic and Negro peoples to the south just as effectively as the deserts and the sea bar Libyan and Semitic peoples to the north, east, and west. In the morning the sun rises in the east, it crosses the sky by day, and it sets in the west in the evening. Of course, you know that; but it is important enough in Egypt to deserve repeated mention, because the daily birth, journey, and death of the sun were dominating features of Egyptian life and thought. In a country essentially rainless, the daily circuit of the sun is of blazing importance. We might think that there was too much sun in Egypt, that shade was a welcome necessity; but the Egyptian hated the darkness and the cold and stretched himself happily to greet the rising sun. He saw that the sun was the source of his life. At night 'the earth is in darkness, as if it were dead.'[4] So the personification of the sun's power, the sun-god, was the supreme god and the creator-god.

It is curious that the Egyptians gave relatively little credit to another force – the wind. The prevailing wind in Egypt comes from the north, across the Mediterranean and then down the trough of the Nile Valley. It mitigates the unceasing heat of the sun and makes Egypt an easier place in which to live; it contrasts with those hot dry winds of late spring, which bring sandstorms and a brittle heat out of Africa to the south. This north wind was good, and the Egyptians expressed their appreciation and made it into a minor divinity; but, relative to the all-pervading power of the sun, the wind was practically ignored.

It is somewhat different in the case of the Nile. The river was so obvious a source of life that it had its appreciated place in the scheme of things, even though it also could not compete with the sun for position. The Nile had a cycle of birth and death on an annual basis, which corresponded to the daily birth and death of the sun. In the summer the river lies quiet and slow between its shrunken banks, while the fields beside it parch and turn to dust and blow away toward the desert. Unless water can be raised by a series of lifts from the river or from very deep wells, agricultural growth comes to a standstill, and people and cattle grow thin and torpidly look upon the face of famine.

Then, just as life is at its lowest ebb, the Nile River stirs sluggishly and shows a pulse of power. Through the summer it swells slowly but with increasing momentum until it begins to race with mighty waters, burst its banks, and rush over the miles of flat land lying on each side. Great stretches of moving muddy water cover the land. In a year of a high Nile they encroach upon the little village islands standing up out of the fields, nibble at the mud-brick houses, and bring some of them tumbling down. From inert, dusty wastes, the land has turned to a great shallow stream, which carries a refertilizing load of silt. Then the peak of the flood passes, and the waters become more sluggish. Out of the flooded stretches there appear little peaks of soil, refreshed with new, fertile mud. The torpor of men disappears; they wade out into the thick mud and begin eagerly sowing their first crop of clover or grain. Life has come again to Egypt. Soon a broad green carpet of growing fields will complete the annual miracle of the conquest of life over death.

These, then, were the two central features of the Egyptian scene: the triumphant daily rebirth of the sun and the triumphant annual rebirth of the river. Out of these miracles the Egyptians drew their assurance that Egypt was the centre of the universe and their assurance that renewed life may always be victorious over death.

It is necessary to make some qualification to a picture which has been presented in terms of a free gift of life and fertility.

Egypt was rich but not prodigal: the fruit did not drop from the trees for indolent farmers. The sun and the Nile did combine to bring forth renewed life, but only at the cost of a battle against death. The sun warmed, but in the summer it also blasted. The Nile brought fertilizing water and soil, but its annual inundation was antic and unpredictable. An exceptionally high Nile destroyed canals, dams, and the homes of men. An exceptionally low Nile brought famine. The inundation came quickly and moved on quickly; constant, back-breaking work was necessary to catch, hold, and dole out the waters for the widest and longest use. The desert was always ready to nibble away at the cultivation and turn fertile silt into arid sand. The desert in particular was a terrible place of venomous serpents, lions, and fabulous monsters. In the broad muddy stretches of the Delta, jungle-like swamps had to be drained and cleared to make arable fields. For more than a third of every year the hot desert winds, the blasting sun, and the low Nile brought the land within sight of death, until the weather turned and the river brought abundant waters again. Thus Egypt was rich and blessed in contrast with her immediate neighbours, but within her own territory she experienced struggle, privations, and dangers which made the annual triumph real. There was a sense that the triumph was not an automatic privilege but that it must be earned at some cost.

We have already suggested that the Egyptians were self-centred and had their own satisfied kind of isolationism. We have said that they used the word 'humans' to apply to Egyptians in distinction from foreigners. The concept that Egypt was the focal centre of the universe set the standard for what was right and normal in the universe in terms of what was normal in Egypt. The central feature of Egypt is the Nile, flowing north and bringing the necessary water for life. They therefore looked at other peoples and other existences in terms of their own scene. The Egyptian word 'to go north' is the Egyptian word 'to go downstream', and the word 'to go south' is the word 'to go upstream', against the current. When the Egyptians met another river, the Euphrates, which flowed south instead of north, they had to express the sense of contrast by calling it 'that circling water which goes downstream in going upstream', which may also be translated 'that inverted water which goes downstream by going south'.[5]

Navigation on the Nile employed the power of the current in moving north. In moving south, boats raised the sail in order to take advantage of the prevailing north wind, which would push them against the current. Since this was normal, it became the ideal for any world, including the afterlife. Into their tombs the Egyptians put two model boats, which might be projected by magic into the next world for navigation there. One boat had the sail down, for sailing north with the current on the waters of the other world; one boat had the sail up for sailing south with that north wind which must be normal in any proper existence, here or hereafter.

So, too, rain could be understood only in terms of the waters which came to Egypt. Addressing the god, the Egyptian worshipper acknowledged his goodness to Egypt: 'Thou makest the Nile in the lower world and bringest it whither thou wilt, in order to sustain mankind, even as thou hast made them.' Then, in an unusual interest in foreign lands, the worshipper went on: 'Thou makest that whereon all distant countries live. Thou hast put (another) Nile in the sky, so that it may come down for them, and may make waves upon the mountains like a sea, in order to moisten their fields in their townships. ... The Nile in the sky, thou appointest it for the foreign peoples and (for) all the beasts of the highland which walk upon feet, whereas the (real) Nile, it comes from the lower world for (the people of) Egypt.'[6] If we reverse our concept that water normally falls from the skies and accept as appropriate a system in which water comes up from caverns below to be the only proper sustainer of life, then we will refer to rain in our own terms. It is then not the case that Egypt is a rainless country but rather it is the case that other countries have their Nile falling from the skies.

In the quotation just given there is a significant grouping of foreign peoples and the beasts of the highland. I do not mean that it is significant in coupling barbarians with cattle, although that has a minor implication. It is rather that these two had their habitat in regions which were similarly conceived in their contrast to the Nile Valley. Egypt was a flat pancake of fertile black soil (⚌). Every foreign country consisted of corrugated ridges of red sand. The same hieroglyphic sign was used for 'foreign country' that was used for 'highland' or for 'desert' (𓈉); a closely similar sign was used for 'mountain' (𓈈), because the mountain ridges which fringed the Nile Valley were also desert and also foreign. Thus the Egyptian pictorially grouped the foreigner with the beast of the desert and pictorially denied to the foreigner the blessings of fertility and uniformity.

Just as people from our own western plains feel shut in if they visit the hills of New England, so the Egyptian had a similar claustrophobia about any country where one could not look far across the plain, where one could not see the sun in all its course. One Egyptian scribe wrote to another: 'Thou hast not trodden the road to Meger (in Syria), in which the sky is dark by day, which is overgrown with cypresses, oaks, and cedars that reach the heavens. There are more lions there than panthers or hyenas, and it is surrounded by Bedouin on (every) side. ... Shuddering seizes thee, (the hair of) thy head stands on end, and thy soul lies in thy hand. Thy path is filled with boulders and pebbles, and there is no passable track, for it is overgrown with reeds, thorns, brambles, and wolf's pad. The ravine is on one side of thee, while the mountain rises on the other.'[7]

A similar sense that a land of mountains, rain, and trees is a dismal place comes out in the words: 'The miserable Asiatic, it goes ill with the land where he is, (a land) troubled with water, inaccessible because of the many trees, with its roads bad because of the mountains.' Just as this land was wrong in every respect, so the miserable Asiatic was unaccountable: 'He does not live in a single place, but his feet wander. He has been fighting since the time of Horus, but he conquers not, nor is he conquered, and he never announces the day in fighting. ... He may plunder a lonely settlement, but he will not take a populous city. ... Trouble thyself not about him: he is (only) an Asiatic.'[8] Our own standard of life is the one which we apply to others, and on the basis of this standard we find them wanting.

There is another topographical feature of the Nile Valley which finds its counterpart in the Egyptian psychology. That is the uniformity of landscape. Down the centre of the land cuts the Nile. On each bank the fertile fields stretch away, with the west bank the counterpart of the east. Then comes the desert, climbing up into two mountain fringes lining the valley. Again, the western mountain desert is the counterpart of the eastern. Those who live on the black soil look out through the clear air and see practically the same scene everywhere. If they travel a day's journey to the south or two days' journey to the north, the scene is much the same. Fields are broad and level; trees are rare or small; there is no exceptional break in the vista, except where some temple has been erected by man, or except in the two mountain ranges, which are really the outer limits of Egypt.

In the broad reaches of the Delta the uniformity is even more striking. There the flat stretches of fields move on monotonously without feature. The only land which matters in Egypt has uniformity and it has symmetry.

The interesting result of uniformity is the way in which it accentuates any exceptional bit of relief that happens to break the monotonous regularity. Out in the desert one is conscious of every hillock, of every spoor of an animal, of every desert duststorm, of every bit of movement. The rare irregular is very striking in an environment of universal regularity. It has animation; it has life within the dominating pattern of non-life. So also in Egypt the prevailing uniformity of landscape threw into high relief anything which took exception to that uniformity. A solitary tree of some size, a peculiarly shaped hill, or a storm-cut valley was so exceptional that it took on individuality. Man who lived close to nature endowed the exceptional feature with animation; it became inspirited to his mind.

The same attitude of mind looked upon the animals which moved through the scene: the falcon floating in the sky with no more apparent motive power than the sun; the jackal flitting ghostlike along the margin of the desert; the crocodile lurking lumplike on the mudflats; or the powerful bull in whom was the seed of procreation. These beasts were forces going beyond the normality of landscape; they were forces which transcended the minimal observed natures of animals. They therefore took on high relief in the scene and were believed to be vested with mysterious or inscrutable force related to an extra-human world.

This may be an oversimplification of ancient man's animistic outlook on nature. Of course, it is true that any agricultural people has a feeling for the force that works in nature and comes to personalize each separate force. And before there were naturalists to explain the mechanism of plants and animals, to reason out the chain of cause and effect in the behaviour of other things in our world, man's only yardstick of normality was humanity: what he knew in himself and in his own experience was human and normal; deviations from the normal were extra-human and thus potentially superhuman. Therefore, as was pointed out in the opening chapter, the human came to address the extra-human in terms of human intercourse. The phenomenal world to him was not 'It' but 'Thou'. It was not necessary that the object become finally superhuman and be revered as a god before it might be conceived in terms of 'Thou'. As extra-human, but not of divine nature, it was accorded the 'Thou' rather than the 'It' by man. The Egyptians might – and did – personify almost anything: the head, the belly, the tongue, perception, taste, truth, a tree, a mountain, the sea, a city, darkness, and death. But few of these were personified with regularity or with awe; that is, few of them reached the stature of gods or demigods. They were forces with which man had the 'Thou' relation. And it is a little difficult to think of anything in the phenomenal world with which he might not have that relation as indicated in scenes and texts. The answer is that he might have the 'Thou' relation with anything in the phenomenal world.

Another aspect of the uniform landscape of Egypt was its symmetry: east bank balancing west bank, and eastern mountain range balancing western mountain range. Whether this bilateral symmetry of landscape was the reason or not, the

Egyptian had a strong sense of balance, symmetry, and geometry. This comes out clearly in his art, where the best products show a fidelity of proportion and a careful counterpoising of elements in order to secure a harmonious balance. It comes out in his literature, where the best products show a deliberate and sonorous parallelism of members, which achieve dignity and cadence, even though it seems monotonous and repetitive to modern ears.

Let us illustrate this literary balance by quotations from a text giving a statement of one of the Egyptian kings:

> Give heed to my utterances / hearken to them.
> I speak to you / I make you aware
> That I am the son of Re / who issued from his body.
> I sit upon his throne in rejoicing / since he established me
>   as king / as lord of this land.
> My counsels are good / my plans come to pass.
> I protect Egypt / I defend it.[9]

The balance sought by the artist could be illustrated by Egyptian sculptures or paintings. Instead, we shall quote from the inscription of a 'chief craftsman, painter, and sculptor', who went into considerable detail with regard to his technical abilities. Of his modelling, he said: 'I know how to work up clay, how to proportion (it) according to rule, how to mould or introduce (it) by taking away or adding to it so that (each) member comes to its (proper) place.' Of his drawing, he said: 'I know (how to express) the movement of a figure, the carriage of a woman, the pose of a single instant, the cowering of the isolated captive, or how one eye looks at the other.'[10] The emphasis of his claimed skill lies in proportion, balance, and poise.

The same balance comes out in the Egyptian's cosmology and his theology, where he sought for a counterpoise to each observed phenomenon or each supernatural element. If there is a sky above, there must be a sky below; each god must have his goddess consort, even though she has no separate divine function but is simply a feminine counterpart of himself. Some of this striving for bilateral symmetry seems to us strained, and undoubtedly artificial concepts did arise in the search to find a counterpoise for anything observed or conceived. However, the psychological desire for balance which drew forth the artificial concept was not itself artificial but was a deeply engrained desire for symmetric poise.

That deep desire for balance will appear to the reader as contradictory to the lack of order which we deplored in the Egyptians' bland acceptance of any new concept, whether it conformed to an old concept or not, and their maintenance of apparently conflicting concepts side by side. There is a contradiction here, but we believe that it can be explained. The ancient Egyptian had a strong sense of symmetry and balance, but he had little sense of incongruity: he was perfectly willing to balance off incompatibles. Further, he had little sense of causation, that *A* leads sequentially to *B* and *B* leads sequentially to *C*. As remarked in the introductory chapter, the ancient did not recognize causality as impersonal and binding. It is an oversimplification to say that the Egyptian's thinking was in terms of geometry rather than in terms of algebra, but that statement may give some idea of his limited virtues. The order in his philosophy lay in physical arrangement rather than in integrated and sequential systematization.

COSMOLOGY

It is now time to consider the terms in which the Egyptian viewed the physical universe, of which his own land was the focal centre. First of all, he took his orientation from the Nile River, the source of his life. He faced the south, from which the stream came. One of the terms for 'south' is also a term for 'face'; the usual word for 'north' is probably related to a word which means the 'back of the head'. On his left was the east and on his right the west. The word for 'east' and 'left' is the same, and the word for 'west' and 'right' is the same.

We were technically incorrect in stating that the Egyptian's orientation was to the south; more precisely we should say that the Egyptian 'australized' himself toward the source of the Nile. It is significant that he did not take his primary direction from the east, the land of the rising sun, the region which he called 'God's Land'. As we shall see, the formulated theology did emphasize the east. But back in the prehistoric days before theology had crystallized, when the terms of the Egyptian language were forming, the dweller on the Nile faced toward the south, the source of the annual refertilization of his land. The theological priority of the sun seems thus to be a later development.

It may be that we are dealing with two separate searchings for direction. In the trough of Upper Egypt, where the Nile so clearly flows from the south as the dominating feature of the land, the compass of man's attention swung to the south. In the Delta, where the broad stretches had no such magnetic pull of direction, the rising of the sun in the east was a more important phenomenon. The worship of the sun may thus have been more important in the north and may have been transferred to the entire land as state theology in some prehistoric conquest of the south by the north. Such a conquest would have established the theological primacy of the sun and made the east, which was the region of the sun's rebirth, the area of religious importance, but it would not affect the words which showed that man's polarity was originally to the south.

The crystallized theology, as we know it in historic times, made the orient, the land of the sun's rising, the region of birth and re-birth, and made the occident, the land of the sun's setting, the region of death and life after death. The east was *ta-netjer*, 'God's Land', because the sun rose there in youthly glory. This general term for the east was even used for specific foreign countries, which were otherwise despised. Syria, Sinai, and Punt, all lying to the east, might be afflicted with mountains, trees, and rain, might be inhabited by 'miserable Asiatics', but they belonged to the youthful sun-god, so that they were designated also as 'God's Land' and enjoyed a reflected glory through geographical accident and not through inner merit. Implicitly the good produce of these eastern countries was ascribed to the sun-god rather than to the inhabitants: 'All good woods of God's Land: heaps of myrrh gum, trees of fresh myrrh, ebony, and clean ivory ... baboons, apes, greyhounds, and panther skins,'[11] or 'cedar, cypress, and juniper ... all good woods of God's Land.'[12]

In the dogma that arose in magnification of the rising sun

the grateful joy of all creation at the renewed appearance of the morning sun was expressed again and again. The contrast between evening and morning was a contrast between death and life. 'When thou settest on the western horizon, the land is in darkness in the manner of death ... (but) when the day breaks, as thou risest on the horizon ... they awake and stand upon their feet ... they live because thou hast arisen for them.'[13] Not only does mankind join in this renewal of life, but 'all beasts prance upon their feet, and everything that flies or flutters,'[14] and 'apes worship him; "Praise to thee!" (say) all beasts with one accord.'[15] The Egyptian pictures show this morning worship of the sun by animals: the apes stretching out limbs which had been cooled at night, in apparent salutation to the warmth of the sun, or the ostriches limbering up at dawn by dancing a stately pavane in the first rays of the sun. Such observed phenomena were visible proofs of the communion of men, beasts, and the gods.

But to return to the Egyptian's concept of the world in which he lived. We are going to try to give this in a single picture, which will have only partial justification. In the first place, we are concerned with something like three thousand years of observed history, with the vestiges of prehistoric development partially visible; and there was constant slow change across this long stretch of time. In the second place, the ancient Egyptian left us no single formulation of his ideas which we may use as nuclear material; when we pick and choose scraps of ideas from scattered sources, we are gratifying our modern craving for a single integrated system. That is, our modern desire to capture a single picture is photographic and static, whereas the ancient Egyptian's picture was cinematic and fluid. For example, we should want to know in our picture whether the sky was supported on posts or was held up by a god; the Egyptian would answer: 'Yes, it is supported by posts or held up by a god – or it rests on walls, or it is a cow, or it is a goddess whose arms and feet touch the earth.' Any one of these pictures would be satisfactory to him, according to his approach, and in a single picture he might show two different supports for the sky: the goddess whose arms and feet reach the earth, and the god who holds up the sky-goddess. This possibility of complementary viewpoints applies to other concepts. We shall therefore pick a single picture, in the knowledge that it tells a characteristic story, but not the only story.

The Egyptian conceived of the earth as a flat platter with a corrugated rim. The inside bottom of this platter was the flat alluvial plain of Egypt, and the corrugated rim was the rim of mountain countries which were the foreign lands. This platter floated in water. There were the abysmal waters below, on which the platter rested, called by the Egyptian 'Nūn'. Nūn was the waters of the underworld, and, according to one continuing concept, Nūn was the primordial waters out of which life first issued. Life still issued from these underworld waters, for the sun was reborn every day out of Nūn, and the Nile came pouring forth from caverns which were fed from Nūn. In addition to being the underworld waters, Nūn was the waters encircling the world, the Okeanos which formed the outermost boundary, also called the 'Great Circuit' or the 'Great Green'. Thus it was clear that the sun, after its nightly journey under the world, must be reborn beyond the eastern horizon out of those encircling waters, just as all the gods had originally come forth out of Nūn.

Above the earth was the inverted pan of the sky, setting the outer limit to the universe. As we have already said, the craving for symmetry, as well as a sense that space is limited, called forth a counterheaven under the earth, bounding the limits of the underworld. This was the universe within which man and the gods and the heavenly bodies operated.

Various qualifications to this picture are immediately necessary. Our picture gives the vault of heaven as suspended by apparent levitation above the earth. That would appeal to the ancient Egyptian as dangerous, and he would ask for some visible means of support. As we have already said, he provided various means of support in various concepts, the incompatibility of which he cheerfully ignored. The simplest mechanism was four posts set on earth to carry the weight of heaven. These were at the outer limits of the earth, as is indicated by such texts as: 'I have set ... the terror of thee as far as the four pillars of heaven,'[16] and the number four suggests that they were placed at the four points of the compass. Fortunately, this arrangement appealed to the Egyptian as being both strong and permanent: '(As firm) as heaven resting upon its four posts' is a simile used more than once.[17]

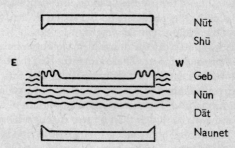

Nūt
Shū

E   W

Geb
Nūn
Dāt
Naunet

But heaven might have other support. Between heaven and earth there was Shū, the air-god, and it was his function to stand firmly on earth and carry the weight of heaven. In the Pyramid Texts (1101) it is said: 'The arms of Shū are under heaven, that he may carry it.' Significantly, another version of this text gives a variant: 'The arms of Shū are under Nūt, that he may carry her,' for heaven was, of course, personified as a deity, the sky-goddess Nūt. She is represented as crouching over earth, with her fingers and toes touching the ground, while the sun, moon, and stars adorn her body. She may carry her own weight in this pose, or the air-god Shū may take some of her weight on his uplifted hands.

Again, the vault of heaven might be represented as the under-belly of a celestial cow, studded with stars, and providing the Milky Way along which the boat of the sun might make its heavenly course. That these concepts are essentially alternatives did not seem to bother the Egyptian. In the course of a single text he might use these differing ideas about heaven; each concept pleased him and had its pertinent value in a universe which was fluid and in which almost all things were possible to the gods. Within his own standards of what is credible and convincing, he had his own consistency. All his concepts of heaven and its supports gave him assurance instead of uncertainty, because they were all stable and enduring and because one concept could be taken as complementing another instead of contradicting it.

Under the vault of heaven were the heavenly bodies, the stars hanging from the inverted pan or else spangling the belly of the cow or of the goddess, and the moon similarly treated. The moon has curiously little weight in Egyptian mythology, or, rather, we should say that it has little weight in the evidence which has descended to us. There are traces that there had been early important centres of moon worship, but this worship became diverted into less cosmic directions in historic times. Thus the moon-god Thoth was more important as a god of wisdom and a divine judge than he was through his heavenly activity. The waning and waxing moon disc as one of the two celestial eyes became a rather formal part of the Osiris story, serving as the injury suffered by Horus in fighting for his father, an injury which was restored every month by the moon-god. Conceivably this idea was taken over from some earlier myth in which the moon had had an importance comparable to that of the sun, the other celestial eye. In historical times there was little comparison between the two bodies.

Similarly, the stars had their importance in the measuring of time, and two or three of the major constellations were deities of some weight; but only one group of stars achieved lasting importance in the Egyptian scene. Again, this importance had to do with triumph over death. In the clear Egyptian air the stars stand out with brilliance. Most of the stars swing across the sky with a scythe-like sweep and disappear below the horizon. But one section of the skies employs a smaller orbit, and there the stars may dip toward the horizon but never disappear. Those are the circumpolar stars swinging around the North Star, stars which the Egyptians called 'those that know no destruction' or 'those that know no weariness'. These undying stars they took as the symbol of the dead who triumphed over death and went on into eternal life. That north section of heaven was in early times an important part of the universe. Visibly there was no death there; therefore, it must be the place of the eternal blessedness for which Egyptians longed. In the early mortuary texts, which we moderns call the Pyramid Texts, the goal of the deceased was the region of Dāt in the northern part of heaven, where he would join the circumpolar stars 'which know no destruction' and thus live forever himself. There were located their Elysian Fields, the 'Field of Reeds' and the 'Field of Offerings', in which the dead would live as an *akh*, an 'effective' spirit.

As time went on, and as the dominant mythology of the sun spread its weight over the nation, the region of Dāt shifted from the northern part of the sky to the underworld. The old texts which tried every conceivable method of boosting the dead into heaven were still reiterated with solemn fervour, but the entry-way into the next world was now in the west, and the two Elysian Fields were below the earth. This was clearly because the sun died in the west, had its spiritual course under the earth, and gloriously was reborn in the east. So, too, the dead must share in this promise of constantly continued life, must be shifted to the proximity of the sun in order to participate in his fate. Thus our picture of the universe must recognize Dāt, the area between earth and the counterheaven as the realm of the immortal dead.

Enough has already been said about the central importance of the sun in this scene. Something must be said about his motive power on his daily journey. Most commonly he is depicted as moving by boat, and the bilateral symmetry which the Egyptian loved gave him a boat for the day and another boat for the night. Various important gods formed the crews of these two boats. This journey might not be all stately and serene: there was a serpent lurking along the way to attack the boat and presumably swallow the sun; battle was necessary to conquer this creature. This is, of course, the common belief in many lands that eclipses occur when a snake or dragon swallows up the sun. But a true eclipse was not the only phenomenon involved; every night an attempt to swallow up the sun was met and conquered in the underworld.

The sun might have other motive power. It seemed to be a rolling ball, and the Egyptians knew a rolling ball in that pellet which the dung beetle pushed across the sand. So a beetle, a scarab, became a symbol for the morning sun, with an afternoon counterpart in an old man wearily moving toward the western horizon. Again, the symbol of the falcon soaring in apparent motionlessness in the upper air suggested that the sun disc also might have falcon wings for its effortless flight. As before, these concepts were felt to be complementary and not conflicting. The possession of many manifestations of being enlarged the glory of the god.

To move the concept of the sun even farther from the physical, from the notion of a fiery disc which swung around the earth every twenty-four hours, we must here note other aspects of the sun-god, Rē. As supreme god, he was a divine king, and legend said that he had been the first king of Egypt in primordial times. He was thus represented in the form of a bearded deity with a disc as his crown. As supreme god, he loaned himself to other gods, in order to enlarge them and give them a primacy within geographical or functional limits. Thus he was both Rē and Rē-Atum, the creator god, at Heliopolis. He was Rē-Harakhte, that is, Rē-Horus-of-the-Horizon, as the youthful god on the eastern horizon. At various localities he became Montu-Rē, a falcon-god, Sobek-Rē, a crocodile-god, and Khnum-Rē, a ram-god. He became Amon-Rē, King of the Gods, as the imperial god of Thebes. As we have said, these separate manifestations enlarged him. He was not simply a solar disc. He had personality as a god. Here we revert again to the distinction between the scientific concept of a phenomenon as 'It' and the ancient concept of a phenomenon as 'Thou' given in chapter I. There it was said that science is able to comprehend the 'It' as ruled by laws which make its behaviour relatively predictable, whereas the 'Thou' has the unpredictable character of an individual, 'a presence known only in so far as it reveals itself.' In these terms the apparently antic and protean character of the sun becomes simply the versatile and ubiquitous reach possible to a very able individual. Surprise at this being's many-sided personality may ultimately give way to an expectation that he will be able to participate in any situation with specialized competence.

COSMOGONY

Now we shall examine some of the Egyptian creation stories. It is significant that a plural should be necessary, that we cannot settle down to a single codified account of the beginnings. The Egyptian accepted various myths and discarded none of them. It is further to be noted that it is easier to observe close parallels between the Babylonian and Hebrew accounts of the genesis than it is to relate the Egyptian accounts to the other two. Within the broad area of general developmental similarity in the ancient Near East, Egypt stood slightly apart.

We have already noted that Nūn, the primordial abyss, was the region out of which life first came. This is, of course, particularly true of the sun, because of his daily re-emergence from the depths, and of the Nile, because it consists of ground waters. But the phrase 'who came forth from Nūn' is used of many other individual gods and of the council of the gods as a group. In large part, we need not seek too seriously for a myth for this idea. The depths or the primordial waters are a concept needing no teleological story; Tennyson's reference to life as 'that which drew from out the boundless deep' needs no explanation.

However, we must give closer attention to one account of life appearing out of the waters, and that has the location of creation on a 'primeval hillock'. We have mentioned how broad sheets of water cover Egypt when the Nile inundation is at its height and how the sinking of the waters brings into view the first isolated peaks of mud, refreshed with new fertile silt. These would be the first islands of promise for new life in a new agricultural year. As these first hillocks of slime lift their heads out of the floodwaters into the baking warmth of the sun, it is easy to imagine that they sputter and crackle with new life. The modern Egyptians believe that there is special life-giving power in this slime, and they are not alone in this belief. A little less than three centuries ago there was a scientific controversy about spontaneous generation, the ability of apparently inorganic matter to produce living organisms. One Englishman wrote that if his scholarly opponent doubted that life came into being through putrefaction which went on in mud or slime, 'let him go to Egypt, and there he will find the fields swarming with mice begot of the mud of Nylus, to the great calamity of the inhabitants.'[18] It is not hard to believe that animal life may come out of this highly charged mud.

The evidence on the Egyptian myth of the origin of life on the primeval hillock is scattered and allusive. The essential point is that the creator-god made his first appearance on this solitary island. At least two different theological systems claimed primacy through the possession of a primeval hillock, and indeed ultimately every temple which had a high place for its god probably considered that high place to be the place of creation. The pyramids themselves borrow this idea of a rising hill as a promise to the deceased Egyptian buried within the pyramid that he will emerge again into new being. As pointed out in chapter I, the concept of the creation hillock is the essential, and its location in space, whether Heliopolis or Hermopolis, was of no concern to the Egyptian.

Let us take a passage from the Book of the Dead, which states this first solitary appearance of Rē-Atum, the creator-god. The text is provided with explanatory glosses.

I am Atum when I was alone in Nūn (the primordial waters); I am Rē in his (first) appearances, when he began to rule that which he had made. What does that mean? This 'Rē when he began to rule that which he had made' means that Rē began to appear as a king, as one who existed before (the air-god) Shū had (even) lifted (heaven from earth), when he (Rē) was on the primeval hillock which was in Hermopolis.[19]

The text then goes on to emphasize the fact that the god was self-created and that he proceeded to bring into being 'the gods who are in his following.'

The Egyptian hieroglyph which means the primeval 'hillock of appearance' means also 'to appear in glory'. It shows a rounded mound with the rays of the sun streaming upward from it (☉), graphically portraying this miracle of the first appearance of the creator-god.

The text which we have cited placed the creation on a mound in the town of Hermopolis, the home of certain gods who were in being before the creation. However, that anomaly of pre-creation existence need not worry us too seriously, for the names of these gods show that they represent the formless chaos which existed before the creator-god brought order out of disorder. We should qualify the term 'chaos' slightly, as these pre-creation gods are neatly paired off into four couples, a god and a goddess for each quality of chaos. That is another example of the love of symmetry. These four pairs of gods persisted in mythology as the 'Eight' who were before the beginning. They were Nūn, the primordial waters, and his consort, Naunet, who came to be the counterheaven; Hūh, the boundless stretches of primordial formlessness, and his consort, Hauhet; Kūk, 'darkness', and his consort, Kauket; and Amūn, that is, Amon, 'the hidden', representing the intangibility and imperceptibility of chaos, with his consort, Amaunet. All this is a way of saying what the Book of Genesis says – that, before creation, 'the earth was waste and void; and darkness was upon the face of the deep.' Hūh and Amūn, boundlessness and imperceptibility, are rough parallels to the Hebrew *tohu wavohu*, 'waste and void'; while Kūk, darkness, and Nūn, the abyss, are clearly similar to the Hebrew *hoshek al-penei tehom*, 'darkness upon the face of the deep waters'. This similarity is interesting but not too alluring, because the Egyptian story and the Hebrew diverge immediately when one comes to the episodes of creation, with Egypt emphasizing the self-emergence of a creator-god, whereas the creator-god of Genesis existed alongside the chaos. You have to begin with some concept, so that primitive man everywhere would try to conceive of a formlessness before form was made. This formlessness might have much the same terms anywhere. We shall revert to the Genesis story later.

At this point we cannot pursue the other emergences of a primeval hillock in other cult centres or the implications of this thought in the beliefs and iconography of Egypt. We wish instead to plunge on to a more developed mythological phenomenon which has its importance in the creation stories.

In early times the sun-god had his own family of gods, which was also the supreme council of the gods. This group, which had its chief centre at the temple of the sun at Heliopolis, was the Ennead, 'the Nine', consisting of four inter-related couples surmounted by one common ancestor. This Ennead or 'Nine' may be placed in contrast to the 'Eight', which we have already discussed, for the 'Eight' comprised elements of cosmic disorder, whereas this 'Nine' contained only progressive steps of cosmic order: air and moisture; earth and sky; the beings on the earth. This says clearly that the creation marks the dividing-line between preceding confusion and present order. It is not implied that the creator-god conquered and annihilated the elements of chaos and set the elements of order in their place. On the contrary, it is obvious that such pre-creation gods as Nūn, the underworld waters, and Kūk, darkness, continued after the creation; but they continued in their proper place and not in universal and formless disorder. In that sense, this creation has similarities with the creation in Genesis: a separation of light from darkness and a separation of waters below from waters above.

The sun-god Atum, as he perched on the primeval hillock, was self-created; as the Egyptian puts it, he 'became, by himself'. Now the name Atum means 'everything' and it means 'nothing'. This is not as paradoxical as it sounds, for the word means 'what is finished, completed, perfected', and all these terms have their positive and their negative. 'Finis', written at the end of a book, means: 'That's all. There isn't any more.' So, too, Atum means all-inclusiveness and it means emptiness, at the beginning rather than at the end. Atum is the inchoation of all. He is like that pregnant stillness which precedes a hurricane.

There are varying accounts of the creation itself. The Book of the Dead (17) states that the sun-god created his names, as the ruler of the Ennead. This is explained as meaning that he named the parts of his body and that 'thus arose these gods who are in his following'. That is delightfully primitive and has a consistency of its own. The parts of the body have separate existence and separate character, so that they may have relation to separate deities. The name is a thing of individuality and of power; the act of speaking a new name is an act of creation. Thus we have the picture of the creator squatting on his tiny island and inventing names for eight parts of his body – or four pairs of parts – with each utterance bringing a new god into existence.

The Pyramid Texts present a different picture. Addressing Atum and recalling the occasion when the god was high upon the primeval hillock, the inscription goes on: 'Thou didst spit what was Shū; thou didst sputter out what was Tefnūt. Thou didst put thy arms about them as the arms of a *ka*, for thy *ka* was in them' (1652–53). This has the creation as a rather violent ejection of the first two gods. Perhaps it was as explosive as a sneeze, for Shū is the god of air, and his consort, Tefnūt, is the goddess of moisture. The reference to the *ka* needs explanation. We shall discuss the *ka* or other personality of an individual later. The concept of the *ka* has something of the alter ego in it and something of the guardian spirit with the protecting arms. That is why Atum puts his arms protectingly around his two children, for his *ka* was in them, an essential part of himself.

Another, more earthy, text makes the production of Shū and Tefnūt an act of self-pollution on Atum's part.[20] This is clearly an attempt to surmount the problem of generation by a god alone, without an attending goddess.

The couple Shū and Tefnūt, air and moisture, gave birth to earth and sky, the earth-god Geb and the sky-goddess Nūt. Or, according to another concept, the air-god Shū lifted and tore asunder earth and sky. Then in their turn Geb and Nūt, earth and sky, mated and produced two couples, the god Osiris and his consort Isis, the god Seth and his consort Nephthys. These represent the creatures of this world, whether human, divine, or cosmic. I shall not take time to argue the exact original significance of these four beings, as we are not precisely certain of any of them.

Atum
Shū – Tefnūt
Geb – Nūt

Osiris – Isis	Seth – Nephthys

Thus in this ruling family of the gods we have a creation story implicitly. Atum, the supercharged vacuum, separated into air and moisture. As if in the operation of the nebular hypothesis, air and moisture condensed into earth and sky. Out of earth and sky came the beings that populate the universe.

We do not here wish to go into some of the other creation stories, such as the god who was himself the 'rising land' on which the miracle took place. It is interesting that we lack a specific account of the creation of mankind, except in the most allusive way. A ram-god, Khnum, is referred to as forming mankind on his potter's wheel, or the sun-god is called the 'discoverer of mankind'.[21] But no story of separate creation of man is necessary, for a reason which we shall discuss more fully later; that reason is that there was no firm and final dividing-line between gods and men. Once a creation was started with beings, it could go on, whether the beings were gods, demi-gods, spirits, or men.

One of the texts which comments incidentally on creation states that mankind was made in the image of god. This text emphasizes the goodness of the creator-god in caring for his human creatures. 'Well tended are men, the cattle of god. He made heaven and earth according to their desire, and he repelled the water monster (at creation). He made the breath (of) life (for) their nostrils. They are his images that have issued from his body. He arises in heaven according to their desire. He made for them plants and animals, fowl and fish, in order to nourish them. He slew his enemies and destroyed (even) his (own) children when they plotted rebellion (against him).'[22] The text is interesting and unusual in making the purposes of creation the interests of humans; normally the myth recounts the steps of creation without indication of purpose. But this particular text happens to have strong moral purpose. Note, for example, the reference to the god's destroying mankind when they rebelled against him. We shall return to this remote parallel to the biblical Flood story in the next chapter.

We must examine at length one final document bearing on the creation. This is an inscription called the Memphite Theology, a context so strange and different from the material we have been discussing that it seems, at first glance, to come from another world. And yet closer examination assures us that the difference is a matter of degree and not of kind, because all the strange elements in the text of the Memphite Theology were present in other Egyptian texts in isolated instances; only in this text were they brought together into a broad philosophical system about the nature of the universe.

The document in question is a battered stone in the British Museum, bearing the name of an Egyptian pharaoh who ruled about 700 B.C.[23] However, this pharaoh claimed that he had simply copied an inscription of the ancestors, and his claim is borne out by the language and typically early physical arrangement of the text. We are dealing with a document which comes from the very beginning of Egyptian history, from the time when the first dynasties made their new capital at Memphis, the city of the god Ptah. Now, Memphis as the centre of a theocratic state was an upstart; it had had no national importance before. To make matters worse, Heliopolis, a traditional religious capital of Egypt, the home of the sun-god Rē and of the creator-god Rē-Atum, was only twenty-five miles from Memphis. It was necessary to justify a new location of the centre of the world. The text in question is part of a theological argument of the primacy of the god Ptah and thus of his home, Memphis.

The creation texts which we have discussed earlier have been more strictly in physical terms: the god separating earth from sky or giving birth to air and moisture. This new text turns as far as the Egyptian could turn toward a creation in philosophical terms: the thought which came into the heart of a god and the commanding utterance which brought that thought into reality. This creation by thought conception and speech delivery has its experiential background in human life: the authority of a ruler to create by command. But only the use of physical terms such as 'heart' for thought and 'tongue' for command relate the Memphite Theology to the more earthy texts which we have been considering. Here, as Professor Breasted has pointed out, we come close to the background of the Logos doctrine of the New Testament: 'In the beginning was the Word, and the Word was with God, and the Word was God.'

Before undertaking this difficult text itself, we should lay out for ourselves the known factors that play into the interpretation of the text. First, the Memphite text takes off from the creation stories which I have already recounted: Atum coming into being out of Nūn, the primeval waters, and Atum bringing his Ennead of gods into existence. The Memphite text is aware that these were prevailing concepts in Egypt. In place of discarding them as competitive, it wishes to subsume them into a higher philosophy, to take advantage of them by pointing out that they belong to a higher system.

That higher system employs *invention* by the cognition of an idea in the mind and *production* through the utterance of a creating order by speech. Now thought and speech are ancient attributes of power in Egypt, personified as deities in our earliest literature. They occur normally as a pair of related attributes of the sun-god: Hū, 'authoritative utterance', that speech which is so effective that it creates, and Sia, 'perception', the cognitive reception of a situation, an object, or an idea. Hū and Sia were attributes that carried governing authority. In the Pyramid Texts the ruling god leaves his shrine and surrenders his office to the deceased king, because the latter 'has captured Hū, has control of Sia' (300). In our Memphite text these two attributes of power are taken in material terms: the heart is the organ which conceives thought, and the tongue is the organ which creates the conceived thought as a phenomenal actuality. All this is credited to the activity of the Memphite god Ptah, who is himself thought and speech in every heart and on every tongue, and thus was the first creative principle, just as he remains now.

The part of the text in which we are interested begins by equating Ptah with Nūn, the primeval waters out of which came Atum, the normally accepted creator-god. This in itself makes Ptah antecedent to the sun-god, and that priority occurs in passing references in other texts. But our text does not leave the priority implicit; it states the mechanism by which Ptah produced Atum.

'Ptah, the Great One; he is the heart and tongue of the Ennead of gods ... who begot the gods ... There came into being in the heart, and there came into being on the tongue (something) in the form of Atum.' This is the invention and production of Atum. Out of nothing, there came into existence the idea of an Atum, of a creator-god. That idea 'became, in the heart' of the divine world, which heart or mind was Ptah himself; then that idea 'became, upon the tongue' of the divine world, which tongue or speech was Ptah himself. The Egyptian uses pictorial, physical language; it says elliptically: 'in-the-form-of-Atum became, in the heart, and became, on the tongue', but there is no question of the meaning. Conception and parturition reside in these terms.

But Ptah's creative power does not stop with the production of the traditional creator-god. 'Great and mighty is Ptah, who has transmitted (power to all gods), as well as their spirits, through this (activity of the) heart and this (activity of the) tongue.' Nor does the creative principle stop with the gods. 'It has come to pass that the heart and tongue control (every) member (of the body) by teaching that he (Ptah) is throughout every body (in the form of the heart) and throughout every mouth (in the form of the tongue), of all gods, of all men, of (all) animals, of all creeping things, and of what (ever) lives, by (Ptah's) thinking (as the heart) and commanding (as the tongue) anything that he wishes.' In other words, we have no single miracle of thought conception and articulation, but the same principles of creation which were valid in the primeval waters to bring forth Atum are still valid and operative. Wherever there is thought and command, there Ptah still creates.

The text even draws an invidious distinction between the traditional creation by which Atum brought forth Shū and Tefnūt and that creation whereby Ptah spoke Shū and Tefnūt and thus brought them into being. Ptah's teeth and lips are the articulating organs of the productive speech. As we mentioned earlier, one version of the Atum story makes Shū and Tefnūt products of the self-pollution of the creator-god. Thus teeth and lips in the case of Ptah are brought into parallelism with the semen and hands of Atum. To our modern prejudice, this makes the Ptah creation a nobler activity; but it is not certain that the ancient meant to belittle the more physical story. Perhaps he was simply expressing the correspondence of alternative myths when he said: 'Now the Ennead of Atum came into being from his seed and by his fingers; but the Ennead (of Ptah) is the teeth and the lips in this mouth which uttered the name of everything and (thus) Shū and Tefnūt came forth from it.' We have already seen how the utterance of a name is in itself an act of creation.

That text goes on to specify in detail the products of the activity of the conceptive heart and creative tongue, without adding anything essentially new. It explains the mechanistic relation of the various senses to the heart and tongue by stating that the function of the sight of the eyes, the hearing of the ears, and the smelling of the nose is to report to the heart. On the basis of this sensory information, the heart releases 'everything which is completed', that is, every established concept, and then 'it is the tongue which announces what the heart thinks'.

Then the text summarizes the range of this creative power of Ptah as heart and tongue. Thus were the gods born; thus came into being all of the divine order; thus were made the directive destinies which supply mankind with food and provisions; thus was made the distinction between right and wrong; thus were made all arts, crafts, and human activities; thus Ptah made provinces and cities and set the various local gods in their governing places. Finally: 'Thus it was discovered and understood that his (Ptah's) power is greater than (that of the other) gods. And so Ptah rested after he had made everything, as well as the divine order'. Admittedly the word 'rested' introduces a parallel to the Genesis story of God's resting on the seventh day. The translation 'rested' is defensible, but it is probably safer to render: 'And so Ptah was satisfied, after he had made everything'.

It is clear that there is some special pleading in this text, the attempt of an upstart theology to establish itself as national and universal against older, traditional ways of thinking. That comes out in a quotation which we have just given, which might be paraphrased: For these reasons, all right-thinking men have come to the conclusion that Ptah is the most powerful of all gods. Undoubtedly that special interest does lie in this text, but that fact need not concern us much. As we have said, the Memphite Theology did not wish to conquer and annihilate the theology of Heliopolis but to conquer and assimilate it. And, after all, we are more interested in the possibility of a developed speculative thought as given in this text than in any controversy between two important shrines.

Perhaps it would be better to call our rendering of the words 'the word of the god' by 'the divine order' a free paraphrase. But we should still justify it. 'The word of the god' can and does mean 'concern of the gods' or what we might call 'divine interests'. But the phrase 'the divine order' implies that the gods have a system into which all the created elements should fit as soon as created. The context enumerates the created elements: gods, fortunes, food, provisions, towns, districts, etc. These are summed up in the term 'everything', after which we have 'as well as the word of the god'. What can this mean other than the directive order?

One can argue this same sense in other Egyptian contexts. For example, an assertion that the righteous man is not wiped out by death but has an immortality because of his goodly memory is indorsed with the words: 'That is the method of reckoning of the word of god'; in freer sense: 'That is the principle of the divine order'.[24]

Because the Egyptians thought of the word in physical, concrete terms and because the priesthood was the interpreter of what was divine, this 'word of god' came to be treated as a body of literature, the sacred writings, but it was still the directive speech given by the gods. A dead noble was promised 'every good and pure thing, in conformance to that writing of the word of god which (the god of wisdom) Thoth made.'[25] In another passage one scribe chides another for the impious presumption of his boasting: 'I am astonished when thou sayest: "I am more profound as a scribe than heaven, or earth, or the underworld!" ... The house of books is concealed and invisible; the council of its gods is hidden and distant. ... Thus I answer thee: "Beware lest thy fingers approach the word of god!"'[26] What the gods have said is in itself directive and controlling; it sets an order within which man and the other elements of the universe operate.

Thus the 'word of the god' is nothing so simple in these contexts as 'divine writing' or hieroglyphic. It is the word or concern or business of the gods which applies to the elements which the gods have created. Not only were material elements created, but there was created for them a 'word', which applied to them and which put them into their appropriate places in the god's scheme of things. Creation was not the irresponsible production of oddly assorted pieces, which might be shaken down in a vast impersonal lottery wheel. Creation was accompanied and directed by a word which expressed some kind of a divine order in order to comprehend the created elements.

In summary, the ancient Egyptian was self-conscious about himself and his universe; he produced a cosmos in terms of his own observation and his own experience. Like the Nile Valley, this cosmos had limited space but reassuring periodicity; its structural framework and mechanics permitted the reiteration of life through the rebirth of life-giving elements. The creation stories of the ancient Egyptian were also in terms of his own experience, although they bear loose general similarity to other creation stories. The most interesting advance lies in a very early attempt to relate creation to the processes of thought and speech rather than to mere physical activity. Even this 'higher' philosophy is given in pictorial terms arising out of Egyptian experience.

NOTES

1. Champollion, *Mon.*, 238–40.
2. Admon., 3:1; 1:9.
3. Wenamon, 2:19–22.
4. Aton Hymn, 3.
5. Tombos, l. 13.
6. Aton Hymn, 9–10.
7. Anast. I, 19:2–4; 24:1–4.
8. Merikarē, 91–98.
9. Med. Habu II, 83, ll. 57–8.
10. Louvre, C 14, 8–10.
11. Urk. IV, 329.
12. *Ibid.*, 373.
13. Aton Hymn, 3–6.
14. Aton Hymn, 5.
15. BD, Introductory Hymn.
16. Urk. IV, 612.
17. *Ibid.*, 183, 843.
18. *Encyclopaedia Britannica* (11th ed.).
19. Urk. V, 6=BD, 17.
20. Pyr. 1248.
21. In Beatty I, p. 24.
22. Merikarē, 130–4.
23. Kurt Sethe, *Dramatische Texte zu altägyptischen Mysterienspielen.*
24. Peasant, B1, 307–11.
25. Cairo 28085; Lacau, *Sarc. ant.*, p. 206.
26. Anast. I, 11:4–7.

CHAPTER III

Egypt: The Function of The State

THE UNIVERSE AND THE STATE

THE FIRST two chapters have attempted to establish the attitude of mind with which ancient man viewed the world around him. Before moving directly to a consideration of the state and its place in the Egyptian scene, we should consider two questions which provide a setting for that consideration. Did the ancient Egyptian see an essential difference in substance between men, society, the gods, plants, animals, and the physical universe? Did he believe the universe to be benevolent, hostile, or indifferent to him? These questions have bearing on the relation of the state to the universe and on the functioning of the state for the benefit of man.

Let us take first the question about difference of substance among men, gods, and other elements of the universe. This problem has vexed Christian theologians for centuries. We can give only a personal answer with reference to ancient Egypt. To be sure, a man seems to be one thing, and the sky or a tree seems to be another. But to the ancient Egyptian such concepts had a protean and complementary nature. The sky might be thought of as a material vault above earth, or as a cow, or as a female. A tree might be a tree or the female who was the tree-goddess. Truth might be treated as an abstract concept, or as a goddess, or as a divine hero who once lived on earth. A god might be depicted as a man, or as a falcon, or as a falcon-headed man. In one context the king is described as the sun, a star, a bull, a crocodile, a lion, a falcon, a jackal, and the two tutelary gods of Egypt – not so much in simile as in vital essence.[1] There was thus a continuing substance across the phenomena of the universe, whether organic, inorganic, or abstract. It is not a matter of black being antipodal to white but rather that the universe is a spectrum in which one colour blends off into another without line of demarcation, in which, indeed, one colour may become another under alternating conditions.

We wish to argue this point further. Our line of argument will be that to the ancient Egyptian the elements of the universe were consubstantial. If that be true, the terms which he knew best – human behaviour – would be the frame of reference for non-human phenomena. It would then be idle to argue whether the universe, or the gods of the universe, were believed to be benevolent, malevolent, or indifferent. They would be just like humans: benevolent when they were benevolent, malevolent when malevolent, and indifferent when indifferent. To put it in active terms, they would be benevolent when benevolence was their stated business and malevolent when malevolence was their stated business. That conclusion would have relation to the business of the state and the forces responsible for the state.

The first claim for the argument that the elements of the universe were of one substance is in the principle of free substitution, interchange, or representation. It was very easy for one element to take the place of another. The deceased wanted bread, so that he might not be hungry in the next world. He made contractual arrangements whereby loaves of bread were presented regularly at his tomb, so that his spirit might return and eat of the bread. But he was aware of the transitory nature of contracts and of the greed of hired servants. He supported his needs by other forms of bread. A model loaf made of wood and left in the tomb would be an adequate representative of an actual loaf. The picture of loaves of bread on the tomb wall would continue to feed the deceased by representation. If other means of presentation were lacking, the word 'bread', spoken or written with reference to his nourishment, might be an effective substitute. This is an easy concept: the physical man was formerly here; now the spiritual man is over there; we must project over to him spiritual, not physical, bread, so that the absolute is not necessary; the name or the idea or the representation will be enough.

Let us carry representation into another area. A god represented something important in the universe: the sky, a district of Egypt, or kingship. In terms of his function that god had extensiveness and intangibility. But he might have a localization in our world, in a place where he might feel at home; that is, a shrine might be specified for him. In that shrine he might have a place of manifestation in an image. This image was not the god; it was merely a mechanism of stone or wood or metal to permit him to make an appearance. This is stated by the Egyptians in one of the creation accounts. The creator-god acted for the other gods, and 'he made their bodies like that with which their hearts were satisfied. So the gods entered into their bodies of every (kind of) wood, of every (kind of) stone, or every (kind of) clay ... in which they had taken form.'[2] These images were provided for them so that they might have places in which to take visible form. Thus the god Amon might be at home in a stone statue of human form, in a specially selected ram, or in a specially selected gander. He remained himself and did not become identical with this form of appearance, and yet he had a different form of appearance for a different purpose, just as humans might maintain different homes or might have different garments.

Of course, we rationalize the image or the sacred animal as being an empty shell of divinity unless divinity were manifest in the shell. However, in another sense the image or the animal was a representative of divinity or was divinity itself. I mean that divinity would be present in his place of manifestation whenever his business placed him there, and his business placed him there when the act of worship before the image called him into residence. So that the image did act for and as the god whenever the worshipper addressed himself to the image. In that sense, the image was the god *for all working purposes*.

There were other substitutes for the gods. The king of Egypt was himself one of the gods and was the land's representative among the gods. Furthermore, he was the one official intermediary between the people and the gods, the one recognized priest of all the gods. Endowed with divinity, the pharaoh had the protean character of divinity; he could merge with his fellow-gods and could become any one of them. In part this was symbolic, the acting of a part in religious drama or the simile of praise. But the Egyptian did not distinguish between symbolism and participation; if he said that the king was Horus, he did not mean that the king was playing the part of Horus, he meant that the king *was* Horus, that the god was effectively present in the king's body during the particular activity in question.

How can the king be the god-king unless the god-king is present in him, so that the two become one? A single text magnifying the king equates him with a series of deities: 'He is Sia,' the god of perception; 'he is Rē', the sun-god; 'he is Khnum', the god who brings mankind into being on his potter's wheel; 'he is Bastet', the goddess who protects; and 'he is Sekhmet', the goddess who punishes.[3] Understanding, supreme rule, building-up of the populace, protection, and punishment were all attributes of the king; the king *was* each of them; each of these attributes was manifest in a god or goddess; the king *was* each of these gods or goddesses.

Carrying the principle of substitution one step further, if the king could represent a god, it is also true that the king could be represented by a man. The business of kingship was too detailed for absolute rule by a single individual so that certain responsibilities must be deputized, even though state dogma said that the king did all. Similarly, state dogma might insist that the king was the sole priest for all the gods; but it was impossible for him to function every day in all the temples; that activity must also be deputized. Here we must admit that there is some difference of representation; the priest or official acted *for* the king, not *as* the king. It was deputizing rather than participating in the nature of the other being. This is an acknowledged difference, but even this difference is not absolute. Those who act in the place of another share somewhat in the personality of that other. Simply the physical grouping of the tombs of Old Kingdom courtiers around the pyramid of pharaoh shows that they wished to share in his divine glory by belonging to him and thus participating in him. Even here they belonged to some portion of the same spectrum and had an ultimate consubstantiality with him, which was partially derived and partially innate. Between god and man there was no point at which one could erect a boundary line and state that here substance changed from divine, superhuman, immortal, to mundane, human, mortal.

The fluidity of Egyptian concepts and the tendency to synthesize divergent elements have led some Egyptologists to believe that the Egyptians were really monotheistic, that all gods were subsumed into a single god. In a moment we shall present a text that would seem to be a prime document for this thesis of essential monotheism, but we wish to preface it by insisting that it is not a matter of single god but of single nature of observed phenomena in the universe, with the clear possibility of exchange and substitution. With relation to gods and men the Egyptians were monophysites: many men and many gods, but all ultimately of one nature.

The text that we mentioned presents an ancient Egyptian trinity: the three gods who were supremely important at one period of history all taken up into a single divinity. The purpose was to enlarge the god Amon by incorporating the other two gods into his being. 'All gods are three – Amon, Rē, and Ptah – and they have no second'. Amon is the name of this single being, Rē is his head, and Ptah is his body. 'Only he is: Amon and Rē (and Ptah), together three.'[4] Three gods are one, and yet the Egyptian elsewhere insists on the separate identity of each of the three.

In another group of hymns which has been called monotheistic[5] the god is addressed as a single personage of composite form, Amon-Rē-Atum-Harakhte, that is, the several sun-, supreme-, and national-gods rolled up into one. The text goes on to break this being down into his several facets as Amon, Rē, Atum, Horus, and Harakhte, and also to equate him with Kherpri, Shū, the moon, and the Nile. Whether this is monotheistic or not depends upon one's definition. It may be hairsplitting, but we prefer to invoke the principles of consubstantiality and free interchange of being and claim that the Egyptians were monophysite instead of monotheistic. They recognized different beings but felt those beings to be of a single essential substance, a rainbow, in which certain colours were dominant under certain conditions and others dominant when the conditions altered. A complete personality includes many different aspects of personality.

One element of consubstantiality lies in the fact that the Egyptian gods were very human, with human weaknesses and varying moods. They could not remain on a high and consistent plane of infallibility. And no god was single-mindedly devoted to a single function. For example, the god Seth is well known as the enemy of the 'good' gods Osiris and Horus; therefore, Seth was the enemy of good; he was roughly like the devil. Yet throughout Egyptian history Seth appeared also as a good god, who functioned beneficently for the dead at times, who fought on behalf of the sun-god, and who acted positively for the enlargement of the Egyptian state. Horus, the good son throughout Egyptian history, once flew into a rage at his mother Isis and chopped off her head, so that the poor goddess was forced to take the form of a headless statue.[6]

The Egyptians apparently delighted in the humanness of their gods. A well-known story tells how Rē, the creator-god, repented that he had created mankind, which had devised evil against him. He decided to destroy them and sent Sekhmet, the 'Powerful', against them. This goddess slew mankind, waded in their blood, and exulted in their destruction. Then Rē relented and regretted his desire to obliterate. Instead of ordering Sekhmet to stop the slaughter, he resorted to a stratagem. Seven thousand jars of red-coloured beer were poured out in Sekhmet's path, so that she might believe that it was blood. She waded lustily into it, became drunken, and stopped her slaughtering.[7]

This childish tale, so different from the biblical story of the Flood because of its lack of moral motivation, is told here only to emphasize the frequent littleness of the Egyptian gods. They changed their minds, and they resorted to tricks to accomplish their ends. And yet – in a neighbouring text – they may be portrayed as noble and consistent.

Another, more sophisticated story tells of a trial in the divine tribunal. A minor deity rose and shouted an insult at the supreme, presiding god; he cried ' "Thy shrine is empty!" Then

Rē-Harakhte was pained at this retort which had been made to him, and he lay down on his back, and his heart was very, very sore. Then the Ennead went out ... to their tents. And so the great god spent a day lying on his back in his arbour, alone, while his heart was very, very sore.' In order to cure his sulks, the other gods sent the goddess of love to him, and she exhibited to him her charms. 'Then the great god laughed at her; and so he arose and sat down (again) with the great Ennead,' and the trial was resumed.[8] This is admittedly a lusty tale for entertainment, but its characterization of the gods accords with the picture given in more sober contexts.

If the gods were so human, it will not be surprising that humans could address them in brusque terms. Not infrequently there are texts in which the worshipper recalls the nature of his services to the gods and threatens those gods who fail to return service for service. One of the famous passages in Egyptian literature is called the 'Cannibal Hymn', because the deceased expresses his intention of devouring those whom he meets in his path, human or divine. It was originally written for the deceased king but was later taken over by commoners. 'The sky is overcast, the stars are beclouded ... the (very) bones of the earth-god tremble ... when they see (this dead man) appear animated as a god who lives on his fathers and feeds on his mothers .... (He) is the one who eats men and lives on gods. ... (He) is the one who eats their magic and devours their glory. The biggest of them are for his breakfast; their middle-sized are for his dinner; and the smallest of them are for his supper. Their old males and females (serve only) for his fuel.'[9]

The effective continuation of that concept is that any human might become so magically potent that he could consume the greatest of the gods and, by consuming them, take their magic and their glory into his own being. That is the ultimate statement of consubstantiality from highest to lowest in the universe. It may sound childish, like the mighty imaginings of a small boy who dreams of becoming Superman and conquering the world. But the small boy is not yet grown up, and it is not beyond the range of his dreams for his future that he may be incredibly great some day. The same range of possibility was present for the Egyptian through the single substance which extended from him up into the vast unknown.

This statement which we are making about the single substance of the Egyptian universe is true of the earlier long period of Egyptian thinking, down to perhaps 1300 B.C. Involved in this concept of consubstantiality is the feeling that there is no ultimate difference between men and gods. It is necessary to make a reservation, however, about the later period of Egyptian history. As shall be seen in the next chapter, there came a time when a gulf developed between weak, little man, and powerful god. In that later period a difference was felt, and the two were no longer of the same substance. For the present, however, we do not wish to stress the later change but rather the earlier unity.

Indeed, the more one examines this hypothesis of consubstantiality, the more exceptions or qualifications one must admit. We gave one in the last chapter when we said that the Egyptians did not accept foreigners as being like themselves. We shall give another later in this chapter, when we point out a difference in administrative freedom between the king, who was a god, and his ministers, who were humans. It is a question whether one is talking about difference qualitatively (difference of substance) or quantitatively (variations of the same substance). We take it to be a quantitative difference of the same substance. In contrast to ourselves and to other peoples, the Egyptians took the universe as being of one continuous substance, without any definite line of demarcation between part and part.

To return, then, to the question about the disposition of the universe towards the Egyptian, whether friendly, hostile, or indifferent. Since there is but one substance reaching from man off into the unknowns, the world of the dead, the world of gods and spirits, the world of organic and inorganic nature, this means that the frame of reference must be human behaviour itself. Are other men friendly, hostile, or indifferent to us? The answer must be that they are not exclusively any of these three dispositions but that interested beings are benevolent or mal-evolent, according to whether their interests are complementary or competitive, and uninterested beings are indifferent. It becomes a matter of the stated concern of the force in question, as well as the particular disposition of the force at a stated time. The sun gives life by warming; but it may destroy life by blasting, or it may destroy life by withdrawing itself and chilling. The Nile brings life, but an unusually low or an unusually high Nile may bring destruction and death.

The modern Egyptian feels himself to be surrounded by unseen personalized forces, the *ginn*, each of them concerned with some phenomenon: a child, a sheep, a house, a tree, running water, fire, etc. Some are friendly, some unfriendly; but most are static unless one offends them, when they become malevolent, or unless one invokes them to benevolence. The ancient Egyptian had a similar sense of a surrounding world of forces. A mother had to croon a protective song over her sleeping child: 'Thou flowing thing that comes in darkness and enters furtively in, with her nose behind her and her face twisted around, who fails in that for which she came – hast thou come to kiss this child? I will not let thee kiss him! Hast thou come to strike dumb? I will not let thee strike dumbness into him! Hast thou come to injure him? I will not let thee injure him! Hast thou come to carry him away? I will not let thee carry him away from me! I have made his magical protection against thee out of clover ... onions ... honey. ...'[10] In an incantation against disease, the malevolent forces which may bring sickness include 'every blessed male, every blessed female, every dead male, and every dead female', that is, the dead who have attained a state of eternal glory, as well as those who have died without certainty of immortality.[11]

However, despite this surrounding world of uncertain spiritual forces, the general rule was that certain beings had a stated function or activity, and that activity was either friendly or hostile. Thus the generally beneficent functions of the sun, the Nile, the north wind, Osiris, or Isis were established; just as the generally dangerous or hostile functions of the Apōphis-demon, Seth, or Sekhmet were established. These functions were general, and at times it might be necessary to protect an individual from the 'good' Osiris or to entrust an individual to the helpful activity of the 'bad' Seth, just as humans in this world have more than one side to their characters.

If this functional authority and responsibility are clear, then we must seek our answer to the functions of the state in those forces which had authority over and responsibility for the state. The speculative thought of the ancient Egyptians will provide no treatise on the philosophy of statecraft or the relation of government to the governed, but their speculative thought will play upon the powers, attributes, and interests of those gods who were primarily concerned with Egypt as a going concern. Ultimately our attention focuses on statements concerning the 'good god' who was king of Egypt. We can best discover the functions of the state by determining the ideals laid down in scattered sources for the one individual responsible for government – the king.

THE KING

The Egyptian's love of symmetrical balance produced an ideal ruler who was nicely composed of graciousness and terror, because rule is nurture and rule is control. Again and again this balance appears in close juxtaposition in the texts. The king is 'that beneficent god, the fear of whom is throughout the countries like (the fear of) Sekhmet in a year of plague'.[12] Poems of praise emphasize the two aspects of his being with bewilderingly sudden shifts of emphasis: 'Exulting is he, a smasher of foreheads, so that none can stand near him. ... He fights without end, he spares not, and there is nothing left over (from his destruction). He is a master of graciousness, rich in sweetness, and he conquers by love. His city loves him more than its own self and takes more joy in him than in its (own local) god.'[13] Here, in two adjacent statements, it is claimed that the king conquers by lustful destruction and that he conquers by kindly love. We are again dealing with a personality of more than one side, a spectrum in which one colour or another may be emphasized. But here speculative thought has its reasons in producing a balance of forces. Government must be gracious but terrible, just as the sun and the Nile are gracious but terrible in their effective power.

The starting-point of our consideration is the fact that the king of Egypt was a god and that he was a god for the purposes of the Egyptian state. This was not stated in a nice compact formulation which made the pharaoh the personification of the land of Egypt or even embodied rule as a personified principle. But the supreme god, Rē, entrusted the land to his son, the king. From the Old Kingdom on, an effective title for the Egyptian pharaoh was the 'Son of Rē'. In mythology the only son of Rē was the air-god Shū, but the pharaoh was made Son of Rē for the specific purpose of ruling Rē's chief concern, the land of Egypt. 'As for Egypt, men say since (the time of) the gods, she is the only daughter of Rē, and it is his son that is upon the throne of Shū.'[14] Implicit in this statement there was a pairing of god and goddess, Egypt as the only daughter of Rē and pharaoh as the Son of Rē, in those brother-sister terms which made up the couples of Egyptian dieties. Just as the husband was urged by the books of wisdom to take kindly care of the wife, because 'she is a field advantageous to her lord',[15] so the king had ownership, authority, and responsibility over his land. It was his to control with power, but if he were wise, he would also nurture with care.

The Egyptian stated repeatedly that the king was the physical son who issued from the body of the sun-god Rē. To be sure, it was recognized that he had been born of a woman in this world. But the father who had begotten him was definitely a god. Rē himself had to ensure the proper divine rule of the land of Egypt. Looking toward the future, he made earthly visits to produce rulers. A story about the origin of the Fifth Dynasty tells of the humble mother of the coming rulers. 'She is the wife of an (ordinary) priest of Rē, Lord of Sakhebu, who is pregnant with three children of Rē, Lord of Sakhebu, and he (Rē) has said of them that they shall exercise this beneficent office (of king) in this entire land.'[16]

Even the problem of the earthly father, in view of the fact that kings did exist and apparently did produce sons who became kings, was not insurmountable. For purposes of procreation the supreme god assumed the form of the living king and gave that seed which was to become the 'Son of Rē'. Hatshepsūt was clearly the daughter of Thutmose I, but the account of that divine birth which permitted her to become pharaoh of Egypt makes it clear that there was a substitution here, and that the supreme god, Amon-Rē, was her effective father. The queen-mother was selected by the gods, and it was recommended that Amon visit her while the pharaoh was still in his youthful vigour. '(Amon took) his form (as) the majesty (of) this her husband, the King (Thutmose I). ... Then he went to her immediately; then he had intercourse with her. ... The majesty of this god did all that he desired with her. The words which Amon, Lord of the Thrones of the Two Lands, spoke in her presence: "Now Khenemet-Amon-Hatshepsūt is the name of this my daughter whom I have placed in thy body. ... She is to exercise this benefi(cent king)ship in this entire land.'"[17] No words could more explicitly state the divine purposes and divine methods. The pharaoh was produced by the supreme deity, masquerading as the ruling king, to be a god in order to rule the land.

In this solar theology the king of Egypt issued out of the body of the sun-god and, on death, returned to the body of his progenitor. Here is the statement of the death of a pharaoh: 'Year 30, third month of the first season, day 9: the god entered his horizon. The King of Upper and Lower Egypt, Sehetepibrē, went up to heaven and was united with the sun-disc, so that the divine body was merged with him who made him.'[18] This is the necessary completion of filial attachment to the supreme god: from conception through life to the final triumph over death, the king was the 'Son of Rē'. As we shall see, an alternative system of thought made the dead king Osiris, ruler of the realm of the dead.

The formal list of titles which denominated the king of Egypt breaks into three groups. We have already seen that he was called the son and successor of the sun-god; we shall shortly discuss his identification with the god Horus; we shall now consider him as incorporating the responsibilities for the two parts of Egypt.

Physically and culturally the land of Egypt breaks into the narrow trough of the Nile Valley and the spreading Delta.

Upper Egypt has ties to the desert and to Africa; Lower Egypt faces out to the Mediterranean Sea and to Asia. From time immemorial these two regions have had a self-conscious separation. Lying so close together and yet apart from neighbours, they are aware of their differences. The old texts bring out this feeling of contrast. One who had impulsively left his office expressed his bewilderment over the forces that had led him to such unaccountable action: 'I do not know what sundered me from my place; it was like a dream, as if a man of the Delta were (suddenly) to see himself in Elephantine.'[19] Just as today, the dialects of these two regions varied enough to cause misunderstanding. An inept writer was chided with these words: 'Thy narratives ... are confused when heard, and there is no interpreter who can unravel them; they are like the speech of a man of the Delta with a man of Elephantine.'[20] These two regions were then disparate, and they were traditionally and continuingly competitive. Yet they were a unity in their isolation from the rest of the world, and they were a unity in their dependence upon the Nile. It was a function of government to make Upper and Lower Egypt an effective single nation. This was done by incorporating authority and responsibility for both regions in a single figure, the god-king.

By his formal titles he was Lord of the Two Lands, that is, owner and master; he was King of Upper Egypt and King of Lower Egypt, the wearer of the double crown which symbolized the union of the two regions; and he was the 'Two Ladies', that is, the incorporation of the two tutelary goddesses who represented the north and the south. A parallel title, the 'Two Lords', expressed the dogma that the two competing gods of Lower and Upper Egypt, Horus and Seth, were also physically resident and reconciled within the person of the king. An important ritual activity of the king's coronation was the 'Uniting of the Two Lands', a ceremony somehow in relation to the throne of a dual kingship.

Now this self-consciousness about two different parts of the land was expressed administratively in a duality of office and officers. There were two viziers, two treasurers, and often two capitals. There had to be a recognition of the separate needs of the two areas, a sort of states' rights in administration. But the two lands had no final rule except in the single person of the pharaoh, who partook of the divinity of each area in exactly balanced measure. This worked. In all stable periods of Egyptian history there was only one king of the united Two Lands. The god-king was a successful expression of national unity.

The third group of formal titles for the pharaoh makes him the incorporation of the god Horus, a falcon whose divine province was the heavens. As in the case of the other two types of titles, the 'Son of Rē', and the embodiment of the deities of the Two Lands, the identification with Horus seems to have made the pharaoh the king of all Egypt. We are not precisely sure how this came to be. It is true that the myths indicate that Horus contested for and won the rule of his dead father, the god Osiris. Thus Horus came to be the living king who had succeeded the dead king, Osiris. Every living king was Horus, and every dead king Osiris. But we moderns would like to reconcile the idea of the kingly Horus as son and successor of Osiris and the idea of the 'Son of Rē', as kingly successor of the sun-god. In consecutive lines of a single text the pharaoh is called the son of Osiris, who issued from the body of Isis, and it is stated that Rē begot his majesty.[21]

Perhaps again we should not seek to sunder ideas which were complementary and thus gave added strength to the throne. Probably we have concentration on two different aspects of the divinity of the pharaoh. The title 'Son of Rē' emphasized the story of his physical birth as a god, whereas the title 'Horus' emphasized his divine credentials to rule in the palace, as the god who had been awarded the kingship by the divine tribunal. At any rate, Horus ruled the entire land and not simply a part. All the titles taught that there was but one being who could hold sway over all Egypt by divine right.

The divine person of the pharaoh was too holy for direct approach. An ordinary mortal did not speak 'to' the king; he spoke 'in the presence of' the king. Various circumlocutions were employed to avoid direct reference to the king: 'May thy majesty hear', instead of 'mayest thou hear', and 'one gave command', instead of 'he gave command'. One of these circumlocutions, *per-aa*, 'the Great House', gave rise to our word 'pharaoh', in somewhat the same way as we modernly say: 'The White House today announced. ...'

It is not clear that this avoidance of verbal contact with awful majesty was paralleled by an avoidance of physical contact with the royal person. To be sure, there is a somewhat obscure tale about a courtier who was touched by the king's ceremonial staff, after which the king gave him firm assurances that he was to suffer no hurt thereby. The mere bumping with a stick is not enough to justify the magnification of the tale into something worth carving on a tomb wall. Arguably the blight of majesty was so terrible that it had to be exorcised by royal words.[22] Possibly we personally over-value this text, as it has been pointed out to us that the king's assurances may be rather an apology than the exorcising of a blight. A royal apology might be a sufficient mark of attention to warrant recording in a tomb.

A similar uncertainty clouds the next example. A late story has a rather puzzling joke. The shadow of the sunshade of a foreign prince fell upon an Egyptian, and there was an ironic warning to the Egyptian to beware, for the shadow of the pharaoh of Egypt had touched him. This sounds as though an intimate part of the royal person like the shadow was too fraught with holiness for human approach.[23] If so, the body of the king will also have been dangerous for the ordinary mortal. But the pharaoh certainly had his personal attendants and body servants, and there must have been means of delivering them from the blight of majesty. The first principle is surely that of Diodorus (i. 70), that the royal servants were selected from the highest classes, close to the king in blood. The second principle will have been that the other gods had their personal attendants, who cared for their most intimate needs, and so the divine king could also have his priestly servants, authorized to act for his person and thus not to be blasted by contact with a god. It is significant that the same epithet, 'pure of hands', was used for the priests who served the gods and for the personal attendants on the king.

As our evidence on the physical unapproachability of the pharaoh is weak, we wish to adduce a few additional points, none of which clinches the case. Certain individuals were granted close access to the king and exempt from any blight of holiness. This was probably implicit in such titles as 'Sole Companion', 'Privy Councillor of the House of the Morning', 'He Who Is Beside the King' (literally, 'under the head of the King'). Some favoured individuals were graciously permitted to kiss the royal foot, instead of kissing the ground before the pharaoh (Urk. I, 41; 53; BAR, I, 260). The uraeus-serpent on the brow of the king was a fire-spitting sorceress, who protected the royal person from any approach of unauthorized persons. Whether these instances fall short of a dogma of unapproachability or not is an open question to us.

Just as the person of the king arguably had a dangerously high voltage, so also his lofty responsibilities involved knowledge and abilities beyond the ken of ordinary man. As one of his chief ministers said: 'Now his majesty knows what takes place. There is nothing at all which he does not know. He is (the god of wisdom) Thoth in everything: there is no subject which he has not comprehended.'[24] Or his grovelling courtiers told him: 'Thou art like Rē in all that thou doest. What thy heart desires flows forth. If thou desirest a plan in the night, at dawn it comes into being quickly. We have seen a multitude of thy marvels since thou didst appear as King of the Two Lands. We cannot hear, nor can our eyes see (how it happens); yet (things) come into being everywhere.'[25] This was superhuman: it was the closely guarded secret of kingship. At a time when the state was overthrown and rule crumbled into anarchy, it was thought to be the release of this 'secret' that permitted the impious fragmentation of divine rule: 'Behold, it has come to (a point where) the land is stripped of the kingship by a few irresponsible people. ... Behold, the secret of the land, whose limits are unknown, is divulged, so that the (royal) residence is overthrown in an hour ... The secrets of the kings of Upper and Lower Egypt have been divulged.'[26]

We cold modern analysts view the doctrines of the divinity, the blighting majesty, and the mystery of the Egyptian king as mere propaganda devices to bolster the person of a man who was solely responsible for the state. But they cannot be brushed aside for that reason. They had the reality of long-continuing success. They were as real in ancient Egypt as in Solomon's Temple at Jerusalem – or as in modern Japan.

He was a lonely being, this god-king of Egypt. All by himself he stood between humans and gods. Texts and scenes emphasize his solitary responsibility. The temple scenes show him as the only priest in ceremonies before the gods. A hymn to a god states: 'There is no one else that knows thee except thy son, (the king), whom thou causest to understand thy plans and thy power.'[27] It was the king who built temples and cities, who won battles, who made laws, who collected taxes, or who provided the bounty for the tombs of his nobles. The fact that the pharaoh might not have heard about a battle until it was reported to the royal court was immaterial; the literary and pictorial myth of Egypt's might demanded that he be shown as defeating the enemy single-handed. An Egyptian in a provincial town might make contractual provision for the delivery of goods to his tomb after death; the reigning pharaoh need have nothing to do with this transaction; in the age-long framework of mortuary activity the goods would come as an 'offering which the king gives', a mark of royal favour.

Only the national gods might intervene in the affairs of the state: the sun-god might ask the king to clear away the sand from the Sphinx, or Amon might commission the king to undertake a campaign against the Libyans. Otherwise pharaoh was the state, because he was himself a national god, specifically charged to carry out the functions of the state.

Because we can penetrate the trappings of divinity and discern the human heart of the pharaoh, we can sympathize with the loneliness of his administration. The other gods might temporarily escape to realms outside this world. He alone was a god who had to live out his solitary life surrounded by humans. Those humans through daily intimacy might dare to encroach upon his omniscience and omnipotence. One aged king has left a weary warning to his son and successor: 'Thou that hast appeared as a god, listen to what I have to say to thee, so that thou mayest be king over the land and ruler over the river banks, so that thou mayest achieve an overabundance of good. Hold thyself together against those subordinate (to thee), lest that should happen to whose terrors no thought has been given. Do not approach them in thy loneliness. Fill not thy heart with a brother, know not a friend, nor create for thyself intimates – that has no (happy) outcome. ... I gave to the poor and brought up the orphan ... (but) it was he who ate my food that raised up troops (against me) ... and they who were clothed in my fine linen looked upon me as (mere) dried weeds.'[28] The penalty of being a god was the removal of divinity from the world of humanity. The gods had sent him forth to tend mankind, but he was not of mankind.

This is perhaps the most fitting picture of the good Egyptian ruler, that he was the herdsman for his people. The functions of the state were to own, control, drive, discipline, and defend; they were also to cherish, nurture, shelter, and enlarge the population. The god-sent controller of the Egyptian people was the herdsman who kept them in green pastures, fought to secure fresh pastures for them, drove off the voracious beasts who attacked them, belaboured the cattle who strayed out of line, and helped along the weaklings.

The Egyptian texts use the same picture. One of the pharaohs stated why the god had made him ruler: 'He made me the herdsman of this land, for he discerned that I would keep it in order for him; he entrusted to me that which he protected.'[29] In a time of distress, men looked toward the ideal king of the future: 'He is the herdsman of every one, without evil in his heart. His herd may be cut down (in numbers), but he will spend the day in caring for them.'[30] Elsewhere the king is called 'the goodly herdsman, watchful for all mankind whom their maker has placed under his supervision.'[31] The sun-god 'appointed him to be shepherd of this land, to keep alive the people and the folk, not sleeping by night as well as by day in seeking out every beneficial act, in looking for possibilities of usefulness'.[32] The antiquity of this concept of the king is visible in the fact that a shepherd's crook is one of the earliest insignia of the pharaoh and is the origin of one of the words meaning 'to rule'.

The concept of the herdsman has its negative pole in the

implication that men are simply cattle, property on a lower stage of existence. This attitude is never given in a single statement, because the view that the pharaoh was the Lord, or Possessor, of the Two Lands was taken for granted, and the texts naturally concentrated attention on the proper care of property rather than on the fact of property itself. For example, one long story deals with an injustice done to a peasant and his protests that those who administer justice have a responsibility to take a constructive rather than a passive attitude toward their clients. It was necessary to reject certain customary expressions of indifference to the fortunes of ordinary men. For example, a proverb, 'The poor man's name is pronounced (only) for his master's sake', is cited as an expression of non-justice against which the peasant is struggling.[33] A magistrate was urged by other officials not to intervene on behalf of the peasant, because the latter had gone over the head of his immediate master. Do not disturb the ordinary disciplinary rights of a master; 'behold, it is what they (normally) do to peasants of theirs who go to others instead of to them'; the operation of justice should not interfere with the control of property.[34] Characteristically this text has an ultimate triumph of justice, because the Egyptians always rejected the narrow belief that the owner has no responsibility to maintain his property. At the positive pole, the herdsman's duty was to nurture and build up his herds.

The herdsman is primarily the pastor, the 'feeder', and a first responsibility of the state was to see that the people were fed. Thus the king of Egypt was the god who brought fertility to Egypt, produced the life-giving waters, and presented the gods with the sheaf of grain which symbolized abundant food. Indeed, an essential function of his kingship was that of a medicine man, whose magic ensured good crops. In one of the ceremonials of kingship, the pharaoh encircled a field four times as a rite of conferring fertility upon the land.[35] He controlled the water which made Egypt and made her fertile. 'The Nile is at his service, and he opens its cavern to give life to Egypt.'[36] As his courtiers told him: 'If thou thyself shouldst say to thy father, the Nile, the father of the gods: "Let water flow forth upon the mountains!" he will act according to all that thou hast said.'[37]

As the pharaoh controlled the water of Egypt, the Nile, so also he was a rainmaker for the foreign countries. One text makes the king of the Hittites say that his land must make overtures to pharaoh, for 'if the god accepts not its offering, it sees not the waters of heaven, since it is in the power of' the king of Egypt.[38] Pharaoh himself was a little more modest; he did not pose as the rainmaker for lands abroad but as the intermediary to the gods for water. Thinking of a diplomatic deputation which he had sent to Syria and Anatolia, 'his majesty took counsel with his own heart: "How will it go with those whom I have sent out, who are going on a mission to Djahi in these days of rain and snow which come in winter?" Then he made an offering to his father, (the god) Seth; then he came praying and said: "Heaven is in thy hands, and earth is under thy feet. ... (Mayest) thou (delay) to make the rain and the north wind and the snow until the marvels reach me which thou hast assigned to me!" ... Then his father Seth heard every word, and the heavens were peaceful, and summer days came for (him).'[39]

All nature that had reference to the prosperity of Egypt was under the sway of the pharaoh. He was the 'lord of the sweet breeze', the cooling wind from the Mediterranean which made Egypt habitable.[40] Nay, even more, as the master-magician he controlled the moon and the stars, so that the months, days, and hours came with regular cadence. A hymn of joy at the accession of one of the kings runs: 'Be gay of heart, the entire land, for the goodly times have come! A lord has been given to all lands! ... The waters stand and are not dried up, and the Nile carries a high (flood). (Now) the days are long, the nights have hours, and the moons come normally. The gods are at rest and happy of heart, and people live (in) laughter and wonder!'[41] By doctrine and by continuing ritual, pharaoh was the god who gave to Egypt its normal times and seasons, who brought the abundant waters, and who gave the fertile crops.

In actual practice there was administrative justification for the dogma of treating pharaoh as a water- and field-god. It seems that the central government also maintained the national astronomical and calendrical offices, although we lack full proof here. As one document in the case we cite a black ebony bar in the collections of the Oriental Institute museum at the University of Chicago. This is part of an astronomical apparatus for charting the movements of the stars, and it was made by the hands of Tūtankhamon himself. Whether this was his royal hobby, or whether the observation of the heavenly bodies was a function of kingship, we cannot be sure. We can say that the dogma that the pharaoh was responsible for food, water, and seasons was carried out by the function of bureaus of the royal government.

Diodorus paints a dreadful picture of the king of Egypt as the slave of regulations which controlled his every hour and every act. 'The hours of both the day and night were laid out according to a plan, and at the specified hours it was absolutely required of the king that he should do what the laws stipulated and not what he thought best' (i. 70–71). Diodorus goes on to state that these regulations covered not only the king's administrative actions but also his own freedom to take a walk, bathe, or even sleep with his wife. He was allowed no personal initiative in his governmental functions but was required to act only in conformance with the established laws. Diodorus insists that the pharaohs of his time were quite happy in this tightly laced straitjacket of prescription because they believed that men who followed their natural emotions fell into error, whereas the kings, in depending rigidly on the law, were personally freed from responsibility for wrongdoing.

Diodorus' hollow shell of a king is paralleled by the empty picture which Herodotus (ii. 37) gives of Egyptian religion at his time, when he says that the Egyptians were more religious than any other nation – the word used is *theosebēs*, 'god-fearing'. It turns out that Herodotus means that they were slavishly devoted to ritual, most scrupulous about ceremonial cleanliness and the prescribed forms, but without the slightest indication of spirituality or of a working ethics.

In the next chapter we wish to draw a distinction between

an earlier and a later period of ancient Egyptian history. In the earlier period the spirit was broadly one of conformance to precept, but the proof was laid upon the individual to show himself worthy by his own actions and his own freedom of decision within general law. In the later period the spirit was solely one of conformance to precept, with the individual charged to exhibit patience and humility in following that which the gods had laid down. It is our belief that Diodorus and Herodotus were both relating a practice and a spirit which were not normal to the Egypt discussed in these chapters. The atmosphere of their times was one of withdrawal into long-hallowed practice; the earlier atmosphere was one of free play of individual initiative within the general framework of human law and what we have called the 'divine order'.

The earlier kings of Egypt, of the period when that culture was developing as a native growth, were encouraged to express individuality as a part of the divine and worldly order to which they belonged. This earlier scene emphasized personal justice rather than impersonal law. We shall take up the concept of justice in the next chapter, which is devoted to an examination of 'The Values of Life'; for the present the reader must accept our word that Egyptian *ma^cat* means 'justice', one of the essential attributes of the Egyptian state, and that this justice does not appear to have been codified in statutes and precedents but was expressed in right-dealing in relation to persons and situations. The ruler who dispensed justice was urged to dispense it in relation to need, indeed, to give more than was due. The state thus did have a responsibility to act with initiative to meet the needs of the nation.

We shall not defend this thesis that rule was personal and flexible – paternalistic, if you please – except to throw out one or two examples of protest against impersonal non-justice. That peasant whom we have mentioned as struggling against injustice did not humbly submit to discipline from a magistrate. Instead he cried out bitterly: 'So then the son of Meru goes on erring!' and went on with a series of bitter charges against the lack of ruling principle in the high official: that he was like a town without a mayor or a ship without a skipper.[42]

Similarly, Rameses II, when abandoned in battle, turned angrily against the imperial god Amon and cried out: 'What is the matter with thee, my father Amon! Has a father ever forgotten his son? Have I ever done anything apart from thee?' and continued to recite his benefits to the god as deserving of better return.[43] There is here no resignation to destiny or to the inscrutable plans of the gods; there is here an indignant sense that personal worth must be rewarded. It would be easy to multiply examples from the earlier period of Egyptian history to show that rulers did not operate in an impersonal mechanism of law and custom but were free-acting individuals.

To be sure, there was a prescribed pattern for the ideal king and there were hallowed precedents; let us examine some of the prescriptions laid down for the good ruler. He turns out to be a composition of love and terror, which the Egyptians took to be complementary colours in the same spectrum. Good rule was paternalistic, and there was a devotion to the principle of disciplinary control. That is not as fantastic as it may seem to a generation given over to a progressive education. The Egyptian word 'to teach' is also the word 'to punish', like our word 'discipline', and it was apparently felt that 'whom the Lord loveth he chasteneth'. The components of good rule were god-given authority and godlike magnanimity.

In the preceding chapter we examined the text of the Memphite Theology, in which the continuing creative principles were the heart which conceived thought and the tongue which produced command. In that connection we mentioned a pair of related attributes of the sun-god, which were themselves personified as deities, Hū, 'authoritative utterance', or the commanding speech which brings a situation into being, and Sia, 'perception', the cognitive reception of an object, idea, or situation. These are god-like qualities, the perception of something in integrated and constructive terms and the consequent authoritative utterance which creates something new.

These two qualities were not confined to the sun-god; they were also attributes of the king. To the pharaoh it was said 'Authoritative utterance is indeed that which is in thy mouth, and perception (is that which) is in (thy heart).'[44] Two other texts may be cited as combining these two qualities of discernment and command as essential kingly characteristics,[45] but we are more interested in the fact that some texts added a third member to the combination which a ruler needed. In the two passages, 'authoritative utterance, perception, and justice are with thee'[46] and 'authoritative utterance is in thy mouth, perception is in thy heart, and thy tongue is the shrine of justice',[47] the word *ma^cat*, 'justice' or 'right-dealing' or 'truth', is added as the moral control which must accompany intelligence and authority.

Justice was the quality which accompanied a good ruler to the throne. In a time of national disorder, it was prophesied that a king would arise to unite the Two Lands, 'and justice will come into its place, and unrighteousness will be driven out.'[48] A poet rejoicing at the accession of a new king cried out: 'Justice has banished deceit!'[49] a consummation of proper times, as is indicated by the accompanying words: 'and normality has come down (again) into its place.'[50] Daily the king offered up justice to the god, symbolically presenting the little hieroglyph of the goddess Ma^cat, 'Truth' or 'Justice'. By this fact of daily ritual offering, justice did tend to become a mere form, which might be delivered through literal conformance to law or ritual.

But there was also a constant insistence that justice is something more positive than mere neutral conformance, that it lies in doing more than is required. The longest discourse on justice referred to divine law in equating justice and goodness: 'But justice (lasts) forever and goes down into the necropolis with him who renders it. When he is buried and joined to the earth, his name is not wiped out on earth, but he is remembered for goodness. That is a principle of the divine order.'[51] The writer related justice to a golden rule of doing unto others what might be expected from them. 'Do to the doer in order to cause him to do (for thee). That is thanking him for what he may do; that is parrying something before it is shot.'[52] Carrying the thought even further, the writer rejected injustice as lying in mere minimal performance of duty, like the ferryman who insisted upon payment before conveying passengers across the stream. Addressing the indifferent magistrate, he said: 'Behold thou art a ferryman who carries over (only) the one who has a fare, a straight-dealer whose straight-dealing is clipped short.'[53] Such impersonal rule, lacking in paternal benevolence, was really the absence of rule: 'Behold, thou art a town without its mayor ... like a ship which has no captain, a company without its leader.'[54] Insistently through the texts ran the obligation of the ruler to render on the basis of need and not on the basis of a *quid pro quo* trade. Intelligent perception of situations, the ability to command with authority, and straightforward justice were three main attributes of rule, and proper justice involved the quality of mercy.

Perhaps we may use a single text to summarize the combination of benevolence and force which characterized good rule as personified in the king. It is the instruction which a high official left for his children.[55] 'Adore ye within your bodies King Nemaatrē, living for ever, and associate his majesty with your hearts. He is perception which is in your hearts, for his eyes search out every body. He is Rē, by whose beams one sees; he is one who makes the Two Lands brighter than (does) the sun-disc. He is one who makes the land greener than (does) a high Nile. (Thus) he has filled the Two Lands with strength and life. Nostrils are chilled if he inclines toward rage, so that he is peaceful in order that the air may be breathed. He gives food to those who follow him and supplies provisions to him who treads his path. The king is the *ka*, and his mouth is abundance. That means that he brings into being him who is to be.'

The equation of the king with the *ka* as a constructing and provisioning force deserves a brief comment. The *ka* was that detached part of the personality which planned and acted for the rest of the person. Pictorially the *ka* was shown in the arms extended for support and protection. It was born with the individual as an identical twin, accompanied him through life as the sustaining, constructing force, and preceded him in death to effect his successful existence in the next world. It is hard to supply a succinct translation for this concept, although we like the term 'vital force', which has been used by some. Elsewhere the king is again called: 'The goodly *ka* that makes the Two Lands festive and meets the needs of the entire land.'[56] The ruler was thus seen as the constructive vital force of Egypt, creating and sustaining.

Resuming our text: 'He is (the fashioning god) Khnum for all bodies, the begetter who brings people into being. He is (the kingly goddess) Bastet, who protects the Two Lands; (but) he who adores him will escape his arm. He is (the punishing goddess) Sekhmet against him who transgresses his command; (but) he is mild towards him who has troubles.' In those last two equations we find the characteristic balance of protection and force, punishment and magnanimity. The text then concludes with the injunction that loyalty to the king means life and success, disloyalty means obliteration. 'Fight for his name; be pure for his life; and ye shall be free from (any) trace of sin. He whom the king has loved will be a revered (spirit), but there is no tomb for him who rebels against his majesty: his corpse shall be cast into the water. If ye do these things, your bodies shall be sound. (So) shall ye find it for ever.'

As there was a constant urging of the ruler toward the positive pole of justice, so there was always an urging him away from the negative pole of the arbitrary use of authority. The punishment of infractions of rule was certainly necessary, but it was also necessary to temper the exercise of force against excess. 'Beware lest thou punish wrongfully. Do not slaughter: that is not to thy advantage; but thou shouldst punish with beatings and with arrests. Thereby this land shall be (well) founded.' The one crime deserving death is treason against the state. 'The exception is the rebel, when his schemes are discovered, for the god knows the treacherous of heart, and the god strikes down his sins in blood.'[57]

THE KING'S OFFICIALS

This statement has been devoted to the ideals of good rule as personified in the king. Only through protest has it appeared that there was a practical situation in which the king had to delegate authority and government to others, and in which the growth of the state led to a venal and job-holding bureaucracy. In part, we could ignore that, as this chapter is devoted to the functions of the state as formulated in the speculation of men, and those functions were summed up in the ideals laid down for the good ruler. But it would be unfair to leave the impression that the Egyptians were so devoted to principle that they carried it successfully into practice. There was a constant fragmentation of rule, breaking it down into the subordinate functions and functionaries, until the minor bureaucrats were far removed from the god-king in whom were embodied the good principles of government.

In a country where offices multiply beyond the limit of personal accountability, the goal becomes office-holding as a sinecure with potentially high rewards. We possess many documents from ancient Egypt urging the young man to become a scribe or government clerk because it is a respectable, clean, and easy job. 'Put writing in thy heart, so that thou mayest protect thine own person from any (kind of) labour and be a respected official.'[58] Other lines of activity were burdensome: 'the scribe, however, he is the one who directs the work of everybody (else). He pays out taxes by writing, so that he has no (real) obligations.'[59]

This implicit contempt for responsibility went along with the feeling that the job should provide left-handed resources. We are given a moving description of the poor man thrust into the law courts without a sponsor; the court squeezes him, and he hears the cry: 'Silver and gold for the clerks of the court! Clothes for the attendants!'[60] In that situation he might well burst out: 'Seizers! robbers! plunderers! officials! – and yet appointed to punish evil! Officialdom is the refuge of the arrogant – and yet appointed to punish falsehood!'[61] Under this weight of cynical and corrupt officials, the ordinary citizen groaned: 'The land is diminished, but its rulers are increased. (The land is) bare, but its taxes are heavy. The grain is little, but the grain measure is large and measured (by the tax officials) to overflowing.'[62]

Of course, there are exaggerations on both sides, the picture of the ideal rule of justice was never one of attainment, and the corruption of the ruling class differed from age to age and from individual to individual. Egypt was never wholly noble or wholly corrupt. The definition of justice and the conflict between a moral justice and the arbitrary exercise of authority were perennial issues in the land.

It is often difficult for us to be sure whether protests against corruption were based on high moral grounds or arose out of politics, the attack of the outs against the ins. For example, an Egyptian official denounced the Twentieth Dynasty tomb robberies, in which high administrators surely played a lucrative part. Was the protesting official activated by sincere indignation against the desecration of holy property and the cynical participation of his colleagues? Or was he one who had not got his 'cut' and was trying 'to put the squeeze on the gang'?[63] Was the lofty revolution of Akhnaton against the all-embracing control of the old imperial gods – a revolution which used the slogan of *ma^cat*, 'justice' – a moral protest against the abuse of power or simply a political move to secure power for a new party? We cannot give final answers to these questions; the situation will never permit a simple arbitrary analysis; and our answers may arise out of personal prejudices. I, for example, am incurably romantic and charitable; whether politics played a part or not, I believe that men were swayed by rightful wrath against abuses. The divine order, which made man one with the gods, demanded that humans have something of the divine in them. And justice was the food upon which the gods lived.

Since the king was the state by official doctrine, and since he had to delegate his authority and responsibility to others, it will be instructive to examine the words in which he deputized rule to his chief officer, the vizier. These words were a formulation of the principles of rule, with one minor qualification. Delegated authority lays a greater emphasis on the how of rule rather than the why. It will operate more in an atmosphere of law and precedent than in an atmosphere of unconstrained and topical justice. To the magistrate law and justice may be the same.

Nevertheless, the vizier was sufficiently highly placed to use his own discretion at times, and there is evidence that the best of viziers would play by ear rather than note. At least, that is our interpretation of ruling the land 'with his fingers'. The text in question is a hymn to the god Amon-Rē as the magistrate to whom the poor and helpless may turn. 'Amon-Rē ... thou vizier of the poor man! He does not accept an unrighteous reward; he does not speak (only) to him who can bring witnesses; he does not give attention (only) to him who makes promises. (No), Amon judges the land with his fingers; his words belong to the heart. He separates the unjust and consigns him to the fiery place, but the righteous to the west.'[64] The divine pattern for the official operated in terms of justice and need rather than law and property.

When the king was installing the vizier in office, he had certain general charges to make about the spirit of rule, as distinct from the practices of administration.

'Look thou to this office of vizier; be vigilant concerning [all] that is done in it. Behold, it is the supporting (post) of the entire land. Now, with regard to the vizierate, behold, it is by no means sweet – nay, it is bitter. ... Behold, it does not mean giving his attention (only) to officials and councillors, nor (yet) making [dependents] of everybody. ... Therefore, see to it for thyself that all [things] are done according to that which conforms to the law and that all things are done according to the precedent therefor in [setting every man in] his just deserts.' The reason given for conformance to law and precedent is that a public official cannot escape public knowledge of his actions. 'Behold, as for the official who is in public view, the (very) waters and winds make report of all that he does; so, behold, his deeds cannot be unknown. ... Now the officials' place of refuge lies in acting in conformance with the regulations, that is, in doing that (concerning) which a commitment has been made [to] the petitioner. ...'[65]

Thus far there has been little moral motivation in the instructions. The vizier is in public view, and the 'bitterness' of his office lies in the rigid application of law. What follows shows the same austerity, although the emphasis shifts to unmoved equity in administering law. 'The abomination of the god is an exhibition of partiality. This is the instruction, and thus shalt thou act: "Thou shalt look upon him whom thou knowest like him whom thou knowest not, upon him who has access to [thy person] like him who is far [from thy household]." ... Do not be severe with a man wrongfully; thou shouldst be severe (only) over that which merits severity. Inspire fear of thyself, so that men fear thee, (for) the official who is feared is a (real) official.' That sounds harsh, and it therefore must be mitigated by words of caution. 'Behold [the respect for an official (comes from the fact) that he dispenses] justice. Behold, if a man inspires the fear of himself a million times, there is something wrong with him in the opinion of the people, and they do not say of him: "[There is] a man!" ... Behold, (thus) thou shouldst attach to thy carrying-out of this office thy carrying-out of justice.'[66]

These are the terms of good government as expressed by the king to his first official. They are somewhat formal; justice lies in the impartial administration of law rather than the redress of human injustice. The words of the vizier himself in commenting on his activities mitigate this impression only slightly: 'When I judged a petitioner, I showed no partiality, I did not incline my brow because of a reward ... but I rescued the timid man from the arrogant.' [67] A trace of mercy does appear here, but there is no insistence on anything except probity and even-handedness. Perhaps the answer is that justice outside the law could not be delegated by one man to another, but each man must discover for himself where he might make exceptions to law in order to achieve justice. Perhaps the answer is that perception, authoritative utterance, and justice were godly characteristics, which were retained by the godly pharaoh. At any rate, it was safer for a human deputy to find his 'place of refuge' in 'conformance with the regulations.' On the other hand, full discretion to operate within or without the legal statutes could be conceded to the divine pharaoh, who was himself 'the lord of destiny and he who creates fortune'.[68] Such a one, in the unimpeded exercise of intelligence, command, and justice, could inspire those twin products of good government: love and fear.

In this chapter we have seen that the universe was of a single substance and that the king was the point of contact between men and gods as the divine ruler vested with concern for the state. We have seen that his responsibility as herdsman for his people implied a balance of force and tender care. We have seen that the king was supposed to exercise a creative intelligence, an ability to issue proper commands, and a justice which was something more than law. His officials were more constrained to law and precedent, but the king's divine qualities permitted him a discretion in the effecting of proper rule.

Involved in all this discussion there are unanswered questions dealing with the moral purposes of the state, outside of the mere aspect of the state as property. Such problems involve the purposes of individual or group life and moral distinctions between right and wrong. Now we shall wrestle with some of those questions.

NOTES

1. Urk. IV, 614–18.
2. Memphite Theology, 60–61.
3. Sehetepibrē.
4. Leyden Amon Hymn, 4:21–26.
5. Beatty IV, Recto.
6. Beatty I, 9:7–10.
7. Destruction, 1–24.
8. Beatty I, 3:10 – 4:3.
9. Pyr. 393–404.
10. Mutter und Kind, 1:9 – 2:6.
11. Smith, 19:6.
12. Sinuhe, B44–45.
13. Ibid., 55–67.
14. Israel, 12–13.
15. Ptahhotep, 330.
16. Westcar, 9:9–11.
17. Urk. IV, 219–21.
18. Sinuhe, R5; cf. Urk. IV, 896.
19. Sinuhe, B224–26.
20. Anast. I, 28:5–6.
21. Nauri, 3–4.
22. Urk. I, 232.
23. Wenamon, 2:45–47.
24. Urk. IV, 1074.
25. Kubban, 13–14.
26. Admon., 7:2–6.
27. Aton Hymn, 12.
28. Amenemhet, 1:2–6.
29. Berlin Leather Roll, 1:6.
30. Admon., 12:1.
31. Dümichen, *Hist. Inschr.*, II, 39:25.
32. Cairo, 34501.
33. Peasant, B18–20.
34. Peasant, B42–46.
35. *Analecta orientalia*, 17:4 ff.
36. *Egyptian Religion*, 1933, p. 39.
37. Kubban, 21–22.
38. Anast. II, 2:4.
39. Marriage, 36–38.
40. *Egyptian Religion*, 1933, p. 41.
41. Sall. I, 8:7 – 9:1.
42. Peasant, B1, 188 ff.
43. Kadesh Poem, 26.
44. Petrie, *Koptos*, xii, 3:4.
45. Pyr. 300, 307.
46. Admon., 12:12.
47. Kubban, 18.
48. Neferrohu, 68–69.
49. Sall. I, 8:9–10.
50. Ibid., 8:8.
51. Peasant, B307–11.
52. Ibid., B109–11.
53. Ibid., B171–73.
54. Ibid., B189–92.
55. Sehetepibrē.

CHAPTER IV

Egypt: The Values of Life

THE NATURE OF THIS ANALYSIS

IN THE two preceding chapters few would quarrel with the generalizations that the ancient Egyptian saw his wider universe in terms of his own immediate environment and experience and that the state had been entrusted to the divine pharaoh so that he might control and nurture it as a herdsman tends his cattle. Now, however, we are to search for the values which the ancient Egyptian attached to life. If our thesis so far is valid, that man was an essential part of a consubstantial universe and that man therefore applied the norm of the human to the non-human, we shall need to know what norm he applied to himself. Here we come to the real problem of speculative thought: What am I here for? Here it is not possible to compound out one nice generalization to cover two thousand years of history. And such generalizations as may be made will not find as wide an acceptance among other scholars, because we inevitably use our own personal philosophies to evaluate the philosophies of others. Our conclusions may be fairly accurate on the nature of the evidence, but on the value of the evidence we shall hang our personal estimates.

What were the purposes of life? In order to secure a visible picture of the possible answers, we might make a visit to Egypt and go down into two structures which should be comparable.[1] Each is the tomb of an Egyptian vizier, that highest official of the land, the first deputy under the king. Near the Step Pyramid at Saqqara we enter the tomb of a vizier of the Old Kingdom, a man who lived about 2400 B.C. The rooms are crammed and packed with vigorous scenes of life and the lust for more life. The vizier is shown spearing fish, while his servants bring a bellowing hippopotamus to bay. The vizier supervises the roping and butchering of cattle, the ploughing and harvesting of the fields, the carpenters and metal-workers in their shops, and the building of boats for his funeral services. He presides over the vigorous punishment of tax delinquents, and he watches the games of children. Even when he is in repose, as when he listens to his wife playing the harp, he gives the impression of high potential, of being ready to spring into action. Non-spiritual and active life is the full account of this tomb. This is his monument for eternity; this is how he wants to be remembered; this is the good life which he wishes to extend into eternity.

We leave this tomb and walk a few hundred yards to the tomb of a vizier of the Late Period, a man who lived about 600 B.C. Eighteen hundred years have brought a quietude, a pious calm. Here we see no exuberant noble, no bellowing hippopotamus, no tumbling children. The walls are covered with ritual and magical texts. There are a few posed and dull pictures of the vizier frozen in hieratic attitude before the god of the dead. There are a few vignettes to illustrate the texts with scenes of the underworld and the genii who live there. The life of this world is completely lacking; the funeral services and the world of the dead are the only concerns of this man. His monument for eternity concentrates on the next world instead of this life. His good consists in magic, ritual, and the favour of his god.

That is our problem. At one pole there is an emphasis on life, on action, and on the material world; at the other pole, an emphasis on death, on repose, and on religion. Clearly our discussion must bridge the gap and must be historical in order to give the change from one stage to the other. We shall see two major periods of Egyptian thought, the aggressive and optimistic earlier times and the submissive and hopeful later times, with a long period of transition between. It was like a hurricane, with strong winds blowing to the east, then a dead centre of uncertain balance, and then the winds blowing just as strongly to the west. The earlier winds to the east were radical and individualistic; the later winds to the west were conservative and communal. But, as we said before, it depends upon who analyses the trends; another man has seen the earlier trend as a compliance to group forms and the later as an interest in personal well-being. Inevitably the discussion involves the religious, political, and social prejudices of the analyst.

THE OLD AND MIDDLE KINGDOMS

The emergence of Egypt into the light of history seems to be a very sudden phenomenon, symbolized in the abrupt appearance of stone architecture of highest technical perfection. Dr. Breasted once dramatized this brilliant flowering in these words:

In the Cairo Museum you may stand in the presence of the massive granite sarcophagus which once contained the body of Khufu-onekh, the architect who built the Great Pyramid of Gizeh. ... Let us in imagination follow this early architect to the desert plateau behind the village of Gizeh. It was then bare desert surface, dotted only with the ruins of a few small tombs of remote ancestors. The oldest stone masonry construction at that time had been erected by Khufu-onekh's great-grandfather. Only three generations of architects in stone preceded him. ... There probably were not many stone masons, nor many men who understood the technique of building in stone as Khufu-onekh took his first walk on the bare Gizeh Plateau, and staked out the ground plan of the Great Pyramid. Conceive, then, the dauntless courage of the man who told his surveyors to lay out the square base 755 feet on each side! ... [He knew that it would] take nearly two and a half million blocks each weighing two and one-half tons to cover this square of thirteen acres with a mountain of masonry 481 feet high. ... The Great Pyramid of Gizeh is thus a document in the history of the human mind. It clearly discloses man's sense of sovereign power in his triumph over material forces. For himself and for his sovereign the pharaoh's engineer was achieving the conquest of immortality by sheer command of material forces.[2]

This vivid picture illustrates the sudden surge of vigour and the zest for action and accomplishment which characterized the Old Kingdom of Egypt. From the same general period come some of Egypt's highest intellectual achievements, such as that philosophy of the Memphite Theology which we discussed previously and the scientific attitude expressed in the Edwin Smith Surgical Papyrus. This raises questions about the antecedents of these daring and forceful people. They hardly seem visible in the modest products of pre-dynastic Egypt. And yet we cannot see that this is a reason for assuming that these achievements must therefore have been introduced by conquering invaders. That simply takes an unknown and thrusts it out into unknown realms. Sometimes the spirit of man soars in dizzy flight beyond the plodding pace which cultural evolution would see as normal, and there is good reason to believe that this whole surge of power was quite local, enjoying only the stimulus of similar wonderful developments known from Mesopotamia. The reasons for this sudden spurt of power are not clear. It was a revolution, the abrupt flowering of a slow development under the influence of some stimulation which remains obscure. One may argue that the stability of state and society which permitted the beginnings of the Egyptian dynasties laid new demands on individual men. They were organized more effectively through the specification of function. One man was charged to be an architect, another to be a seal-cutter, another to be a record clerk. These functions had previously been avocations in a more simple society. Now they were important enough to be vocations and called forth the accumulation of abilities which had been latent but growing in the earlier periods. For centuries the Egyptians had been gathering slow strength within the Nile Valley until their day arrived, and they sprang upward with a suddenness which is miraculous to us. The Egyptians also had a sense of something very wonderful. They found themselves capable of great accomplishment. Material success was their first goal of the good life.

We can feel the relish with which a noble of the Old Kingdom relates his advances in station: (The King) made me Count and Overseer of Upper Egypt. ... Never before had this office been conferred upon any servant, but I acted for him as Overseer of Upper Egypt to satisfaction. ... I filled an office which made my reputation in this Upper Egypt. Never before had the like been done in this Upper Egypt.'[3] The attitude was a frontier spirit of visible accomplishments, of the first success in a new line. This was a youthful and self-reliant arrogance, because there had been no setbacks. Man was enough in himself. The gods? Yes, they were off there somewhere, and they had made this good world, to be sure; but the world was good because man was himself master, without need for the constant support of the gods.

Man's world was not completely devoid of god, because the rules under which the world operated had been laid down by god, or the gods, and any man who trangressed those rules was accountable to god. Even in this early time, the word 'god' is used in the singular in referring to his system, his desires for man, or his judging violations of the system. It is not quite clear in the Old Kingdom what god is involved in this singular use. Sometimes it is certainly the king, sometimes it is certainly the creator or supreme god, who had laid down the broad, general rules for the game of life. But sometimes there appear to be unification and personification of correct and efficient behaviour summed up in the will of 'the god' who is not as august or as distant as the king or the creator-god. If the hypothesis of consubstantiality is valid, this unification and universality of deity is a problem which we have already faced. It was not monotheism; it was monophysitism applied to deity.

Where the principles of proper behaviour concern table etiquette or administrative procedure, it is likely to be 'the *ka*' that has a governing interest as 'the god'.[4] As we explained in the previous chapter, the *ka* was the detached part of the human personality which protected and sustained the individual. As such it could well be the divine force within man which governed his proper and successful activity. The frequency of Old Kingdom names like 'Rē-is-my-*ka*' and 'Ptah-is-my-*ka*' suggests that, through the principles of consubstantiality and free substitution, the *ka* was thought to be a man's god, sometimes godship in general, and sometimes a specific god, like a name saint or a patron saint.

We are here referring to the Old Kingdom, when the gods of the pantheon were more remote from common man, although not necessarily from his intermediating *ka*. That situation changed later. In the latter part of the Empire an Egyptian expressed a close personal relation to a specifically named god, who was his protector and controller. That direct relation to a personal god may be visible before the Empire in the 'town god', the equivalent of the local saint. In the early Eighteenth Dynasty, for example, a wish for a noble runs: 'Mayest thou

spend eternity in gladness of heart and in the favour of the god
who is in thee,'[5] for which a variant runs: 'in the favour of thy
town god'.[6] However, (a) these concepts are rarely clear cut or
firmly identifiable; and (b) in certain contexts 'the god' is the
king or a specific god of universal control, like the creator-
god.

The independent self-reliance of the Egyptian of the Pyramid Age is indicated by the physical decentralization of the
tombs of the nobles of the period. At first the high officials
were buried in close juxtaposition to the god-king whom they
had served; through his certainty of eternity their hopes for
continued existence would be realized. Very soon, however,
they exhibited sufficient self-confidence to move away from the
king and seek their own eternity in their own home districts.
Within the general framework of divine rule they were inde-
pendently successful in this life; they had assurance that this
success was applicable to the future. Under their own momentum they could carry on into future life, join their *ka*'s over
there, and become *akh*'s, 'effective beings', for a vigorous
eternal life. Their own accumulation of worldly success guaranteed, by legal contract and by precedent, a conquest over
death. In that sense there was a decided democratic – or,
more precisely, individualistic – trend throughout the Old
Kingdom.

'Individualism' is a better term than 'democracy' for this
spirit, because it applied chiefly to personal rule of conduct
and not to political government. A sense of personal adequacy
may lead to decentralization of government and thus bring
a limited sense of democratic ambition. But we do not see in
ancient Egypt that political democracy which chapter V will
indicate for Mesopotamia. The dogma of the divinity of the
Egyptian pharaoh was a cohesive force too strong to be fractured by individualistic forces.

No servile dependency upon a god was necessary in this
early period for the greatest goods of life: success in this world
and continued life in the next. Man was generally accountable
to the king, to the creator-god, and to his own *ka*, but he was
not humbly suppliant to a named god of the pantheon, and he

was not formally responsible to Osiris, the later ruler of the dead. His wealth and position in this life gave him confidence that he was fully effective now and later, and – as the lively tomb scenes show – he wanted a next world just as gay and exciting and successful as this world.

We want to emphasize just as strongly as we can that the Egyptians of these times were a gay and lusty people. They relished life to the full, and they loved life too fully to surrender its hearty savour. That is why they denied the fact of death and carried over into the next world the same vigorous and merry life which they enjoyed here.

We possess for this early period a book of etiquette for an official, 'the utterances of beautiful speech ... as the instruction of the ignorant in knowledge and in the rules of good speech, which are of advantage to him who will listen and of disadvantage to him who may abuse them.'[7] This contains the gospel of the 'go-getter', the bald rules for a young man who is on the make. It has been summarized as follows:

The ideal picture is that of a correct man, who wisely avoids impulse and fits himself by word and deed into the administrative and social systems. An assured career as an official awaits him. No moral concepts like good and bad come into discussion here; rather the standard lies in the characteristics of the knowing man and the ignorant man, perhaps best given in the words 'smart' and 'stupid'. Smartness can be learned. ... So rules are provided for a man's career. If he pays attention, he will be smart; he will find the right way in all life's situations through this smartness; and through his correct attitude he will bring his career to success.[8]

This book contains precepts for getting on with superiors, equals, and inferiors. Thus one who comes into competition with a speaker who is better at argument is advised to 'cut down on bad talk by not opposing him'; one who meets an equal is to show his superiority by silence so that the attending officials may be impressed; and an inferior opponent is to be treated with indulgent disregard, for thus 'thou shalt smite him with the punishment of the (truly) great.'[9] He who sits at the table of a superior is urged to maintain a sedate countenance, to take only what he is offered, and to laugh only when his host laughs; thus the great one will be pleased and will

accept whatever one may do.[10] An official who must listen to
the pleas of clients should listen patiently and without rancour,
because 'a petitioner wants attention to what he says (even)
more than the accomplishing of that for which he came'.[11] It
is seemly to found a household, to love and cherish a wife,
because 'she is a field of advantage to her master'; and one
must be careful to hold her from gaining mastery in the household.[12] There is a practical, materialistic wisdom in the injunction: 'The wise man rises early in the morning to establish himself',[13] or in the advice to be generous to one's hangers-on,
because no one can foresee the exigencies of the future, and it
is wise to build up the insurance of a body of grateful
supporters.[14]

It would be unfair to leave the impression that the entire
text is opportunistic and materialistic. There is one passage
which urges on the official that honesty is the best policy, but
even this arises out of experience rather than principle. 'If thou
art a leader who directs the affairs of a multitude, seek for thyself every benevolent opportunity until thy conduct shall be
without fault. Justice is of advantage, and its utility lasts. It
has not been disturbed since the time of its maker, whereas
there is punishment for him who passes by its laws. ... It is
(true that) evil may gain wealth, but the (real) strength of justice is that it lasts, for a man can say: "It was the property of
my father (before me)."'[15] Here lay the values of that age:
a transmittable property and the experience that a man 'got on'
in the world if he was smart enough to follow certain com-
mon-sense principles. A success visible to all men was the great
good. These were the supreme values of the Old Kingdom, and
they continued in value throughout Egyptian history.

It was easy to worship success as long as success conferred
its benefits on all men, as long as well-tended pyramids and
tombs were the visible symbols of the lasting power of worldly
success. But that happy state did not last. The Old Kingdom of
Egypt collapsed into turmoil heels over head. The old values
in position and property were swept away in an anarchy of
force and seizure. The Egyptians ascribed their woes in part to
a dissolution of their own character, but also to the violent

presence of Asiatics in the Egyptian Delta. However, it is doubtful whether the Asiatics came in as an invading and suppressing horde; it is much more likely that an inner breakdown of rule in Egypt permitted small groups of Asiatics to come in and settle but that these insignificant penetrations were result rather than cause of the breakdown.

The real source of the collapse was a progressive decentralization. Rulers other than the dynastic pharaohs felt their individual capacity for independence and set up competitive government until the strain fractured Egypt into a lot of warring factions. This was part of the individualistic, self-seeking trend which had been gaining momentum throughout the Old Kingdom. Now, with the single, central control dissipated, there was anarchy in the competing grabs for power, which went right down to the lowest strata of society. Egypt has been moving away from autarchy in the direction of separatism based on individual capacity to act, but the nation was unprepared to take advantage of the breakdown of autarchy by the immediate institution of a system of rule on a broader basis. In the confusion there was no rule.

We have many expressions of the bewilderment of the Egyptian at the overturn of his old world. Instead of the prized stability and security, the land whirled around dizzily like a potter's wheel. The former rich and powerful were now in rags and hunger, whereas the former poor had property and power. We of the present day read with a wry amusement the protests that there was a thoroughgoing cheapening of the high court of justice and a disregard for the statutes of the law, that poor men were now able to wear fine linen, that servant girls were insolent to their mistresses, and the laundryman arbitrarily refused to carry his bundle. The visible continuity of life through the care and preservation of the tombs of the great was abruptly fractured; tombs were plundered, including the pyramids of the pharaohs, and the treasured dead lay exposed upon the desert plateau. The crisp frontier lines which had given geometric order to Egypt were erased; the red desert pushed its way into the fertile black soil, the provincial states were 'hacked to pieces', and foreigners from abroad had entered Egypt. When the provinces refused to pay taxes, the central control of agriculture broke down, and no one would plough even when the Nile was in beneficial flood. The old profitable commerce with Phoenicia and Nubia had disappeared, so that the appearance of a few miserable traders from the desert offering herbs and birds was now a remarkable phenomenon.[16]

Egypt may have been moving steadily toward individualism and decentralized power, but it had still had the single keystone of the kingship. When this had been removed, the whole arch had fallen. 'Behold, it has come to a point where the land is robbed of the kingship by a few irresponsible men. ... Behold, the secret of the land, unknowable in its extent, has been exposed, and the (royal) residence has been overthrown within an hour.'[17] We have seen in the earlier wisdom literature that the norm for the good life had been the successful official. Now the officials were in hunger and want. 'Behold, no office at all is in its (proper) place, like a stampeded herd without its herdsman.'[18] 'Changes have taken place, so that it is no (longer) like last year, but one year is more burdensome than another.'[19] The old values of a successful individual career, which showed to the world property, administrative position, and a tomb provisioned unto eternity had been swept away. What values could be found to replace them?

In the upset, some found only the negative answers of despair or scepticism. Some turned to suicide, and we read that the crocodiles of the river were sated because men went to them of their own accord.[20] One of the finest documents of Egyptian literature records the debate of a would-be suicide with his own *ka*, or soul. Life was too much for him, and he proposed to seek his death by fire. It was symptomatic of the times that the soul, which should have exhibited the consistent and directing attitude towards death, was the wavering member to the debate and could find no satisfactory answer to the man's melancholy. It first was inclined to accompany him no matter what his end might be; then it shifted and tried to hold him back from violence. Still it had no constructive arguments for realizing a good life on this earth and could only urge the man to forget his cares and seek sensual enjoyment. Finally, after the man had contrasted the miseries of this life with the sober pleasures of the next world, the soul agreed to make a home with him no matter what his fate might be. There was no answer except that this world was so bad that the next must be a release.

This document carries a philosophy of pessimism worth our study. The man presented his argument to his soul in four poems of uniform tristichs contrasting life with the release of death. The first poem urged that the man's name would be in bad odour if he followed the advice of his soul to give himself up to pleasure. He had his own standards still, and he would not permit his good name to be damaged.

> Behold, my name will reek through thee
> More than the stench of fishermen,
> More than the stagnant swamps where they have fished.

> Behold, my name will reek through thee
> More than the stench of bird-droppings,
> On summer days when the sky is hot.[21]

In six more stanzas the man presented the evil odour of his reputation if he followed the cowardly advice of his soul. Then in a second poem he turned to a lament over the breakdown of standards in the society of his day. Three of the stanzas in this poem run as follows:

> To whom can I speak today?
> (One's) fellows are evil;
> The friends of today do not love.

> (To whom can I speak today?)
> The gentle man has perished,
> But the violent man has access to everybody.

> To whom can I speak today?
> No one remembers (the lessons of) the past;
> No one at this time does (good in return) for doing (good).[22]

From these evils of life the man turned to contemplate death as a blessed release.

> Death (stands) before me today
> (Like) the recovery of a sick man,
> Like going out-doors (again) after being confined.

> Death (stands) before me today
>> Like the fragrance of myrrh,
>> Like sitting under a shade on a breezy day.

> Death (stands) before me today
>> As a man longs to see his house,
>> After he has spent many years held in captivity.[23]

Finally, the man urged the high privileges of the dead, who had the power to oppose evil and who had free access to the gods.

> Nay, but he who is yonder
>> Shall be a living god,
>> Inflicting punishment upon the doer of evil.

> Nay, but he who is yonder
>> Shall be a man of wisdom,
>> Not stopped from appealing to Rē when he speaks.[24]

This man was ahead of his day in rejecting the active values of this life in favour of the passive values of future blessedness. As we shall see, such submissiveness characterized a period a thousand years later. This was a tentative move in the pessimism of the period – that one should seek death as a release instead of emphasizing the continuance of the life as known here.

In this debate the man's soul at one point urged upon him the futility of taking life seriously and cried out: 'Pursue a holiday (mood) and forget care!'[25] This theme of non-moral hedonism occurs again in another text of the period, where the argument is: The old standards of property and position have broken down; we have no certainty about future happiness, so let us grasp what happiness we can in this world. The past shows only that this life is brief and transitory – but transitory to an unknowable future.

'Generations pass away and others go on since the time of the ancestors. ... They that build buildings, their places are no more. What has been done with them?

'I have heard the words of (the past sages) Imhotep and Hardedef, with whose sayings men speak so much – (but) what are their places (now)? Their walls are crumbled, their places are non-existent, as if they had never been.

'No one returns from (over) there, so that he might tell us their disposition, that he might tell us how they are, that he might still our hearts until we (too) shall go to the place where they have gone.'[26]

Since that wisdom which was so highly prized in the earlier age had not guaranteed for the wise a visible survival in well-kept tombs, and since it was impossible to tell how the dead fared in the other world, what was left for us here? Nothing, except to snatch at the sensual pleasures of the day.

'Make holiday and weary not therein! Behold, it is not given to a man to take his property with him. Behold, no one who goes (over there) can come back again!'[27]

Thus the first two reactions to the defeat of a successful and optimistic world were despair and cynicism. But they were not the only reactions. Egypt had still a spiritual and mental vigour which refused to deny the essential worth of individual man. He was still an object of value to himself. If his old standards of value in physical and social success had proved to be of ephemeral nature, he began to grope for other standards which might have a more lasting nature. Dimly and uncertainly he became aware of the great truth that the things which are seen are temporal but that the things which are unseen may be of the very stuff of eternity. And eternal life was still his great goal.

Now the words which we have just used and the words which we are going to use prejudice the discussion in terms of modern ethical judgments. That is deliberate. We consider the Egyptian Middle Kingdom to have reached moral heights in its search for the good life. This is a personal prejudice, in which we follow Professor Breasted, although our own analysis of the factors differs slightly from his. A counterview has been urged by others. They point out that the Egyptians of the earliest fully visible period, the Old Kingdom, reached heights which were never surpassed later – in technical ability (as in the Great Pyramid and in sculpture), in science (as in a remarkable surgical papyrus and in the institution of a calendar), and in philosophy (as in the Memphite Theology). This view would deny any assumption of progress beyond those points. Indeed, it would protest at the claim of progress at all and would insist that we see change only and that this change is within the limits of a culture very largely static from the beginnings. The more it changes, the more it exhibits itself to be the same. There is undoubted truth to this. The materialism which we stressed as characterizing the Old Kingdom was still an important factor in this new period. The social-moral advances which we shall claim for this new period were already indicated in the Old Kingdom (increasing democratization, concept of justice, etc.). This view would also protest at the imposing of our consciously self-righteous standards of moral judgment upon the ancient Egyptians. Have we the right to translate *ma^cat* as 'justice', 'truth', or 'righteousness', instead of 'order', 'regularity', or 'conformity'? Have we the right to hail increasing democracy of viewpoint in ancient Egypt as 'an advance', which was 'good'?

We insist that one has the right to make moral judgments and to talk in terms of progress or decline. These are subjective matters, not strictly scientific. But any generation has the right – nay, even the duty – of presenting the evidence objectively and then of giving a subjective valuation to the evidence. We know that objectivity cannot be completely divorced from subjectivity, but a scholar can attempt to show just what the evidence is and just where his personal criticism comes in. In the period which we are going to examine now, we would agree that a hard practical materialism still continued strong, that the anti-ethical force of magic played a large role, and that the moral impulses which we shall stress had been present earlier and continued later. But we are satisfied that there were changes of emphasis in this period and that these shifts of emphasis look like advances to a modern Westerner.

The two great changes which we can see are a decline in the emphasis on position and material property as being the good of this life, with a corresponding shift of emphasis to proper social action as being the good, and a continuation of the individualistic trend of the Old Kingdom to the point where all good things were potentially open to all men. These two trends are ultimately the same: if the good in life is within the quest of any man, rich or poor, then power and wealth are not ultimates, but right relations to other men are strongly recommended.

Three quotations will give us the new emphasis. A struggle of the previous period had been to build and maintain a tomb, an imposing funerary monument lasting to eternity. The Middle Kingdom continued the physical establishment but introduced a new note: 'Do not be evil, (for) kindliness is good. Make thy monument to be lasting through the love of thee. ... (Then) the god will be praised by way of rewarding (thee).'[28] Here the monument which lasted came through other men's grateful reaction to benevolence. A second passage gives clearly the statement that the god delighted more in good character than in elaborate offerings; the poor man could thus have as good a title to god's interest as the rich. 'More acceptable is the character of a man just of heart than the ox of the evildoer.'[29]

The most remarkable passage of the period is one which occurs only here and – as far as we know – was not repeated later. It stands isolated, and yet it was not foreign to the highest aspiration of the times; it is a reason for prizing the spirit of this age beyond those which preceded or followed. It stated simply that all men were created equal in opportunity. In these words the supreme god gave the purposes of creation.

> I relate to you the four good deeds which my own heart did for me ... in order to silence evil. I did four good deeds within the portal of the horizon.

> I made the four winds that every man might breathe thereof like his fellow in his time. That is (the first) of the deeds.

> I made the great flood waters that the poor man might have rights in them like the great man. That is (the second) of the deeds.

> I made every man like his fellow. I did not command that they might do evil, (but) it was their hearts that violated what I had said. That is (the third) of the deeds.

> I made that their hearts should cease from forgetting the
> west, in order that divine offerings might be made to
> the gods of the provinces. That is (the fourth) of the
> deeds.[30]

The first two passages of this text state that wind and water
are equally available to all men of any degree. In a land where
prosperity depended upon securing a proper share in the inundation waters and where water control must have been a powerful factor in setting one man in domination over another, an
assurance of equal access to water meant basic equality of opportunity. The statement, 'I made every man like his fellow',
that is, 'all men are created equal', was coupled with the god's
insistence that he had not intended that they do evil, but that
their own hearts had devised wrong. This juxtaposition of
equality and wrongdoing says that social inequality is no part
of god's plan, but man must bear that responsibility alone.
This is a clear assertion that the ideal society would be fully
equalitarian. Certainly, ancient Egypt never came near that
ideal, except as we moderns do in the pious postponement of
full equality to the future life. But it was still a valid sublima-
tion of the highest aspirations of the time. Wistfully it says:
'All men should be equal; the creator-god did not make them
different.'

The final good deed of the supreme god was to call men's
attention to the west, the region of eternal life, and to urge
upon them pious service of their local gods in order to attain
the west. These were important changes of this period, the
democratization of the next world and closer attachment to the
gods. All men might now enjoy eternity in the same terms as
had the king alone in the previous period. We do not know
just what kind of continued existence the ordinary man of the
Old Kingdom had been conceded. He was to continue with
his *ka*, and he was to become an *akh*, an 'effective' personality.
The pharaoh of the Old Kingdom, however, was to become
a god in the realm of the gods. Now that future of the pharaoh
was open also to commoners. They were to become gods as he
had become a god. Whereas only the dead king had become
Osiris in the earlier period, now every deceased Egyptian be-

came the god Osiris. Further, his becoming an Osiris and attaining eternal blessedness was put in relation to an after-life judgment in which his character was assessed by a tribunal of gods.

Pictorially, this judgment of character was already a weighing of justice. In the future this was to become a judgment before Osiris as the god of the dead, with the man's heart placed in the scales against the symbol for justice. Those elements were already present in the Middle Kingdom, Osiris as god of the dead and a judgment of the deceased in terms of justice, but they were not yet put together into a single consistent scene. Instead there was still a carry-over of the older order in which the supreme god, the sun-god, was the judge. There was democratization of the next world and Osirianization, but the entry to the eternal life was not wholly within the control of Osiris. We have reference to 'that balance of Rē, in which he weighs justice';[31] and the deceased was assured that 'thy fault will be expelled and thy guilt will be wiped out by the weighings of the scales on the day of reckoning characters and it will be permitted that thou join with those who are in the (sun)-barque',[32] and that 'there is not a god who will contest a case with thee, and there is not a goddess who will contest a case with thee, on the day of reckoning characters'.[33] It was a tribunal of the gods, presumably under the presidency of the supreme god, to whom the deceased must make his report. 'He shall reach the council of the gods, the place where the gods are, his *ka* being with him and his offerings being in front of him, and his voice shall be justified in the reckoning up of the surplus: though he may tell his faults, they will be expelled for him by all that he may say.'[34] All this shows that there was a judging of the dead in terms of weighing the excess or deficiency of his good against his bad and that a favourable outcome of the weighing was a prerequisite to eternal blessedness. This weighing was a calculation of *ma^{c}at*, justice.

We have met *ma^{c}at* before. Basically, it is probably a physical term, 'levelness, evenness, straightness, correctness', in a sense of regularity or order. From that it can be used in the

metaphorical sense of 'uprightness, righteousness, truth, justice'. There was a real emphasis on this *ma*^c*at* in the Middle
Kingdom in the sense of social justice, righteous dealing with
one's fellow-men. That was the main theme of the story of the
eloquent peasant, which comes from this period. Throughout
his pleadings the peasant demanded from the high official
simple justice as a moral right. Just dealing had its minimum
in the conscientious carrying-out of responsibilities. 'Cheating
diminishes justice, (but) filling (to good (measure) – neither
too low nor overflowing – is justice.'[35] But, as we saw in the
preceding chapter, justice was not simply legal commerce but
was the seeking-out of good in relation to need: ferrying
across the river the poor man who could not pay and doing
good in advance of any known return. And a theme of the
Middle Kingdom was social responsibility: the king was a
herdsman who cherished his herds; the official had a positive
duty toward the widow and the orphan; in short, every man
had rights which imposed responsibilities upon other men.
Even the sculptures of the time sought to bring out this
emphasis on conscientious character and moved from a deli-
neation of majesty and force to a portrayal of concern for
obligations. Such careworn portraits of the pharaohs of the
Middle Kingdom are well known.

All this has been eloquently urged by Breasted, and we need
not document it in further detail. If one seeks to state his
argument differently, it would simply be in a difference of
definition of 'conscience' or of 'character' and a failure to give
the story the simple and straightforward emphasis which he
achieves. In the previous period there had been a demand for
justice in this world and for the next,[36] and there had certainly
been character in the forceful personalities who had built a
great state. But here in the Middle Kingdom greater emphasis
in some lines and lesser emphasis in others permitted an age of
real social conscientiousness, in which the psychological and
moral basis was the belief that every man is the care-worthy
creation of the god.

Up to this time, the Middle Kingdom, the trend in ancient
Egypt had been centrifugal and atomistic: individual man had

been the valued unit. First his individual abilities had been marked out for value, then his individual rights had been recognized. Egypt had been moving somewhat blindly along the road from theocratic autarchy towards democracy of a kind. The spirit was still an encouragement to fill this life with activity, and each man was given an opportunity to realize the bustling, practical, important life here. Consequently, they continued to love this life and defy death. The definition of success may have shifted slightly, but it was still true that a successful life carried over and repeated itself happily in the next world. Consequently, the tombs, which were the bridges between two existences, continued to stress the abundance of life. The scenes of hunting, shipbuilding, and merrymaking were as vigorous as ever. Only an increased attention to scenes of the burial and a few representations of religious feasts suggest to us a new sobriety. It was still the case that the greatest good lay in the good life here and not an escape from this life to a different future life or a resigned submission to the gods. Individual man still enjoyed himself.

THE EMPIRE AND LATER

We come now to the cause of the great transition in the Egyptian ethos. We come to the second political revolution, the Second Intermediate Period, lying between the Middle Kingdom and the Empire, between the eighteenth and sixteenth centuries B.C. Again the central government broke down; again there was competition for the rule by a number of small princelings. Probably a weakening of personal force and character in the central government unleashed the self-seeking individualism of local princes. But the great difference this time was the forceful and conquering incursion of foreigners. Asiatic princes, whom we call the Hyksos, established themselves in armed camps within Egypt and dominated the land with a firmness which was repressive to the still flowering Egyptian spirit. For the first time Egypt as a whole suffered a setback in that philosophy which said: We are the centre and summit of the world; we are free to permit expansion of spirit to the individuals of our community. Now, for the first time, that community was aware of a serious threat from the outside world. Now, for the first time, that community had to draw together into a unity in order to meet and avert that threat.

Egypt did unite and throw out the 'vagabonds', who had dared to rule the land 'in ignorance of Rē'.[37] But the threat was not met by driving them out of Egypt; it was necessary to pursue them into Asia and to keep on pounding them so that they might never again threaten the land of the Nile. There was built up a psychosis for security, a neuropathic awareness of danger similar to that which has characterized Europe in modern times. That common sentiment for security welded the Egyptians into a self-conscious nation. It has been pointed out that only in this period of liberation do the Egyptians speak of their troops as 'our army', instead of crediting the forces to the king.[38] There was a patriotic fervour which put the country's interests before the interests of the individual.

Such a unified spirit was born of the sense of common peril. The common desire for security need not have survived after the Egyptian Empire extended the military frontier of Egypt well into Asia and thus removed the peril from the immediate frontier. That should have given the external security which would relieve the need for communal solidarity. However, it was a restless age, and there were perils on the distant horizon which could be invoked to hold the community together, since unity was to the advantage of certain central powers. When the threat of the Hyksos had subsided, the threat of the Hittites appeared and endangered the Asiatic Empire of Egypt. Thereafter came the Sea Peoples, the Libyans, and the Assyrians. A fear psychosis, once engendered, remained present. And there were forces in Egypt which kept alive this fear psychosis in order to maintain the unified purpose of Egypt.

The course of empire is justified in terms of a crusade, the acceptance of a 'manifest destiny' to extend one culture in domination over another. Whether empire is basically economic or political, it must have a religious, spiritual and intellectual vindication. In Egypt that sanction came through the god-king who stood for the state, and it came through the other national gods who participated in the removal of a threat to Egypt by supporting the extension of the frontiers of the land. The national gods commissioned the pharaoh to march forth and widen the land; indeed, they marched with him at the head of the divisions of his army. The extension of the nation was their own extension.

In how far the gods invested in Egyptian victory in a strictly economic sense is uncertain. We do not know whether the temples acted as bankers to finance foreign conquest and empire. They probably did so when they became wealthy and had extensive assets, because empire constantly increased their wealth. At any rate, they did invest in Egyptian victory in a spiritual-propagandistic sense, in giving a divine blessing and a divine guarantee to empire. For this they received an economic return. This is rather explicitly stated in the monuments; the pharaoh erected buildings, established and endowed feasts, and presented land and serfs to the god who had given the victory. The previously modest temples in Egypt grew in physical size, in personnel, in land, and in total property, until they became the dominating factor in Egyptian political, social, and economic life. It has been estimated that, after the Empire had had three hundred years of active life, the Egyptian temples owned one out of every five inhabitants of the nation and owned almost one-third of the cultivable land.[39] Naturally the temples were interested in perpetuating and tightening a system which was so greatly to their advantage. In order to secure their advantage, they had to insist on the group solidarity of the people for the national interest which had made the temples rich and strong. Ultimately they swallowed up not only the people but also the pharaoh.

Now look at the implications of this history in terms of the individual human. The previous tendency from the Old Kingdom up to the Empire had been centrifugal, atomistic, individualistic: the good life was to be found in the fullest expression of each person. Now the tendency was centripetal, nationalistic, communal: the good life was to be found in the group interest, and the individual was called upon to conform to the asserted needs of the group. Any wavering and tentative approach to an individualistic expression was cancelled out; any sense that the Egyptian community was a thing of value in itself was a cardinal doctrine.

A revolution of this spiritual and intellectual kind is not established by a congress which draws up a manifesto of change; it takes place so gradually as to be perceptible only over the centuries. Even a rebellion against the change, such as characterized the Amarna Revolution, was perhaps as much an unsystematized protest against the power mechanics of the change as a protest against the principles of the change. For centuries the Egyptian texts went on reiterating the older formulas, while the Egyptian tombs repeated the older lusty enjoyment of the manifold opportunities of this life. It is just as if Americans should turn gradually to a socialistic government and a rationalistic ethics while repeating the slogans of democracy and Calvinistic Protestantism; they would be unaware of the change for a long time after it had been effective.

Thus there were centuries of empire before the force of the change became visible in Egyptian literature and art. Only gradually were the old stereotypes replaced by new formulas. When the revolution was complete, we find that the goals of life had shifted from a vigorous, individualistic existence in this world, which would be rewarded by repetition in the next world, to a conforming and formalistic life in this world. As far as the individual Egyptian was concerned, his horizon of opportunity had become circumscribed; he was advised to submit because he was presented with an escape from this world's limitations by a promise of better things in the next world. Those better things were now less of his own agency and more the gift of the gods. There was thus not only a shift from the individual to the group but also a shift from an enjoyment of this world to the promise of the next world. That will explain the contrast between those two tombs which we outlined previously in this chapter, where the earlier monument presented gay and vigorous depictions of field, shop, and market place, whereas the later monument concentrated on the ritual approach to afterlife.

Let us try to document this thesis from the literature and particularly from the wisdom literature. One's first impression is that the late instructions in correct behaviour are just like the earlier instructions; in much the same Polonius language they tell the young official how to get on in his profession. Effective practical etiquette – at table, in the street, or in the law court – is the continuing theme. But gradually one is aware of differences. The reasons given for the injunctions have changed. Back in the older days a man had been advised to take good care of his wife, because 'she is a field of advantage to her master'. Now the man was told to remember the patience and devotion of his own mother and to treat his wife in accordance with his loving gratitude to his mother.[40] Whereas the older texts had enjoined patience and impartiality upon the official when dealing with poor clients, now he was to take positive action on behalf of the poor. 'If thou findest a large debt against a poor man, make it into three parts, throw out two, and let one remain.' Why should one take such an uneconomical action? The answer is that he cannot live with his own conscience unless he does. 'Thou wilt find it like the ways of life. Thou wilt lie and and sleep (soundly). In the morning thou wilt find it (again) like good news. It is better to be praised as one whom people love than (to have) riches in the storehouse. Better is bread when the heart is happy than riches under (the weight of) troubles.'[41] This was a change from the older texts; position and property were not so important now as the sense of right relations with other men. A man belonged to society, not to himself alone.

The key word for the developed spirit of this period was 'silence', which we may render also with 'calm, passivity, tranquillity, submission, humility, meekness'. This 'silence' is linked with weakness or poverty in such contexts as 'Thou art Amon, the lord of the silent, who comes at the voice of the poor',[42] and 'Amon, the protector of the silent, the rescuer of the poor'.[43] Because of that equation these characteristic expressions of humility have been designated as a religion of the poor.[44] It is true that meekness has always been a virtue recommended to the dispossessed, but our essential point is that every Egyptian of this period was dispossessed in terms of a right to self-expression; he had been cut off from the encouragement to voluntary self-development and was now constrained to a deterministic submission to the needs of the group. In proof of this assertion that the spirit of humility was not confined to the poverty-stricken, we would point out that a very high-placed official was at pains to describe himself as 'truly silent'[45] and that even the high priest of Amon might insist that he was 'properly and truly silent'.[46] In the spirit of the times the active and successful official found it necessary to emphasize his conformance to the national pattern of obedience.

As the objectionable contrast to the silent man, the texts offered the 'heated' or 'passionate' man, who was 'loud of voice'. In terms reminiscent of the First Psalm, the contrast is drawn (also Jer. xvii, 5–8):

As for the passionate man in the temple, he is like a tree growing in the open. Suddenly (comes) its loss of foliage, and its end is reached in the shipyards; (or) it is floated far from its place, and a flame is its burial shroud.

(But) the truly silent man holds himself apart. He is like a tree growing in a garden. It flourishes; it doubles its fruit; it (stands) before its lord. Its fruit is sweet; its shade is pleasant; and its end is reached in the garden.[47]

Now silence had often been enjoined in the earlier period, but it had been a topical silence: do not speak or resist unless you are smart enough.[48] Indeed, it had been emphasized that eloquence might be found in the lowest grades of society and that it should be encouraged there when found.[49] Now, in this changed spirit, the continuing injunction was silence alone. In dealings with superiors or in the government offices, it was submissive silence which would give you ultimate success.[50] This was related to the designs of the god, 'who loves the silent man more than him who is loud of voice',[51] and whose protection would confound one's opponents.[52] 'The dwelling of god, its abomination is clamour. Pray thou with a loving heart, all words of which are hidden. Then he will supply all thy needs; he will hear what thou sayest and will accept thy offering.'[53] The well of wisdom is not free for all who wish to drink therefrom; 'it is sealed to him who can discover his mouth, (but) it is open to him who is silent'.[54]

The new deterministic philosophy was rather definitely stated in terms of the will of god, placed over against man's helplessness. 'The god is (always) in his success, (whereas) man is (always) in his failure.' This statement of man's essential need of god was continued in an early expression of *Homo proposuit sed Deus disponit*: 'One thing are the words which men say, (but) another thing is what the god does.'[55] Gone was the earlier reliance upon man himself within the general pattern of the world order; now he specifically and always failed unless he conformed to that which the god directed.

Thus this period came to have a strong sense of fate or external determining force. One may say that this had not been entirely absent in earlier times in some magical force or other. The *ka* had been a semi-detached part of personality which had affected a man's career. But now the god Fate and the goddess Fortune stood outside the personality in remote but firm control. One could not pursue one's own interest without regard to these regulators on behalf of the gods. 'Cast not thy heart in pursuit of riches, (for) there is no ignoring Fate and Fortune. Place not thy heart upon externals, (for) every man belongs to his (appointed) hour.'[56] Man was charged not to search too deeply into the affairs of the gods, because the deities of destiny were his controlling limitation. 'Do not (try to) find for thyself the powers of the god himself, (as if) there were no Fate and Fortune.'[57]

It is possible to emphasize the role of fate exclusively in this period. There was still some voluntarism within the determined scheme of things. The young man was warned against a fatalism which prevents his searching for wisdom: 'Beware lest thou say: "Every man is according to his (own) nature. Ignorant and wise are of one piece (only). Fate and Fortune are carved on the nature (of a man) in the writings of the god himself. Every man passes his lifetime in an hour." (Nay), teaching is good, and there is no wearying in it, and a son should answer with the utterances of his father. I cause thee to know what is right in thy (own) heart, so that thou do what is correct in thy sight.'[58]

If success lay only with god and man was doomed to failure, we should expect to find expressions of the sense of personal shortcoming, ultimately stated as a consciousness of sin. Such expressions do appear at this time. To be sure, the nature of sin is not always clear, and it may involve only ritual irregularity rather than ethical wrongdoing. But we can insist upon an acknowledgment of error when a man says: 'Though the servant is normally (disposed) to do evil, yet the Lord is normally (disposed) to be merciful.'[59] In another case it was the specific crime of perjury that led a man to say of his god: 'He caused men and gods to look on me as if I were a man that does abominations against his Lord. Righteous was Ptah, Lord of Truth, toward me, when he disciplined me.'[60]

What is left for men when they are denied voluntary self-expression and are put into a rigid framework of conformance? Well, there was an escape from the limitations of this world in the promise of the next world, and it is possible to see an intensification of the desire for escape in Egypt, leading ultimately to monasticism and apocalyptic promise. But the promise of something distant is an uncertain thing in the day-by-day activity of a person; he wants something warmer right now. Thus the sense of personal wrongdoing called forth its antidote in a sense of divine nearness and mercy. The individual was swallowed up in a great impersonal system and felt lost. Very well, there was a god who was interested in him, who punished his transgressions, and who then healed him with mercy. Again and again the texts call upon a god or goddess to come in compassion to suffering man. 'I cried out to my Mistress; (then) I found that she came to me with sweet airs. She showed mercy to me, (after) she had made me behold her hand. She turned about again to me in mercy; she caused me to forget the sickness that had been [upon] me. Yea, the peak of the West is merciful if one cries out to her.'[61]

Thus, in compensation for the loss of individual voluntarism and the imposition of group determinism, there emerged a warmer personal relation between an Egyptian and his own god, and the period of the late Empire has been characterized by Breasted as the 'age of personal piety'. There was love and trust on the part of the worshipper; there was justice and mercy on the part of the god. In the revolution of Egyptian feeling, the good life lay no longer in cultivation of personality but in the surrender of personality to some greater force, with the recompense for surrender a security offered by that greater force.

It would take too long to argue the full development of this changed psychology of a people. The substitution of god's mercy for the encouragement of the individual spirit did not prove satisfactory. The joy went out of life. The Egyptian was called upon to rest content in humility and faith. Humility he did show. But faith is 'assurance of things hoped for, a conviction of things not seen'. He might and did still hope for better things in the world to come, but his conviction of things not seen was limited by the experience of things seen. He saw that his own personal god, who showed him mercy in his weakness, was also little and weak like himself. He saw that the great gods of Egypt, the national gods, were rich, distant, powerful and demanding. The priesthood of Egypt was still growing in power and control and demanded blind conformance to the system that gave the temples power and control. Individual man was caught in a strait jacket of rites and obligations, and his only comfort lay in soothing words and distant promises. He turned from a lusty appreciation of this life to means of escape from this life.

In the desire for escape from the present, the Egyptian turned not only to the afterworld future but also to the happy past. As we saw in chapter i, the Egyptians had always had a strong sense of the achievement, power, and dignity of earlier times. Constantly they invoked the good models of their past, whether the mythological times of the rule of the gods or the hazily historical times of the earliest kings.

Earlier in this chapter we quoted an old bit of agnosticism, in which the writer said in effect: The former sages Imhotep and Hardedef are much quoted, but they were unable to protect their tombs or their physical property; what did their wisdom avail them, after all? In later times the expression about these ancestors was different: Their wisdom did avail them, for they had left a memorial worthy of reverence. 'As for those learned scribes since the times which came after the gods ... their names have come to be lasting forever, although they (themselves) have gone. ... They did not make for themselves pyramids of metal, with tombstones of iron. They were not able to leave heirs in children. ... But they made heirs for themselves in writings and in the wisdom literature which they left. ... Books of wisdom were their pyramids, and the pen was their child. ... Is there (anyone) here like Hardedef? Is there another like Imhotep? ... They are gone and forgotten, but their names through (their) writings cause them to be remembered'.[62]

This strong sense of a rich and proud past comforted an age which felt uncertainty in its present. Ultimately this nostalgia for earlier times grew into archaism, with a rather blind and ignorant copying of the forms of a distant past. Personal piety was not able to make the concept of a single fatherly god adequate. The search for the spiritual support of religion went instead over to a recourse to oracles and over to strict ritualistic observance, until religion became as empty as Herodotus saw it. Within the confinement of a system of national conformance even the god-king became a mere puppet of the laws, as Diodorus saw him. Egypt had not had the opportunity or the capacity to work out the inter-relation of man and god in terms satisfactory to both. To put it in a different context, Egypt had not had the opportunity or the capacity to work out the inter-relation of the individual and the community in terms of benefit to both. There the Hebrews went farther, but there we are still struggling at the present day.

THE INTELLECTUAL ROLE OF EGYPT

Did ancient Egypt contribute any significant element to the continuing philosophy, ethics, or world-consciousness of later times? No, not directly in fields which one may specify, as in the case of Babylonian science, Hebrew theology, or Greek or Chinese rationalism. One might critically say that the weight of ancient Egypt was not consonant with her size, that her intellectual and spiritual contributions were not up to her length of years and her physical memorial, and that she herself was unable to realize on her promising beginnings in many fields.

But the very size of Egypt left its mark on her neighbours. The Hebrews and the Greeks were deeply conscious of a past power and a past stability of this colossal neighbour and had a vague and uncritical appreciation of 'all the wisdom of the Egyptians'. This high appreciation gave them two factors for the stimulation of their own thinking: a sense of high value outside their own times and places, so that their philosophies had the benefit of some historical setting, and a curiosity about the more obvious Egyptian achievements: accomplishments in art and architecture, governmental organization, and a sense of geometric order. If in gratifying that curiosity about Egypt they came across intellectual or ethical advances made by Egypt, these could only be valid to them in terms of their own experiences, because they were already ancient history in Egypt. The Hebrews or Greeks had to rediscover for themselves any elements which had already lost persuasive force in Egypt. That culture had reached her intellectual and spiritual heights too early to develop any philosophy which could be transmitted in cultural heritage to the ages. Like Moses, she had had a distant glimpse of the Promised Land, but it was left to others to cross the Jordan and begin the Conquest.

NOTES

1. The two tombs are those of Mereruka, a vizier of the Sixth Dynasty, and of Bekenrenef, a vizier of the Twenty-sixth Dynasty. References in Porter and Moss, *Topographical Bibliography*, Vol. III: *Memphis*, pp. 140 ff., 171 ff.

2. 'Dedication Address', December 5, 1931.   3. Urk. I, 105–6.

4. Ptahhotep, *passim*.   5. Urk. IV, 117.   6. *Ibid.*, 499.

7. Ptahhotep, 42–50.

8. Anthes, *Lebensregeln und Lebensweisheit der alten Ägypter*, pp. 12–13.

9. Ptahhotep, 60–83.   10. *Ibid.*, 119–33.   11. *Ibid.*, 264–69.

12. Ibid., 325–32.   13. Ibid., 573.   14. Ibid., 339–49.

15. Ibid., 84–98.   16. Admon., passim.   17. Ibid., 7:2–4.

18. Ibid., 9:2.   19. Khekheperresonbu, 10.   20. Admon., 2:12.

21. Leb., 93–95; 86–88.   22. Ibid., 103–16.   23. Ibid., 130–42.

24. Ibid., 142–47.   25. Ibid., 68.   26. Harris 500, 6:2–9.

27. Ibid., 7:2–3.   28. Merikarē, 36–37.   29. Ibid., 128–29.

30. Coffin Texts, B3C, ll. 570–76; B6C, ll. 503–11; B1Bo, ll. 618–22; see Breasted, Dawn of Conscience, p. 221.

31. TR 37; Rec., 30:189.   32. Coffin Texts, I, 181.

33. Bersheh, II, xix, 8:8–9.

34. BIFAO, 30:425 ff.; 'thou' changed to 'he' in last clause.

35. Peasant, B, 250–52.

36. E.g., Pyr. Spr. 260; cf. Sethe, Kommentar, I, 394: 'Der rote Faden in dem Texte ist: Gerechtigkeit, in dem was dem Toten im Leben zuteil wurde und in dem, was er selbst nach seinem Tode thut.'

37. Urk. IV, 390.   38. Breasted, Ancient Records, Vol. II, §39, n. d.

39. Schädel, Die Listen des grossen Papryus Harris, p. 67.

40. Anii, 7:17 – 8:3.   41. Amenemope, 16:5–14.

42. Berlin 20377; Erman, Denksteine, pp. 1086 ff.

43. Berlin 6910, Äg. Inschr., II, 70.   44. JEA, 3:83 ff.

45. Urk. IV, 993; cf. ibid., 66; BIFAO, 30:504 – all Eighteenth Dynasty.

46. Bibl. Eg., IV, 279, 281; Cairo 42155; both Bekenkhonsu of Nineteenth Dynasty.

47. Amenemope, 6:1–12

48. Prisse, 1:1–3; 8:11–12; 11:8–11; Peasant, B, 298–99; B, 313–16; Khekheperresonbu, Verso, 4; Sall. II, 9:9 – 10:1.

49. Ptahhotep, 58–59; Peasant, B, 74–80.

50. Anii, 3:17 – 4:1; 9:10; Amenemope, 22:1–18; 22:20 – 23:11.

51. Beatty IV, Recto, 5:8; cf. Beatty IV, Verso, 5:1–2.

52. Amenemope, 23:10–11.   53. Anii. 4:1–4.   54. Sall. I, 8:5–6.

55. Amenemope, 19: 14–17   56. Ibid., 9: 10–13.

57. Ibid., 21:15–16.   58. Beatty IV, Verso, 6:5–9.

59. Berlin 20377.   60. British Museum 589.   61. Turin 102.

62. Beatty IV, Verso, 2:5 – 3:11.

SUGGESTED READINGS

The references given in the notes to chapters ii–iv are of an abbreviated character known to Egyptologists who may wish to check our translations, normally referring to source documents. No work on ancient Egypt covers the same ground as do these chapters. However, certain titles may be listed for valuable discussion along similar lines. James H. Breasted, *Development of Religion and Thought in Ancient Egypt* (New York: Scribner's, 1912), was a brilliant pioneer work, which still has high value. There are useful chapters in George Steindorff and Keith C. Seele, *When Egypt Ruled the East* (Chicago, 2nd ed., 1957), in *The Legacy of Egypt*, edited by S. R. K. Glanville (Oxford, 1942), and in John A. Wilson, *The Burden of Egypt* (Chicago, 1951; which the same University of Chicago Press has issued as a Phoenix paperback under the title, *The Culture of Ancient Egypt*). Readers wishing translations of Egyptian texts are referred to *Ancient Near Eastern Texts relating to the Old Testament*, edited by James B. Pritchard (Princeton: 2nd ed., 1955), and to Adolf Erman, *The Literature of the Ancient Egyptians* (London, 1927). Two introductions to the religion are Jaroslav Černý, *Ancient Egyptian Religion* (London, 1952), and Henri Frankfort, *Ancient Egyptian Religion. An Interpretation* (New York, 1948). The functions of rule in Egypt and Mesopotamia are treated in Henri Frankfort, *Kingship and the Gods* (Chicago, 1948).

MESOPOTAMIA

Thorkild Jacobsen

CHAPTER V

Mesopotamia : The Cosmos as a State

INFLUENCE OF ENVIRONMENT IN EGYPT AND MESOPOTAMIA

IN PASSING from ancient Egypt to ancient Mesopotamia, we are leaving a civilization whose enduring monuments still stand, 'proud pyramids of stone proclaiming man's sense of sovereign power in his triumph over material forces'. We are moving on to a civilization whose monuments perished, whose cities – in the words of the prophet – 'have become heaps'. There is scant reminder of ancient grandeur in the low grey mounds which represent Mesopotamia's past.

It is altogether fitting that this should be so. It suits the basic moods of the two civilizations. Were the Egyptian to come back today, he would undoubtedly take heart from the endurance of his pyramids, for he accorded to man and to man's tangible achievements more basic significance than most civilizations have been willing to do. Were the Mesopotamian to return, he could hardly feel deeply disturbed that *his* works have crumbled, for he always knew, and knew deeply, that as for 'mere man – his days are numbered; whatever he may do, he is but wind'.[1] To him the centre and meaning of existence always lay beyond man and his achievements, beyond tangible things in intangible powers ruling the universe.

How the Egyptian and the Mesopotamian civilizations came to acquire these very different moods—one trusting, the other distrusting, man's power and ultimate significance—is not an easy question. The 'mood' of a civilization is the outcome of processes so intricate and so complex as to defy precise analysis. We shall therefore merely point to a single factor which would seem to have played a considerable role – the factor of environment. Chapters ii–iv have already stressed the active role of the environment in shaping the outlook of early Egypt. Egyptian civilization arose in a compact country where village lay reassuringly close to village, the whole ringed around and isolated by protecting mountain barriers. Over this sheltered world passed every day a dependable, never failing sun, calling Egypt back to life and activity after the darkness of night; here rose every year the trusty Nile to fertilize and revivify the Egyptian soil. It is almost as though Nature had deliberately restrained herself, as though she had set this secure valley apart so that man could disport himself unhindered.

It is small wonder that a great civilization arising on such a scene should be filled with a sense of its own power, should be deeply impressed with its own – with human – accomplishments. Chapter iv defined the attitude of early Egypt as 'a frontier spirit of visible accomplishments, of the first success in a new line. There was a youthful and self-reliant arrogance, because there had been no setbacks. Man was enough in himself. The gods? Yes, they were off there somewhere, and they had made this good world, to be sure; but the world was good because man was himself master, without need for the constant support of the gods'.

The experience of Nature which gave rise to this mood found direct expression in the Egyptian notion of the cosmos. The Egyptian cosmos was eminently reliable and comforting. It had – to quote chapter ii – 'reassuring periodicity; its structural framework and mechanics permitted the reiteration of life through the rebirth of life-giving elements'.

Mesopotamian civilization grew up in an environment which was signally different. We find there, of course, the same great cosmic rhythms – the change of the seasons, the unwavering sweep of sun, moon, and stars – but we also find an element of force and violence which was lacking in Egypt. The Tigris and Euphrates are not like the Nile; they may rise unpredictably and fitfully, breaking man's dykes and submerging his crops. There are scorching winds which smother man in dust, threaten to suffocate him; there are torrential rains which turn all firm ground into a sea of mud and rob man of his freedom of movement: all travel bogs down. Here, in Mesopotamia, Nature stays not her hand; in her full might she cuts across and overrides man's will, makes him feel to the full how slightly he matters.

The mood of Mesopotamian civilization reflects this. Man is not tempted to overrate himself when he contemplates powers in nature such as the thunderstorm and the yearly flood. Of the thunderstorm the Mesopotamian said that its 'dreadful flares of light cover the land like a cloth'.[2] The impression which the flood made on him may be gathered from the following description:

> The rampant flood which no man can oppose,
> Which shakes the heavens and causes earth to tremble,
> In an appalling blanket folds mother and child,
> Beats down the canebrake's full luxuriant greenery,
> And drowns the harvest in its time of ripeness.
>
> Rising waters, grievous to eyes of man,
> All-powerful flood, which forces the embankments
> And mows mighty *mesu*-trees,
> (Frenzied) storm, tearing all things in massed confusion
> With it (in hurtling speed).[3]

Standing amidst such powers, man sees how weak he is, realizes with dread that he is caught in an interplay of giant forces. His mood becomes tense; his own lack of power makes him acutely aware of tragic potentialities.

The experience of Nature which produced this mood found direct expression in the Mesopotamian's notion of the cosmos in which he lived. He was in no way blind to the great rhythms of the cosmos; he saw the cosmos as order, not as anarchy. But to him that order was not nearly so safe and reassuring as it was to the Egyptian. Through and under it he sensed a multitude of powerful individual wills, potentially divergent, potentially conflicting, fraught with a possibility of anarchy. He confronted in Nature gigantic and wilful individual powers.

To the Mesopotamian, accordingly, cosmic *order* did not appear as something given; rather it became something achieved – achieved through a continual integration of the many individual cosmic wills, each so powerful, so frightening. His understanding of the cosmos tended therefore to express itself in terms of integration of wills, that is, in terms of social orders such as the family, the community, and, most particularly, the state. To put it succinctly, he saw the cosmic order as an order of wills – as a state.

In presenting this view here, we shall discuss first the period in which it may be assumed to have originated. We shall then take up the question of what the Mesopotamian saw in the phenomena of the world around him, in order to show how it could be possible for him to apply an order from the social sphere, the state, to the basically different world of Nature. Lastly, we shall discuss that order in detail and comment on those forces which played the most prominent part in it.

DATE OF THE MESOPOTAMIAN VIEW OF THE WORLD

The Mesopotamian's understanding of the universe in which he lived seems to have found its characteristic form at about the time when Mesopotamian civilization as a whole took shape, that is, in the Proto-literate period, around the middle of the fourth millennium B.C.

Thousands of years had already passed since man first entered the valley of the Two Rivers, and one prehistoric culture had followed another – all basically alike, none signally different from what one might have found elsewhere in the world. During those millenniums agriculture was the chief means of support. Tools were fashioned from stone, rarely from copper. Villages, made up of patriarchal families, seem to have been the typical form of settlement. The most conspicuous change from one such culture to another, surely not a very profound one, seems to have been in the way pottery was made and decorated.

But with the advent of the Proto-literate period the picture changes. Overnight, as it were, Mesopotamian civilization crystallizes. The fundamental pattern, the controlling framework within which Mesopotamia is to live its life, formulate its deepest questions, evaluate itself and evaluate the universe, for ages to come, flashes into being, complete in all its main features.

In the economic sphere appeared *planned large-scale irrigation by means of canals*, a form which forever after was to be characteristic of Mesopotamian agriculture. Concurrent with this and closely inter-related with it was a spectacular increase in population. The old villages expanded into cities; new settlements were founded throughout the country. And, as village grew into city, the political pattern of the new civilization emerged – *Primitive Democracy*. In the new city-state ultimate political power rested with a general assembly of all adult freemen. Normally the everyday affairs of the community were guided by a council of elders; but in times of crisis, for instance, when war threatened, the general assembly could confer absolute powers on one of its members and proclaim him king. Such kingship was an office held for a limited term; and, as the assembly could confer it, so it could also revoke it when a crisis was past.

The centralization of authority which this new political pattern made possible may have been responsible, along with other factors, for the emergence of a truly *monumental architecture* in Mesopotamia. Imposing temples now began to rise in the plain, often built on gigantic artificial mountains of sun-dried bricks, the famous *ziqqurats*. Works of such imposing proportions clearly presuppose a high degree of organization and direction in the community which achieved them.

As these things were happening in the economic and social fields, new peaks of achievement were attained in the more spiritual fields of endeavour. *Writing* was invented, at first serving to facilitate the ever more complicated accounting which had become necessary with the expansion of city and temple economy. Eventually it was to become the vehicle of a most significant literature. Moreover, Mesopotamia produced *art* worthy of the name; and the works of these early artists compare very well with the best of later periods.

In economics, in politics, and in the arts Mesopotamia thus found at this early stage its guiding forms, created set ways in which to deal with the universe in its various aspects as they confronted man. It would not be surprising, therefore, to find that the view taken of the universe as a whole should likewise have clarified and taken form at that time. That this actually happened is indicated by the world view itself. As we have already mentioned, Mesopotamian civilization interpreted the universe as a state. However, the basis of interpretation was not the state that existed in historic times but the state as it had been before history – a Primitive Democracy. We have therefore the right to assume that the idea of a cosmic state crystallized very early, when Primitive Democracy was the prevalent type of state – indeed, with Mesopotamian civilization itself.

THE MESOPOTAMIAN ATTITUDE TOWARD THE PHENOMENA OF NATURE

Assuming, then, that the Mesopotamian view of the universe was as old as Mesopotamian civilization itself, we must next ask how it could be at all possible to take such a view. Certainly for us it has no meaning whatever to speak of the universe as a state – of stones and stars, winds and waters, as citizens and as members of legislative assemblies. Our universe is made up largely of things, of dead matter with neither life nor will. This leads us to the question of what the Mesopotamian saw in the phenomena which surrounded him, the world in which he lived.

The reader will remember from the first chapter that 'the world appears to primitive man neither inanimate nor empty but redundant with life'. It was said of primitive man that 'any phenomenon may at any time face him not as "It" but as "Thou". In this confrontation "Thou" reveals individuality, qualities, will'. Out of the repeated experience of the 'I-Thou' relationship a fairly consistent personalistic view may develop. Objects and phenomena in man's environment become personified in varying degrees. They are somehow alive; they have wills of their own; each is a definite personality. We then have what the late Andrew Lang disapprovingly described as 'that inextricable confusion in which men, beasts, plants, stones, stars are all on one level of personality and animated existence'.[4]

A few examples may show that Lang's words well describe the Mesopotamian's approach to the phenomena around him. Ordinary kitchen salt is to us an inanimate substance, a mineral. To the Mesopotamian it was a fellow-being whose help might be sought if one had fallen victim to sorcery and witchcraft. The sufferer would then address it as follows:

> O Salt, created in a clean place,
> For food of gods did Enlil destine thee.
> Without thee no meal is set out in Ekur,
> Without thee god, king, lord, and prince do not smell incense.
> I am so-and-so, the son of so-and-so,
> Held captive by enchantment,
> Held in fever by bewitchment.
> O Salt, break my enchantment! Loose my spell!
> Take from me the bewitchment! – And as my Creator
> I shall extol thee.[5]

As Salt, a fellow-creature with special powers, can be approached directly, so can Grain. When a man offered up flour to conciliate an angry deity, he might say to it:

> I will send thee to my angry god, my angry goddess,
> Whose heart is filled with furious rage against me.
> Do thou reconcile my angry god, my angry goddess.

Both Salt and Grain are thus not the inanimate substances for which we know them. They are alive, have personality and a will of their own. So had any phenomenon in the Mesopotamian world whenever it was approached in a spirit other than that of humdrum, practical, everyday pursuits: in magic, in religion, in speculative thought. In such a world it obviously gives better sense than it does in our world to speak of the relations between phenomena of nature as social relations, of the order in which they function as an order of wills, as a state.

By saying that the phenomena of the world were alive for the Mesopotamian, that they were personified, we have made things simpler than they actually are. We have glossed over a potential distinction which was felt by the Mesopotamian. It is not correct to say that each phenomenon was a person; we must say that there was a will and a personality in each phenomenon – in it and yet somehow behind it, for the single concrete phenomenon did not completely circumscribe and exhaust the will and personality associated with it. For instance, a particular lump of flint had a clearly recognizable personality and will. Dark, heavy, and hard, it would show a curious willingness to flake under the craftsman's tool though that tool was only of horn softer than the stone against which it was pressed. Now, this characteristic personality which confronts one here, in this particular lump of flint, may meet one also over there, in another lump of flint, which seems to say: 'Here I am again – dark, heavy, hard, willing to flake, I, Flint!' Wherever one met it, its name was 'Flint', and it would suffer itself to flake easily. That was because it had once fought the god Ninurta, and Ninurta had imposed flaking on it as a punishment.[6]

We may consider another example – the reeds which grew in the Mesopotamian marshes. It is quite clear from our texts that, in themselves, they were never divine. Any individual reed counted merely as a plant, a thing, and so did all reeds. The concrete individual reed, however, had wonderful qualities which inspired awe. There was a mysterious power to grow luxuriantly in the marshes. A reed was capable of amazing things, such as the music which would come out of a shepherd's pipe, or the meaningful signs which would take form under the scribe's reed stylus and make a story or a poem. These powers, which were to be found in every reed and were always the same, combined for the Mesopotamian into a divine personality – that of the goddess Nidaba. It was Nidaba who made the reeds thrive in the marshes; if she were not near, the shepherd could not soothe the heart with music from his reed pipe. To her would the scribe give praise when a difficult piece of writing had come out from under his stylus and he saw it to be good. The goddess was thus the power in all reeds; she made them what they were, lent them her mysterious qualities. She was one with every reed in the sense that she permeated it as an animating and characterizing agent; but she did not lose her identity in that of the concrete phenomenon and was not limited by any or even all existing reeds.[7] In a crude but quite effective manner the Mesopotamian artists suggested this relationship when they depicted the reed-goddess. She is shown in human form as a venerable matron. But the reeds also are there: they sprout from her shoulders – are bodily one with her and seem to derive directly from her.

In a great many individual phenomena, such as individual lumps of flint or individual reeds, the Mesopotamian thus felt that he was confronted by a single self. He sensed, as it were, a common power-centre which was charged with a particular personality and was itself personal. This personal power-centre pervaded the individual phenomena and gave them the character which they are seen to have: 'Flint' all lumps of flint, Nidaba all reeds, etc.

Even more curious than this, however, is the fact that one such self might infuse itself into other different selves and, in a relation of partial identity, lend them of its character. We may illustrate by quoting a Mesopotamian incantation by which a man sought to become identical with Heaven and Earth:

> I am Heaven, you cannot touch me,
> I am Earth, you cannot bewitch me![8]

The man is trying to ward off sorcery from his body, and his attention is centred on a single quality of Heaven and Earth, their sacred inviolability. When he has made himself identical with them, this quality will flow into him and merge with his being, so that he will be secure from attacks by witchcraft.

Very similar is another incantation in which a man endeavours to drench every part of his body in immunity by such identification with gods and sacred emblems. It reads:

> Enlil is my head, my face is the day;
> Urash, the peerless god, is the protecting spirit leading my way.
> My neck is the necklace of the goddess Ninlil,
> My two arms are the sickle of the western moon,
> My fingers tamarisk, bone of the gods of heaven;
> They ward off the embrace of sorcery from my body;
> The gods Lugal-edinna and Latarak are my breast and knees;
> Muhra my ever-wandering feet.[9]

Here again the identity sought is only partial. Qualities of these gods and sacred emblems are to infuse the man's members and make him inviolable.

As it was thought possible for a man to achieve partial identity with various gods, so could one god enjoy partial identity with other gods and thus share in their natures and abilities. We are told, for instance, that the face of the god

Ninurta is Shamash, the sun-god; that one of Ninurta's ears is the god of wisdom, Ea – and so on through all of Ninurta's members.[10] These curious statements may be taken to mean that Ninurta's face derived its dazzling radiance from, and thus shared in, that brilliance which is characteristically the sun-god's and concentrates itself in him. In similar manner, his ear – for the Mesopotamians believed the ear, not the brain, to be the seat of intelligence – shares in that supreme intelligence which is the outstanding characteristic of the god Ea.

Sometimes such statements of partial identity take a slightly different form. We are told, for instance, that the god Marduk is the god Enlil when there is question of ruling and taking counsel, but that he is Sîn, the moon-god, when he acts as illuminer of the night, etc.[11] This apparently means that the god Marduk, when he rules and makes decisions, partakes of the personality, qualities, and abilities of the divine executive par excellence, the god Enlil. When, on the other hand, Marduk, as the planet Jupiter, shines in the nightly skies, he shares in those special powers which characterize the moon-god and have their centre in him.

Any phenomenon which the Mesopotamian met in the world around him was thus alive, had its own personality and will, its distinct self. But the self which revealed itself, for example, in a particular lump of flint, was not limited by that particular lump; it was in it and yet behind it; it permeated it and gave it character as it did all lumps of flint. And as one such 'self' could permeate many individual phenomena, so it might also permeate other selves and thereby give to them of its specific character to add to the qualities which they had in their own right.

To understand nature, the many and varied phenomena around man, was thus to understand the personalities in these phenomena, to know their characters, the direction of their wills, and also the range of their powers. It was a task not different from that of understanding other men, knowing their characters, their wills, the extent of their power and influence. And intuitively the Mesopotamian applied to nature the experience he had of his own human society, interpreting it in social terms. A particularly suggestive example will illustrate this. Under our eyes, as it were, objective reality assumes the form of a social type.

According to Mesopotamian beliefs, a man who had been bewitched could destroy the enemies who had bewitched him by burning images of them. The characteristic self of the enemy stared up at him from the image. He could get at it and harm it there, as well as in the person. And so he consigned the images to the fire while addressing it as follows:

> Scorching Fire, warlike son of Heaven,
> Thou, the fiercest of thy brethren,
> Who like Moon and Sun decidest lawsuits –
> Judge thou my case, hand down the verdict.
> Burn the man and woman who bewitched me;
> Burn, O Fire, the man and woman who bewitched me;
> Scorch, O Fire, the man and woman who bewitched me;
> Burn them, O Fire;
> Scorch them, O Fire;
> Take hold of them, O Fire;
> Consume them, O Fire;
> Destroy them, O Fire.[12]

It is quite clear that the man approaches the fire for the destructive power he knows to be in it. But the fire has a will of its own; it will burn the images – and in them his enemies – only if it so chooses. And in deciding whether to burn the images or not, the fire becomes a judge between the man and his enemies: the situation becomes a lawsuit in which the man pleads his cause and asks the fire to vindicate him. The power which is in fire has taken definite form, has been interpreted in social terms; it is a judge.

As the fire here becomes a judge, other powers take form in similar pregnant situations. The thunderstorm was a warrior; he flung deadly lightning, and one could hear the roar emitted by the wheels of his war chariot. The earth was a woman, a mother; she gave birth each year to the new vegetation. In such cases the Mesopotamians did only what other people have done throughout the ages. 'Men,' as Aristotle says, 'imagine not only the forms of the gods but their ways of life to be like their own.'[13]

If we were to try to single out a typically Mesopotamian feature, we should perhaps point to the degree to which this people found and emphasized organized relationships of the powers they recognized. While all the people tend to humanize non-human powers and frequently visualize them as social types, Mesopotamian speculative thought seems to have brought out and systematized to an unusual degree the implications of social and political function latent in such typifying and to have elaborated them into clear-cut institutions. This particular emphasis would seem to be closely bound up with the nature of the society in which the Mesopotamian lived and from which he derived his terms and his evaluation.

When the universe was taking form for the Mesopotamian, he lived, we have argued, in a Primitive Democracy. All great undertakings, all important decisions, originated in a general assembly of all the citizens; they were not the affair of any single individual. It is accordingly natural that, in trying to understand how the great cosmic events were brought about, he should be especially intent upon the ways in which the individual forces of the cosmos co-operated to run the universe. Cosmic institutions would naturally come to loom important in his view of the universe, and the structure of the universe would stand out clearly as the structure of a state.

THE STRUCTURE OF THE COSMIC STATE

The commonwealth of the Mesopotamian cosmos encompassed the whole existing world – in fact, anything that could be thought of as an entity: humans, animals, inanimate objects, natural phenomena, as well as notions such as justice, righteousness, the form of a circle, etc. How such entities could all be seen as members of a state we have just shown; they had in them will, character, and power. But though all things that could be imagined were members of the cosmic state, they were not all members on the same political level. The criterion of differentiation was power.

In the state on earth there were large groups of people who had no share in the government. Slaves, children, and perhaps women had no voice in the assembly. Only the adult freemen met there to decide on public affairs; they alone were citizens in the true sense. Quite similarly in the state which the universe constituted.

Only those natural forces whose power inspired the Mesopotamian with awe, and whom he therefore ranked as gods, were considered full citizens of the universe, were thought to have political rights and to exercise political influence. The general assembly in the cosmic state was therefore an assembly of gods.

We hear about this assembly often in Mesopotamian literature, and we know in general how it functioned. It was the highest authority in the universe. Here the momentous decisions regarding the course of all things and the fates of all beings were made and were confirmed by the members of the assembly. Before that stage was reached, however, proposals were discussed, perhaps even heatedly, by gods who were for or against them. The leader of the assembly was the god of heaven, Anu. At his side stood his son Enlil, god of the storm. One of these usually broached the matters to be considered, and the gods would then discuss them. Through such discussions (the Mesopotamians called it 'asking one another') the issues were clarified, and the consensus would begin to stand out.

Of special weight in the discussion were the voices of a small group of the most prominent gods, 'the seven gods who determine destinies'. In this way, full agreement was finally reached, all the gods assented with a firm 'Let it be', and the decision was announced by Anu and Enlil. It was now 'the verdict, the word of the assembly of the gods, the command of Anu and Enlil'. The executive duties (the task of carrying out the decisions) seem to have rested with Enlil.

LEADERS OF THE COSMIC STATE

We have seen that the gods who constituted the divine assembly were powers which the Mesopotamians recognized in and behind the various phenomena of nature. Which of these powers, then, played the most prominent roles in the assembly, influenced most the course of the universe? In a sense we may answer: 'The powers in those elements of the cosmos which were seen to be the greatest and most prominent'.

Anu, the highest of the gods, was god of the sky, and his name was the everyday word for 'sky'. The dominant role which the sky plays – even in a merely spatial sense – in the composition of the visible universe, and the eminent position which it occupies, high above all other things, may well explain why Anu should rank as the most important force in the cosmos.

Enlil, the second highest of the gods, was god of the storm. His name means 'Lord Storm', and he personifies the essence of the storm. No one who has experienced a storm in flat, open Mesopotamia can possibly doubt the might of this cosmic force. The storm, master of all free space under the sky, ranked naturally as the second great component of the cosmos.

As third basic component of the visible universe comes the earth. Earth, so near to man, so vitally important to him in so many of its aspects, was difficult to view and hold fast within the scope of a single concept. We meet it as 'Mother Earth', the fertile giver of blessings to man, and as the 'queen of the gods' and 'lady of the mountains'. But the earth is also the source of the life-giving waters in rivers, canals, and wells; waters which stream from a vast sea within. And as the source of these waters the earth was viewed as male, as *En-ki*, 'lord of the earth', more originally perhaps 'Lord Earth'. The third and fourth in rank of the Mesopotamian gods were these two aspects of the earth, Ninhursaga and Enki. They round off the list of the most important cosmic elements that must rank highest and exercise the greatest influence on all that is.

A. THE POWER IN THE SKY: AUTHORITY

But considerations of size and position alone could hardly have suggested the specific character and the function which these powers were assumed to have in the universe. The Mesopotamian conceived both character and function in direct confrontation with the phenomena when they 'revealed' themselves and deeply affected him.

The sky can, at moments when man is in a singularly receptive mood, reveal itself in an almost terrifying experience. The vast sky encircling one on all sides may be felt as a presence at once overwhelming and awesome, forcing one to his knees merely by its sheer being. And this feeling which the sky inspires is definite and can be named: it is that inspired by majesty. There is in it the experience of greatness or even of the tremendous. There comes a keen realization of one's own insignificance, of unbridgeable remoteness. The Mesopotamians express this well when they say, 'Godhead awesome as the faraway heavens, as the broad sea'. But, though a feeling of distance, this feeling is not one of absolute separation; it has a strong element of sympathy and of the most unqualified acceptance.

Beyond all, however, the experience of majesty is the experience of power, of power bordering on the tremendous, but power at rest, not consciously imposing its will. The power behind majesty is so great that it need not exert itself. Without any effort on its part it commands allegiance by its very presence; the onlooker obeys freely, through a categorical imperative rising from the depths of his own soul.

This majesty and absolute authority which can be experienced in the sky the Mesopotamians called Anu. Anu was the overpowering personality of the sky, the 'Thou' which permeated it and could be felt through it. If the sky was considered apart from him, as it could be, it receded into the category of things and became a mere abode for the god.

The 'Thou' which met the Mesopotamian when he confronted the sky was so powerfully experienced that it was felt to be the very centre and source of all majesty. Wherever else he found majesty and authority he knew it to be that power in the sky, to be Anu. And he did find it elsewhere; indeed, authority, the power which produces automatic acceptance and obedience, is a basic constituent in all organized human society. Were it not for unquestioning obedience to customs, to laws, and to those 'in authority', society would dissolve in anarchy and chaos. So in those persons in whom authority resided – the father in the family, the ruler in the state – the Mesopotamian recognized something of Anu and Anu's essence. As the father of the gods, Anu was the prototype of all fathers; as the 'pristine king and ruler', he was the prototype of all rulers. To him belong the insignia in which the essence of royalty was embodied – the sceptre, the crown, the headband, and the shepherd's staff – and from him did they derive. Before any king had yet been appointed among men these insignia already were, and they rested in heaven before Anu.

From there they descended to earth. Anu also calls to kingship; and when the king commands and the command is unquestioningly and immediately obeyed, when it 'comes true', it is again the essence of Anu which manifests itself. It is Anu's command that issues through the king's mouth; it is Anu's power that makes it immediately efficacious.

But human society was to the Mesopotamian merely a part of the larger society of the universe. The Mesopotamian universe – because it did not consist of dead matter, because every stone, every tree, every conceivable thing in it was a being with a will and character of its own – was likewise founded on authority; its members, too, willingly and automatically obeyed orders which made them act as they should act. These orders *we* call laws of nature. So the whole universe showed the influence of the essence peculiar to Anu.

When in the Babylonian creation story the god Marduk is given absolute authority, and all things and forces in the universe automatically conform themselves to his will so that whatever he orders immediately comes to pass, then his command has become identical in essence with Anu and the gods exclaim: 'Thy word is Anu.'

We see thus that Anu is the source of and active principle in all authority, both in human society and in the larger society which is the universe. He is the force which lifts it out of chaos and anarchy and makes it into a structure, an organized whole; he is the force which ensures the necessary voluntary obedience to orders, laws, and customs in society and to the natural laws in the physical world, in short, to world order. As a building is supported by, and reveals in its structure the lines of, its foundation, so the Mesopotamian universe is upheld by, and reflects in *its* structure, a divine will. Anu's command is the foundation of heaven and earth.

What we have said here at some length about the function of Anu is said briefly and concisely by the Mesopotamians themselves. When the great gods address Anu in the 'Myth of the Elevation of Inanna', they exclaim:

> What thou hast ordered (comes) true!
>> The utterance of prince and lord is (but)
>> what thou hast ordered, (that with which) thou art in agreement.
> O Anu! thy great command takes precedence,
>> who could say no (to it)?
> O father of the gods, thy command,
>> the very foundation of heaven and earth,
>> what god could spurn (it)? [14]

As the absolute sovereign of the world, the highest power in the universe, Anu is described in such words as these:

> Wielder of the sceptre, the ring, and the *palu*
>> who callest to kingship,
> Sovereign of the gods, whose word prevails
>> in the ordained assembly of the great gods,
> Lord of the glorious crown, astounding
>> through thine enchantment,
> Rider of great storms, who occupies the dais of sovereignty,
>> wondrously regal –
> To the pronouncements of thy holy mouth
>> are the Igigi attentive;
> In fear before thee move the Anunnaki,
> Like storm-swept reeds bow to thy orders
>> all the gods. [15]

B. THE POWER IN THE STORM: FORCE

Turning from Anu, god of the sky, to Enlil, god of the storm, we meet a power of a somewhat different cast. As his name *En-lil*, 'Lord Storm', suggests, he was in a sense the storm itself. As the storm, the undisputed master of all space between heaven and earth, Enlil was palpably the second greatest power of the visible universe, second only to the sky above him.

In the storm he 'reveals' himself. The violence, the force, which fills it and is experienced in it was the god, was Enlil. It is thus through the storm, through its violence and force, that we must seek to understand the god and his function in the universe.

The city of Ur had long held sway over Babylonia. Then it fell before a merciless attack by Elamitic hordes which swept down upon it from the eastern mountains. The utter destruction of the city was wrought, in our terms, by the barbaric hordes which attacked it. Not so in terms of the Mesopotamian's own understanding of his universe: the wild destructive essence manifest in this attack was Enlil's. The enemy hordes were but a cloak, an outward form under which that essence realized itself. In a deeper, truer sense the barbaric hordes were a storm, Enlil's storm, wherewith the god himself was executing a verdict passed on Ur and its people by the assembly of the gods; and as that storm the enemy attack is seen and described:

> Enlil called the storm.
>   The people mourn.
> Exhilarating winds he took from the land.
>   The people mourn.
> Good winds he took away from Shumer.
>   The people mourn.
> He summoned evil winds.
>   The people mourn.
> Entrusted them to Kingaluda, tender of storms.
>
> He called the storm that will annihilate the land.
>   The people mourn.
> He called disastrous winds.
>   The people mourn.
> Enlil – choosing Gibil as his helper –
> Called the (great) hurricane of heaven.
>   The people mourn.
>
> The (blinding) hurricane howling across the skies,
>   – The people mourn –
> The shattering storm roaring across the land,
>   – The people mourn –
> The tempest which, relentless as a floodwave,
> Beats down upon, devours the city's ships,
> All these he gathered at the base of heaven.
>   The people mourn.

times one, sometimes another, god. There can be little doubt, however, that the myth, in its original form, centred around Enlil. As such, it describes the dangers which once beset the gods when they were threatened with attack from the powers of chaos: how neither the command of Enki nor that of Anu, reinforced by the authority of the assembly of gods, could stay them; how the gods assembled and chose young Enlil to be their king and champion; and how Enlil vanquished the enemy, Tiᵓamat, by means of the storms, those forces which express the essence of his being.

Thus, in the society which the Mesopotamian universe constitutes, Anu represents authority, Enlil force. The subjective experience of the sky, of Anu, is, as we have seen, one of majesty, of absolute authority which commands allegiance by its very presence. The onlooker obeys it not through any outward pressure but through a categorical imperative which rises within his own soul. Not so with Enlil, the storm. Here, too, is power; but it is the power of force, of compulsion. Opposing wills are crushed and beaten into submission. In the assembly of the gods, the ruling body of the universe, Anu presides and directs the proceedings. His will and authority, freely and voluntarily accepted, guide the assembly much as a constitution guides the actions of a law-making body. Indeed, his will is the unwritten, living constitution of the Mesopotamian world state. But whenever force enters the picture, when the cosmic state is enforcing its will against opposition, then Enlil takes the centre of the stage. He executes the sentences imposed by the assembly; he leads the gods in war. Thus Anu and Enlil embody, on a cosmic level, the two powers which are the fundamental constituents of any state: authority and legitimate force; for, while authority alone may suffice to hold a community together, such a community becomes a state only when it develops organs to back up its authority with force, when its staff, to quote Max Weber, 'successfully displays the monopoly of a legitimate physical compulsion.' For this reason we can say that, while it is the powers of Anu that make the Mesopotamian universe an organized society, it is the complementary powers of Enlil that define this society as a state.

Because Enlil is force, his character is one of peculiar quality: he is at one and the same time the trust and the fear of man. He is force as legitimate force, upholder of the state, a rock of strength even to the gods. Man greets him in words like these:

> O Thou who dost encompass all heaven and earth, fleet god,
> Wise instructor of the people,
> Who dost survey the regions of the world;
> Prince, counsellor, whose word is heeded,
> Whose spoken word ... gods cannot alter,
> The utterance of whose lips no god may spurn;
> Great Lord, ruler of gods in heaven,
> Counsellor of gods on earth, judicious prince.[19]

Yet, because Enlil is force, there lie hidden in the dark depths of his soul both violence and wildness. The normal Enlil upholds the cosmos, guarantees order against chaos; but suddenly and unpredictably the hidden wildness in him may break forth. This side of Enlil is truly and terribly the abnormal, a scattering of all life and of life's meaning. Therefore, man can never be fully at ease with Enlil but feels a lurking fear which finds expression frequently in the hymns which have come down to us:

> What has he planned ... ?
> What is in my father's heart?
> What is in Enlil's holy mind?
> What has he planned against me in his holy mind?
> A net he spread: that is the net of an enemy.
> A snare he set: that is the snare of an enemy.
> He has stirred up the waters, and will catch the fishes.
> He cast his net, and will (bring) down the birds.[20]

This same fear shows in other descriptions of Enlil, who may let his people perish in the merciless storm. The god's rage is almost pathological, an inner turmoil of the soul which renders him insensate, inaccessible to all appeals:

> O father Enlil, whose eyes are glaring (wildly),
> How long – till they will be at peace again?
> O thou who covered up thy head with a cloth – how long?
> O thou who laid thy head upon thy knees – how long?
> O thou who closed thy heart like an earthen box – how long?
> O mighty one who with thy fingers sealed thine ears – how long?
> O father Enlil, even now they perish![21]

C. The Power in the Earth: Fertility

The third great component of the visible cosmos is the Earth, and the Mesopotamians acknowledged it as the third most important power in the universe. Their understanding of this power and its ways was gained, as with sky and storm, in direct experience of it as inner will and direction. Correspondingly, the ancient name of this deity, *Ki*, 'Earth', had difficulty in maintaining itself and tended ever more to give way to other names based on significant characteristics. The earth revealed itself to the Mesopotamians before all as 'Mother Earth', the great inexhaustible mysterious source of new life, of fertility in all its forms. Every year she gives birth anew to grass and plants.

The arid desert becomes green overnight. The shepherds drive out their flocks. Ewes and goats give birth to lambs and kids. Everything thrives and increases. On the good fields of Shumer 'grain, the green maiden, lifts her head in the furrow'; soon a rich harvest will fill granaries and storehouses to overflowing. Well-fed humanity, full of beer, bread, and milk, will feel abundant life surge through their bodies in a wave of profound well-being.

The force active in all this – the power manifesting itself in fertility, in birth, in new life – is the essence of the earth. The earth, as a divine power, is *Nin-tu*, 'the lady who gives birth'; she is *Níg-zi-gál-dím-me*, 'the fashioner of everything wherein is the breath of life'. Reliefs show her as a woman suckling a child; other children are tucked away under her dress and peep out wherever they can; embryos surround her. As the incarnation of all reproductive forces in the universe, she is the 'mother of the gods' and also the mother and creator of mankind; indeed, she is – as an inscription states – the 'mother of all children'. If she so wills, she may deny an evildoer offspring or even stop all birth in the land.

As the active principle in birth and fertility, in the continual renewal of vegetation, the growth of crops, the increase of flocks, the perpetuation of the human race, she holds with right her position as a dominant power, takes her seat with

Anu and Enlil in the assembly of the gods, the ruling body of the universe. She is *Ninmah*, 'the exalted queen'; she is 'queen of the gods', 'queen of kings and lords', the 'lady who determines fates', and the 'lady who makes decisions concerning (all) heaven and earth'.

D. THE POWER IN THE WATER: CREATIVITY

But the earth, so near to man, so varied and manifold in characteristics, is – as we have mentioned – not easily comprehended as an entity by the mind. It is too rich and diverse for any single concept to express fully. We have just described one of its basic aspects, the fertile soil, the active principle in birth and procreation, Mother Earth. But from the earth also come the life-giving sweet waters, the water in wells, in springs, in rivers; and in very early times these 'waters which wander in the earth' seem to have been considered as part of its being, an aspect among many aspects under which it might be viewed. If so viewed, however, the power manifest in it was male, *En-ki*, 'lord of the earth'. In historical times only Enki's name and the role he plays in certain myths give any indication that he and the sweet water for which he stands were once merely an aspect of the earth as such. The waters and the power in them have emancipated themselves, have their own independent individuality and peculiar essence. The power which revealed itself to the Mesopotamian in his subjective experience of water was a creative power, a divine will to produce new life, new beings, new things. In this respect it was akin to the powers in the earth, in the fertile soil. And yet there was a difference – that between passive and active. The Earth, Ki, Ninhursaga, or whatever else we may choose to call her, was immobile; hers is the passive productivity, fertility. Water, on the other hand, comes and goes. It flows out over the field, irrigating it; then it trickles away and is gone. It is as though it were possessed of will and purpose. It typifies active productivity, conscious thought, creativity.

Moreover, the ways of water are devious. It avoids rather than surmounts obstacles, goes around and yet gets to its goal. The farmer, who works with it in irrigation, easing it along from canal to canal, knows how tricky it can be, how easily it slips away, takes unforeseen turns. And so, we may assume, the idea of cunning, of superior intelligence, came to be imparted to Enki. This aspect of his being would be further developed by contemplation of the dark, brooding, impenetrable waters of wells and lagoons, which suggested perhaps the more profound intellectual qualities, wisdom and knowledge. In the functioning of the universe the powers which are peculiarly Enki's manifest themselves often and in many places. They are directly active in the roles played by water everywhere: when it falls from heaven as rain, when it comes flowing down in the rivers, when it is led through canals out over fields and orchards where it produces the crops of the country and the prosperity of the people. But Enki's essence is also manifest in all knowledge.

It is the creative element in thought, whether it produces new effective patterns of action, such as wise counsel (Enki is the one who gives to rulers their broad intelligence and 'opens the door of understanding') or produces new things, as in the skill of the craftsman (Enki is the god of the craftsmen par excellence). Beyond all, however, his essence, his powers, show themselves in the powerful spells of the incantation priests. It is he who gives the powerful orders which constitute the priest's spells, orders which will assuage angry forces or drive away evil demons that have attacked man.

The range of the forces which are Enki's, the place which they occupy in the organized universe, is expressed with great precision in the office which Enki holds in the world state. He is a *nun*, that is, a great nobleman of the realm outstanding by experience and wisdom – a councillor, not unlike the Anglo-Saxon *witan*. But he is not a king, not a ruler in his own right. The position he holds in the world state he holds by appointment. His authority derives from Anu and Enlil; he is their minister. In modern terms one might perhaps call him Secretary of Agriculture in the universe. He is charged with overseeing rivers, canals, and irrigation and of organizing the productive forces of the country. He smooths out such difficulties as may arise by wise counsel, by arbitration, and by reconcilia-

tion. We may quote from a Sumerian hymn which describes
him and his office clearly and well:

> O Lord, who with thy wizard's eyes, even when wrapped in thought,
>   immobile, yet dost penetrate all things,
> O Enki, with thy limitless awareness, exalted counsel
>   of the Anunnaki,
> Very knowing one, who dost exact obedience when turning his wit
>   to conciliation and decision,
> Settling of legal strife; counsellor
>   from sunrise until sunset,
> O Enki, master over prudent words, to thee
>   I will give praise.
> Anu thy father, pristine king and ruler
>   over an inchoate world,
> Empowered thee, in heaven and on earth, to guide and form,
>   exalted thee to lordship over them.
> To clear the pure mouths of the Tigris and Euphrates,
>   to make verdure plentiful,
> Make dense the clouds, grant water in abundance
>   to all ploughlands,
> To make corn lift its head in furrows and to make
>   pasture abundant in the desert,
> To make young saplings in plantations and in orchards
>   sprout, where planted like a forest –
> These acts did Anu, king of gods, entrust to thee;
>   while Enlil granted thee his potent awesome name. ...
> As ruler over all that has been born
>   thou art a younger Enlil,
> Younger brother of him, thou art, who is sole god
>   in heaven and on earth.
> To fix, like him, the fates of North and South
>   he truly has empowered thee.
> When thy righteous decision and pronouncement cause
>   deserted cities to be reinhabited,
> When, O Sabara, countless people have been settled
>   throughout the country far and wide,
> Thou dost concern thee with their sustenance,
>   a father, in truth, thou art to them.
> They praise the greatness of their Lord and God.[22]

SUMMARY: THE COSMIC STATE AND ITS STRUCTURE

With Enki we may halt the detailed presentation of entities and
powers in the Mesopotamian's universe. The list is long; some
are powers within things and phenomena in nature, others – at

least to our way of thinking – represent abstract concepts.
Each of them influenced the course of the world in one particular way, within one well-defined sphere of action. All derived
their authority from some power higher up in that hierarchy of
powers which constituted the universe. In some cases, as in
that of Enki, it was the highest authority, Anu, or Enlil, who
had conferred the office in question. Frequently, however, it
was somebody lower down in the scale; for just as a human
state embodies many different subsidiary power structures at
various levels – families, great estates, etc. – each with its own
organization but all integrated with the larger structure of the
state, so did the cosmic state. It, too, had such minor power-
groups: divine families, divine households, divine estates with
stewards, overseers, servants, and other attendants.

But the basic lines of the view which the Mesopotamians
took of their universe have, we hope, become clear. We may
summarize as follows: The Mesopotamian universe did not,
like ours, show a fundamental bi-partition into animate and
inanimate, living and dead, matter. Nor had it different levels
of reality: anything that could be felt, experienced, or thought
had thereby established its existence, was part of the cosmos.
In the Mesopotamian universe, therefore, everything, whether
living being, thing, or abstract concept – every stone, every
tree, every notion – had a will and character of its own.

World order, the regularity and system observable in the
universe, could accordingly – in a universe made up exclusively of individuals – be conceived of in only one fashion: as
an order of wills. The universe as an organized whole was
a society, a state.

The form of state under which the Mesopotamians viewed
the universe, furthermore, was that of Primitive Democracy,
which seems to have been the form of state prevalent in the
age when Mesopotamian civilization itself came into being.

In the Primitive Democracy of early Mesopotamia – as in
the fully developed democracies of the classical world – participation in government belonged to a large part of, but by no
means to all, the members of the state. Slaves, children, and
women, for instance, had no share in government in democratic

Athens; neither had similar groups in the Mesopotamian city-states any voice in the popular assembly. Correspondingly, in the universal state there were many members who had no political influence, no share in its government. To these groups belonged, to mention one example, man. Man's position in the state of the universe precisely paralleled that of the slave in the human city-state.

Political influence was wielded in the universe only by those members who, by virtue of the power inherent in them, could be classed as gods. They alone were truly citizens in the political sense. We have mentioned a few of the most important: sky, storm, earth, water. Each god, furthermore, was seen as the expression or manifestation of a will and power to be thus and act thus. Enlil, for instance, is the will and power to rage in a storm and als o the will and power to destroy a populous city in an attack by barbaric mountaineers; both storm and destruction were seen as manifestations of one and the same essence. But the realization of these many wills does not produce anarchy or chaos. Each power has limits within which it functions, task and office which it performs. Its will is integrated with those of other powers in the total pattern of conduct which makes the universe a structure, an organized whole.

The basic integration is traceable to Anu. The other powers voluntarily adapt themselves to his authority. He gives to each its task and office in the world state; and so his will is the 'foundation' of the universe, reflected throughout its structure.

But, as any state *must* be, the Mesopotamian universe is dynamic, not static. Mere assignment of tasks and offices does not make a state. The state is, and functions through, the co-operation of the wills that hold the offices, in their readjustment to one another, in their alignment for concerted action in a given situation, in questions of general concern. For such alignment of wills the Mesopotamian universe has a general assembly of all citizens. In this assembly Anu presides and directs proceedings. Questions are discussed by the members pro and con until a consensus begins to stand out; the scales are weighted for it by assent from the seven most prominent gods, among them Anu and Enlil; and thus destinies, the great coming events, are shaped, are agreed to, are backed by the united wills of all the great powers of the universe, and are carried into effect by Enlil. Thus functions the universe.

REFLECTIONS OF THE WORLD VIEW IN EARLY MYTHS

The philosophy which we have outlined, the apprehension of reality as a whole under the aspect of a state, originated, we have argued, with Mesopotamian civilization itself around the middle of the fourth millennium before our era.

As a philosophy of existence as a whole, as the fundamental view of a civilization, this view must have had in large measure the character of an axiom. And just as the science of mathematics is very little concerned with its axioms because they are not problems but the patent, the immediately obvious verities from which it starts out, so Mesopotamian thought of the third millennium takes no particular interest in its philosophic basis. We have – and that is undoubtedly more than an accident – no early Sumerian myth which sets as its theme the basic questions: Why is the universe a state? How did it come to be one? Instead, we find the world state taken for granted. It forms the generally known and generally accepted background against which other stories are set and to which they have reference, but it is never the main theme. The main theme is some detail: some question about fitting one or a group of individual features into the over-all pattern is asked and answered by the myth. We are dealing with the products of an age which has solved the big questions, an age of interest in details. Only much later, when the 'cosmic state' was perhaps not quite so self-evident, were the fundamental issues in that view of the world taken up for consideration.

The questions which the prolific and varied mythological literature of the third millennium posed and answered may be summed up, for the greater part, under three heads. There are, first, *myths of origin* which ask about the origin of some particular entity within the cosmos or some group of such entities: gods, plants, men. The answer given is usually in terms of birth, more rarely in terms of creation or craftsmanship. The second group consists of *myths of organization*. The myths of this group ask how some feature within, or some area of, the existing world order was brought about: how some god or other obtained his function and offices, how agriculture became organized, how certain freak classes of human beings came to be and were assigned their status. The myths answer: 'By divine decree.' Lastly, in a sense a sub-group under the myths of organization, there are *myths of evaluation*. The myths of this group ask by what right something or other holds its position in the world order. Such myths will weigh the farmer against the shepherd or, in a different approach to the same question, grain against wool; they will inquire into the relative merits of the costly gold and the lowly, but more useful, copper, etc. The evaluations implicit in the existing order are affirmed and traced to divine decision. We turn first to myths which deal with details of origins.

A. DETAILS OF ORIGINS

We can comment upon only a few typical examples of stories dealing with origins and shall choose mostly such stories as we have already referred to while summing up the current types.

'THE MYTH OF ENLIL AND NINLIL': THE MOON AND HIS BROTHERS

'The Myth of Enlil and Ninlil' answers the question: How did the moon originate, and how did this bright celestial deity come to have three brothers, all connected with the nether world? The myth takes us to the city of Nippur in central Babylonia, at the beginning of time, names the city by its time-honoured names, Duranki and Durgishimmar, and identifies the river flowing by it, its quay, harbour, well, and canal, as the Idsalla, Kargeshtinna, Karusar, Pulal, and Nunbirdu, respectively, all localities in historical Nippur and well known to the listeners. Then the myth identifies the inhabitants of the city. They are the deities Enlil, Ninlil, and Ninshebargunu.

> We are living in that very city, (in) Duranki,
> We are living in that very city, (in) Durgishimmar.
> This very river, the Idsalla, was its pure river,
> This very quay, the Kargeshtinna, was its quay,
> This very harbour, the Karusar, was its harbour,

> This very well, the Pulal, was its well of sweet water,
> This very canal, the Nunbirdu, was its sparkling canal.
> No less than ten *iku* each – if measured – were its tilled fields.
> And the young man therein was Enlil;
> And the young maiden therein was Ninlil;
> And the mother therein was Ninshebargunu.[23]

Ninshebargunu warns her young daughter about going to bathe alone in the canal; prying eyes might see her; a young man might violate her.

> In those days did the mother who had borne her instruct the young maiden, did Ninshebargunu instruct Ninlil:
>   'In the pure stream, O woman, in the pure stream do not bathe!
>   In the pure stream, O Ninlil, in the pure stream, O woman,
>   do not bathe!
>   O Ninlil, do not climb onto the bank of the canal Nunbirdu.
>   With his shining eyes will the lord, with his shining eyes
>   will he espy thee;
>   With his shining eyes will he espy thee, the great mountain,
>   father Enlil;
>   With his shining eyes will he espy thee, the ... shepherd, the
>   determiner of fates.
>   Forthwith he will embrace thee, he will kiss thee!''

But Ninlil is young and headstrong.

> Did she listen to the instructions which she gave her?
> In that very stream, the pure one, in that very stream, the pure one,
>   does the (young) woman bathe.
> On to the bank of the canal, the bank of Nunbirdu, does Ninlil climb.

Everything goes as Ninshebargunu had feared. Enlil sees Ninlil, tries to seduce her, and, when she refuses, takes her by force. He leaves her pregnant with Sîn, the moon-god.

But Enlil's crime has not gone unnoticed. On his return to town, while he is walking across the square – thus we must visualize Kiur, the large open court in the temple – he is arrested and taken before the authorities. The assembly of the gods, the fifty great gods and the seven whose opinion carries special, decisive weight, condemns him to banishment from the city as guilty of rape. (The meaning of the word which we translate 'ravisher' is somewhat more general: 'one who is under a taboo relating to matters of sex'.)

> Enlil came walking into Kiur,
> And while Enlil was passing through Kiur
> The fifty great gods
> And the seven gods whose word is decisive
>   caused Enlil to be arrested in Kiur:
> 'Enlil, the ravisher, must leave the town;
> This ravisher Nunamnir, must leave town.'

In compliance with the penalty which has been imposed upon him, Enlil then leaves Nippur and makes his way out of the land of the living toward the sinister realm of Hades. But Ninlil follows him.

> Enlil, (in obedience) to the verdict which was given,
> Nunamnir, (in obedience) to the verdict which was given, went.
> And Ninlil followed.

Then Enlil, who is not willing to take her with him outright, begins to fear that other men on the road may misuse the unprotected girl as he himself has done. The first man he meets is the gatekeeper at the town gate. So Enlil stops, takes the place and assumes the likeness of the gatekeeper, and orders him not to say anything if Ninlil should ask.

> Enlil calls unto the gatekeeper:
> 'O man of the gate, O man of the bolt,
> O man of the lock, O man of the sacred bolt,
> Thy queen Ninlil is coming.
> If she asks thee about me,
> Do thou not tell her where I am.'
> Enlil called unto the gatekeeper:
> 'O man of the gate, O man of the bolt,
> O man of the lock, O man of the sacred bolt,
> Thy queen Ninlil is coming.
> The maiden so sweet, so beautiful,
> Thou shalt, O man, not embrace, thou shalt,
>   O man, not kiss!
> To Ninlil, so sweet, so beautiful,
> Has Enlil shown favour; he has looked upon her
>   with shining eyes.'

Accordingly, when Ninlil arrives, she finds Enlil in his disguise. She does not recognize him but thinks he is the gatekeeper. He says that his king Enlil has recommended her to him, and she in turn declares that, since Enlil is his king, she is his queen and that she carries Enlil's child, Sîn, the moon-god, under her heart. Enlil as the gatekeeper then pretends – this seems to be understood – to be profoundly perturbed at the thought that she is taking with her to Hades the bright scion of his lord, and he proposes union with her to beget a son who may belong to Hades and take the place of his king's son, the bright moon.

> Let the precious scion of (my) king go to heaven;
>   let my (own) son go to the nether world.
> Let my (own) son go to the nether world as (changeling for)
>   the precious scion of (my) king.

He then embraces Ninlil and again leaves her with child, the god Meslamtaea (who we know was considered a brother of Sîn, the moon). Enlil then continues his way toward Hades, and Ninlil takes up her pursuit. Two more times he stops, the first time when he comes to 'the man of the river of Hades' whom he similarly impersonates, engendering the god Ninazu, also a god of the underworld, and the second time when he comes to the ferryman at the river of Hades. In the ferryman's guise he engenders a third god of the nether world, but, as the name of this god is damaged in the text, he cannot yet be identified. Here – very abruptly to our way of thinking – the story comes to a close with a short hymn of praise to Enlil and Ninlil, ending:

> Enlil is lord, Enlil is king.
> Enlil's word cannot be altered;
> Enlil's impetuous word cannot be changed.
> Praise be to mother Ninlil,
> Praise! (to) father Enlil.

The story here told cannot, we think, be considered a pleasant one. Even though it is always extremely dangerous to apply one's own moral standards to cultures and people so remote in time and in space, there seems to be a particularly unwholesome air round this tale and the way it is told. Yet, we must not forget two things. First, this story comes from a society in which woman's honour was an unknown concept.

Violation of an unmarried woman was an offence against her guardian; violation of a married woman was an offence against her husband; and both were offences against society and its laws. In no case, however, were they offences against the woman. She and her feelings simply did not count. For that reason there is a moral conflict involved when Enlil breaks the laws of society in raping Ninlil. In what happens to her after that, only Enlil's honour could be injured; and he avoids that by his handling of the men she meets. Second, and far more important, we must make clear to ourselves that Ninlil, whose plight cannot help appealing to us, and who seems a central character, holds almost no interest to the storyteller. His sole concern is with the children she is to bear – with the origin of the moon-god and his three divine brothers. Ninlil exists for him merely as the potential mother of these children, not as a human being interesting in herself. For that reason the story ends in a manner which seems to us abrupt. But for the story-teller there was nothing of interest to relate after the last divine child was in existence. It is only we who wonder about what further happened between Ninlil and Enlil and should like to be told that Ninlil was finally accepted by Enlil as his wife.

It is from the point of view of the children, then, that the myth is to be understood and interpreted. Why does the bright celestial moon-god come to have three brothers, all powers of the lower, infernal regions? Why does Enlil, the storm, a cosmic force which belongs to the world above, have children who belong to the nether world? The myth answers in psychological terms. It seeks the cause in Enlil's own nature with its curiously dark and violent strains. It is this element of wildness and violence which makes him break the laws and taboos of society of the world above when he takes Ninlil by force and Sin is engendered. The consequences are banishment, imposed by the forces which uphold that world and its fundamental order, by the assembly of the gods.

Enlil's later children are engendered after he has been put beyond the pale of the world of light, when he is on his way to Hades and under its sinister shadow. Therefore, the children he now engenders belong in Hades, and their infernal affinities are confirmed by the words Enlil speaks to induce Ninlil to unite with him. For such is the power of Enlil's word that it is binding, that it comes true however and whenever it is spoken. Therefore, and very aptly, the myth ends in a paean to Enlil's word which cannot be altered, cannot be changed.

The immediate answer to the question of the myth: 'Why are Enlil's children so different?' is thus, 'Because Enlil so decreed!' But the myth, in giving that answer, is not yet satisfied. It probes behind the immediate answer: tells of the events and of the situation which caused Enlil to speak as he did. And it shows that these events were in no sense accidental but were precipitated by a fundamental contrast in Enlil's own nature. Background for the myth is the view of the universe as a state. Enlil, Ninlil, Sîn, and all the other characters in the story are forces in nature. But, since the myth-maker sees these forces as 'Thou's', as members of a society, his endeavour is to understand them through psychological analysis of their character and through their corresponding reaction to the laws which govern the state of the universe.

THE TILMUN MYTH: THE INTERPLAY OF EARTH AND WATER IN COSMOS AND ITS RESULTS

An origin myth of a different character, and in a sense far less sophisticated, is the Tilmun myth.[24]

The myth of Enlil and Ninlil was concerned with a single, seemingly anomalous fact: the difference in character of the sons of Enlil. It traced their origin to find that difference ultimately grounded in constrasts within Enlil's own nature. The Tilmun myth is not in that sense wrestling with a problem. It endeavours to trace a causal unity between a great many disparate phenomena and shows their common origin in a conflict of two natures, male and female. It tells the story of a battle of wills in their mutual attraction and mutual antagonism, of constant Mother Earth, Ninhursaga, and Enki, god of the fickle waters.

The story opens in the island of Tilmun – modern Bahrein in the Persian Gulf. This island was allotted to Enki and Ninhursaga when the world was divided among the gods. After Enki, at Ninhursaga's suggestion, has provided the island with fresh water, he proposes to her, and, though she at first refuses, she finally accepts him. Their daughter is the goddess Ninsar, the plants, born of the marriage of soil, Ninhursaga, and water, Enki. But, as the waters of the yearly inundation in Mesopotamia recede and return to the river bed before vegetation comes up, so Enki does not stay to live with Ninhursaga as her husband but has already left her before the goddess of the plants is born. And, as vegetation in the late spring clusters around the rivers, so Ninsar comes to the river's edge where Enki is. But Enki sees in the goddess of the plants just another young girl. He unites with her, but he does not go to live with her. The goddess of the plants gives birth to a daughter representing – we would guess – the plant fibres used in the weaving of linen. Such fibres are obtained by soaking plants in water until the soft matter rots away and only the tough fibres remain. They are, therefore, in a sense the child of plants and water. Then the story repeats itself; the goddess of the dyestuff, with which cloth is dyed, is born, and she in turn gives birth to the goddess of cloth and weaving, Uttu. By now, however, Ninhursaga has realized how fickle Enki is and puts Uttu on her guard. Forewarned, Uttu insists on marriage: Enki must bring gifts of cucumbers, apples, and grapes – apparently to serve as the customary marriage-gift – and only then will she be his. Enki complies and when, as a regular suitor, he presents himself at the house with the gifts, Uttu joyfully lets him in. The wine which he gives her makes Uttu intoxicated, and he takes his pleasure of her. A lacuna interrupts the story at this point and obscures the course of events. Eight plants have sprouted forth, and Ninhursaga has not yet announced what their names, nature, and qualities shall be. Then she suddenly discovers that Enki has already determined all this on his own and has eaten the plants. At this final slight, Ninhursaga is seized with a burning hatred, and she curses the god of the waters. At her terrible curse – which apparently typifies the banning of the fresh waters to darkness underground and to slow death when wells and rivers dry up in the summer season

– all the gods are thoroughly disturbed. But the fox appears and promises to bring Ninhursaga to them. It makes good its promise. Ninhursaga comes, relents, and finally heals the sick Enki by helping to give birth to eight deities, one for each ailing part of his body. It has been suggested that these deities are the plants which Enki had swallowed and which had thus become lodged in his body. The myth ends with the assigning of stations in life to these deities.

As we have stated, this myth endeavours to trace a causal unity among many disparate phenomena; but it is a unity causal in the mythopoeic sense only. When plants are seen as born of soil and water, we can still follow, although with reservations. Toward the end of the myth, however, the deities born that Enki may be healed have no intrinsic connection either with soil, who bears them, or with water. Their names, however, happen to contain elements which recall the words for certain parts of the body, those parts of Enki's body which are healed. For instance, the deity A-zi-mu_4-a, whose name can be understood as 'the growing straight of the arm', was born to heal Enki's arm. And here is the connection. We must remember that in mythopoeic thought a name is a force within the person propelling him in a certain direction. Since the name A-zi-mu_4-a can be understood as meaning 'the growing straight of the arm', though this deity – as far as we know – had nothing to do with arms, the question could not but present itself: 'Whose arm did this deity cause to grow straight?' The myth is ready with an answer: 'Enki's'. It is here satisfied with establishing a connection; it does not probe for a deeper relationship of nature between the two forces, the two gods, involved.

Seen on its own terms, however, and viewed with mythopoeic logic, the myth greatly deepens our understanding of two great forces in the universe, earth and water; for in the Mesopotamian universe understanding means psychological insight. In the myth we get to know the deep antithesis which underlies the fruitful interplay of these forces in nature; we follow it as it rises to its climax in an open break threatening to destroy water forever; and we end on a note of relief with reconciliation, with restoration of harmony in the universe. We also learn, in following the interaction of these forces, their importance as sources of life: From them come plants, from them come weaving and clothing, to them are due numerous potent and beneficial forces in life – numerous minor gods. An area of the universe has become intelligible.

Before we leave this myth, we should call attention to an interesting bit of speculation which it contains, to the picture it gives of the world when it was young. The definite and identifiable character of things in the world came late. In the dawn of time the world was as yet only a world of promise, a world in the bud, not settled in definite form. Neither animals nor men had yet acquired their habits and characteristics; they had not yet their defining traits. They were only potentially what they now are. The raven did not yet croak; the lion did not kill; the wolf did not snatch lambs. Disease and old age had as yet no existence as such, had not acquired their recognizable symptoms and characteristics, and could therefore not identify themselves as 'disease' and 'old age', definite forms which they were only later to assume.

The first lines of the opening section of the myth are addressed directly to Enki and Ninhursaga; these deities are the 'you' of the text. Then the story lapses into ordinary narrative style:

> When you were dividing the virgin earth (with your fellow-gods)
>   – you – the land of Tilmun was a region pure;
> When you were dividing the pure earth (with your fellow-gods)
>   – you – the land of Tilmun was a region pure.
> The land of Tilmun was pure, the land of Tilmun was fresh,
> The land of Tilmun was fresh, the land of Tilmun was bright.
> When they lay down on the ground all alone in Tilmun –
>   Since the place where Enki lay down with his spouse
>   was a fresh place, a bright place. ...
> When they lay down on the ground all alone in Tilmun –
>   Since the place where Enki lay down with his spouse
>   was a fresh place, a bright place –
> The raven in Tilmun did not croak (as the raven does nowadays),
> The cock (?) did not utter the crow of a cock (as the cock does nowadays),
> The lion did not kill,
> The wolf did not seize lambs,

The dog knew not (how) to make the kids crouch down,
The donkey foal knew not (how) to eat grain,

. . . .

Eye disease did not say, "I, eye disease,"
Headache did not say, "I, headache,"
The old woman there did not say, "I, old woman,"
The old man there did not say, "I, old man," ...

B. Details of World Order

Of the next group of myths, those which deal with the establishment of some facet of world order rather than with the origins of things and forces as such, we shall give only two examples. The first of these is a myth, unfortunately in a rather damaged condition, which tells how the natural economy of Mesopotamia became organized.

ENKI ORGANIZES THE WORLD MANOR[25]

The beginning of this myth, now lost, probably related how Anu and Enlil appointed Enki. Where the text becomes readable, Enki is making a tour of inspection in his territory, which includes most of the world as then known, and visiting the larger administrative units in it.

Enki stops in each country, blesses it, and by his blessing endows it with prosperity and affirms its special functions. Next he organizes all the bodies of water and what has to do with water. He fills the rivers Euphrates and Tigris with clear water and appoints a god to oversee them. Then he fills them with fish and sets out canebrakes. To care for these, he appoints another divine overseer. Then he regulates the sea and appoints a divine overseer who is to run it. From the sea Enki turns to the winds which bring the rains and then to agricultural pursuits. He looks after the plough, opens up the furrows, and lets grain grow on the field. He also ranges granaries side by side. From the fields he moves on to town and village, appoints the brick-god to take care of brick-making; he lays foundations, builds walls, and appoints the divine master-builder, Mushdama, as overseer of such works. Finally, he organizes the wild life of the desert under the god Sumukan, while he builds pens and sheepfolds for the tame animals, placing the latter in charge of the shepherd-god Dumuzi or Tammuz. Enki has instituted every important function in the economic life of Mesopotamia; he has set it going; and he has appointed a divine overseer to keep it going. Order in nature is seen and interpreted exactly as if the universe were a large, smoothly running estate organized by a capable manager.

ENKI AND NINMAH: INTEGRATION OF ODDITIES[26]

The order of the universe, patent and obvious to the human mind and generally admirable as well, is, nevertheless, not always and in every detail the order man would have preferred. Even the optimistic Alexander Pope, as the reader will recall, thought he could go no further in his praise than to call this 'the best possible world', which is obviously a far cry from calling it 'the ideal world'. The ancient Mesopotamians likewise found things in the world which they considered unfortunate, or at least queer; and it puzzled them that the gods had arranged it that way. Problems of this kind are dealt with in the myth which we shall now consider. It offers an answer well in keeping with the Mesopotamians' social and psychological approach to forces in the universe: the gods, for all their power, have their human sides. Their emotions, especially after too much beer, are likely to get the better of their judgment; and, when that happens, they are in danger of being tripped up by their own power, by the binding force of their own commands.

The myth deals – as do so many Sumerian tales – with Enki, the god of the sweet waters, and Ninhursaga, the goddess of the earth. In this myth she is called by her epithet Ninmah, 'the exalted lady', and we shall keep this name in recounting the story. We begin once more in the days when the world was young;

> In the days of yore, the days when sky had been
> separated from earth,
> In the nights of yore, the nights when sky had been
> separated from earth.

In those remote times the gods themselves had to work for

a living. All the gods had to use the sickle, the pickaxe, and the other agricultural implements; to dig canals; and generally to earn their bread by the sweat of their brows. And they hated it. The very wise one, he of broad understanding, Enki, lay in deep slumber upon his couch without ever rising from it. To him the gods turned in their misery; and his mother Nammu, the goddess of the watery deep, took their complaints before her sleeping son. Nor did she go in vain. Enki ordered Nammu to get all in readiness to give birth to 'the clay that is above the *apsu*'. ('Above the *apsu*' means below the earth but above the watery deep which lies under the earth and is more or less identical with the goddess Nammu herself.) This clay was to be severed from Nammu as one severs a human infant from its mother. The goddess Ninmah, the earth, was to stand above her – the earth, is of course, above the subterranean waters – and help her when she gave birth, and eight other goddesses were to assist.

In this fashion, we must assume, the clay above the *apsu* was born, and from it man was fashioned. However, a serious gap in the text interrupts the story at this point and prevents us from knowing with certainty how mankind came into being. When the text again becomes readable, Enki is preparing a feast for Ninmah and for his mother, presumably to celebrate her delivery. All the great gods are invited, and all praise Enki highly for his cleverness; but, as the party gets under way, Ninmah strikes a sour note:

> As Enki and Ninmah drink much beer, their hearts become elated,
>   and Ninmah calls over to Enki:
> 'How good or how bad is man's body (really)?
> As my heart prompts me, I can make its lot good or (make it) bad.'

Enki is not slow to accept the challenge: 'The lot thou hast in mind, be it good or bad, verily I will balance (?) it.'

So Ninmah takes of the clay above the *apsu* and models it into a freak human being, one with some bodily defect: a man who cannot hold back his urine, a woman who is unable to bear children, a being who has neither male nor female organs. All in all, six such beings take form under her fingers; but for every one of them Enki is ready with a special lot or fate. He finds a place in society for all of them, a way in which they can gain a living. The being with neither male nor female organs, presumably a eunuch, Enki destines to wait on the king, the barren woman is placed among the ladies-in-waiting to the queen, etc. There can be little doubt that these six freaks formed by Ninmah correspond to definite classes of persons in Sumerian society who, for one reason or another, differed bodily from normal human beings and therefore posed a problem.

But now the contest is on in earnest. Enki has shown that his perspicuity is a match for even the worst Ninmah can think up. Now he proposes that they change sides. He will make freaks, and she shall figure out what to do with them. And so Enki sets to work. We do not know about his first effort, for the text of the myth is damaged at this place; but we hear about the second, a being by the name of U_4-*mu-ul*, 'my day is remote' – that is, a very old man whose birthday lies far back in the past. The eyes of this unfortunate are diseased, his life is ebbing, his liver and heart give him pain, his hands tremble – to mention just a few of the things wrong with him. This creature Enki presents to Ninmah.

Enki calls over to Ninmah:

> I determined the lot for the men thou didst fashion,
> whereby they might subsist.
> Do thou now determine a lot for the man I have fashioned,
> whereby he may subsist.

This, however, is entirely beyond Ninmah. She approaches the creature and puts a question to him, but he cannot answer; she proffers him a piece of bread she has been eating, but he is too feeble to stretch out his arm to take it, etc. Angrily she upbraids Enki: the creature he has fashioned is not a live man. But Enki only tauntingly reminds her how he was able to cope with anything she could think up and find ways for her creatures to make a living.

Another break in the text prevents us from following the details of their quarrel. When the text again is preserved, the quarrel has reached its climax. Through the second of the two creatures which Enki created, he brought into the world sickness and all the other miseries attendant upon old age. Undoubtedly his first creature, whose description is lost in a lacuna, carried a similar load of human evils. With neither of them could Ninmah cope. She was unable to integrate them with the world order, unable to find a useful place for them in society. But they are here to stay, an unmitigated evil. It is possible that it was the effect of these creatures alone (of old age and of the earlier, as yet unknown, evils) on Ninmah's land and city that drove her to desperation; it is also possible that she suffered still further humiliations at Enki's hand. She complains:

> My city is destroyed, my house is wrecked, my children
> have been taken captive.
> I have been forced to leave Ekur, a fugitive (?); even
> I escape not from thy hand.

So she curses him: 'Henceforth thou shalt not dwell in heaven, thou shalt not dwell on earth.' This confines the god of the sweet waters to the dark regions below the earth. The curse is reminiscent of another which she pronounced upon Enki in the Tilmun myth and is seemingly intended to explain the same puzzling feature of the universe: Why are the beneficent sweet waters banned to live in eternal darkness below the earth? For that is where one finds them if one digs deep enough. Enki can do nothing once the curse has been uttered, for it has behind it all the decisive force inherent in a command of one of the great gods. He answers Ninmah: 'A command issuing from thy mouth, who could change it?'

Nevertheless, it seems possible that this frightening sentence was somehow alleviated and that, as in the Tilmun myth, a reconciliation was brought about. The text of the myth becomes extremely fragmentary and difficult at this point, so we cannot tell for certain. However, the very fact that the myth does go on at some length shows that Ninmah's curse was not the final and decisive result of the conflict.

The myth which we have here retold undertakes to explain a number of puzzling features in the world order: the curious abnormal groups – eunuchs, hierodules, etc. – which formed part of Mesopotamian society; the unpleasant, seemingly unnecessary evils which accompany old age; etc. In rendering its account, however, the myth not only explains; it passes judgment. These features do not really belong in the world order; they were not part of the plan. They came in in a moment of irresponsibility, when the gods were in their cups and succumbed momentarily to envy and a desire to show off. Moreover, the myth analyses and evaluates the various features differently. While the freaks which Ninmah made were comparatively harmless and could still be integrated with the social order by the clever Enki, there was no hope whatever when Enki turned his nimble brain to mischief.

In this implicit evaluation of the features whose origin it describes, our myth forms a connecting link, as it were, with the third large group of myths: that which takes as its main theme the evaluation of features in the world order.

C. DETAILS OF EVALUATION

Some of the myths within this group take almost the same form as hymns of praise. They are concerned with a single element in the universe – a deity, an object, or whatever it may be – and extol its qualities in a minute analysis of all its features. Such a myth, for instance, is the 'Myth of the Pickaxe', which tells how Enlil made that indispensable implement and explains its qualities and uses. Other myths within the group, however, are concerned with two entities of the universe, balancing one against the other in a reasoned effort to understand and justify their relative positions in the existing order. These myths frequently take the form of a dispute between the two elements involved, each extolling its own virtues until the dispute is adjudicated by some god. A single passage may serve as illustration. It comes from a myth in which copper, useful but less highly valued, disputes with silver the latter's right to stand in a place of honour as courtier in the royal palace. The copper argues the 'uselessness' of silver:

> When the cold weather has set in, you cannot provide an adze
> which can cut firewood (?);
> When harvest time has come, you cannot provide a sickle which
> can cut the grain.
> Therefore man will take no interest in thee, ...[27]

In a country like Mesopotamia, in which the chief industries were sheep-herding and farming, it is only natural that these two modes of life should form favourite subjects of comparison and evaluation. Which is the better, the more important, the more useful? We possess no less than three myths which take up this theme. One tells the origin of 'sheep' and 'grain' from the very beginning, when the gods alone enjoyed them, and goes on to recount a long dispute which they had as to which should take precedence over the other. Another myth relates the dispute between two divine brothers, Enten and Emesh, sons of Enlil, one seemingly typifying the farmer, the other the shepherd. Their quarrel is settled by Enlil in favour of the farmer. The liveliest treatment of the theme, however, is given in a myth entitled 'The Wooing of Inanna'.

'THE WOOING OF INANNA': RELATIVE MERITS OF SHEPHERD AND FARMER[28]

This myth tells how both the divine farmer Enkimdu and the divine shepherd Dumuzi sued for the hand of the goddess Inanna, who is here seen not as the spouse of Anu and queen of heaven but merely as a young marriageable girl. Her brother and guardian, the sun-god Utu, is in favour of the shepherd and tries to influence his sister.

> Her brother, the warrior, the hero, Utu,
>   says to holy Inanna:
> 'The shepherd ought to marry thee, my sister.
> Why, O maiden Inanna, art thou not willing?
> His butter is good, his milk is good;
> All the shepherd's products are splendid.
> Dumuzi ought to marry thee, Inanna.'

But the brother's words fall on deaf ears. Inanna has made up her mind; she wants a farmer:

> Never shall the shepherd marry me;
> Never shall he drape me in his tufted cloth;
> Never shall his finest wool touch me.
> Me, the maiden, shall the farmer,
> And he only, take in marriage –
> The farmer who can grow beans,
> The farmer who can grow grain.

So the farmer it is, and the poor shepherd feels despondent. He has not only lost his suit; he has been rejected in favour of a farmer, and that wounds his pride deeply. So he begins to compare himself with the farmer. For everything the farmer makes, the shepherd finds some of his own products which will match the farmer's in value:

> In what does the farmer surpass me? A farmer me! A farmer me!
> In what does the farmer, does Enkimdu, the man of dyke and canal
> ... surpass me?
> If he should give me his black cloth, I would give the farmer
> my black wool for it;
> If he should give me his white cloth, I would give the farmer
> my white wool for it.
> If he should pour out for me his prime beer, I would pour out for the
> farmer my yellow milk in return.

The myth continues through all the products of grassland and farm, milk as a match for beer, small cheeses as a match for beans, cottage cheese with honey as a match for bread. And then, the shepherd feels, he would even have a surplus of butter and milk.

The situation which the shepherd here imagines is a typically oriental contest of gifts. He who gives most is the better man; he owes the other nothing, the other is in his debt. And so, as the shepherd proceeds with his soliloquy, he feels better and better and gets in really high spirits. Brazenly, he drives his sheep to the very bank of the river into the heart of the cultivation. There suddenly he sees the farmer and Inanna and, abashed at what he has been doing, immediately takes to his heels to escape into the desert. Both Enkimdu and Inanna run after him, and – if we interpret the text rightly – Inanna calls out to him:

> Why must I race with thee, O shepherd, I with thee,
> shepherd, with thee?
> Thy sheep are free to eat grass on the bank;
> Thy sheep are free to pasture (?) in my stubble (?) field.
> They may eat grain in the fields of Uruk;
> Thy lambs and kids may drink water in my Adab canal.

Though she prefers a farmer for a husband, she harbours no ill feeling toward the shepherd:

> While thou, a shepherd, canst not – just to become my husband –
>   be turned into a farmer, (the kind of man) I befriend,
> Canst not be turned into my friend, the farmer Enkimdu, into my
>   friend the farmer,
> I will bring thee wheat, I will bring thee beans. ...

And so the story ends with a reconciliation. It has compared farmer and shepherd; it has by implication given preference to the farmer, for it is he whom the goddess marries. However, it is at pains to show that putting the farmer ahead of the shepherd is really a matter of personal preference only, the whim of a young girl. Actually one is as good as the other, both are equally useful and necessary members of society; the produce of one balances that of the other. Though there is rivalry between them, there should not be enmity. The farmer must know that Inanna liked the shepherd well enough to throw open the stubble fields to his flocks and permit him to water his sheep at the farmer's canals. Farmer and shepherd must try to get along well together.

With this we may conclude our survey of the older mythological material from Mesopotamia. The bulk of this material is known to us from copies written at the end of the third and the early part of the second millenniums B.C. But the myths themselves are undoubtedly much older. They show clearly for what they are: answers to questions of detail. They treat such varied problems as the origin, the place, and the relative value of all kinds of specific entities or groups of entities within the cosmos. They are one, however, in the underlying view which they take of the world. Their cosmos is a state, an organization of individuals. And the myths are one also in the approach which they take to the problems. It is a psychological approach: the key to understanding the forces which one meets in nature is felt to lie in the understanding of their characters, exactly as the key to understanding men lies in understanding their characters.

REFLECTION OF THE WORLD VIEW IN LATER MYTHS: 'ENUMA ELISH'

But though the view of the universe as a state thus underlies all these tales – or precisely because it underlies them, is the very soil from which they grow – there is little effort to present that view as a whole. A proper cosmogony treating of the fundamental problems of the cosmos as it appeared to the Mesopotamians – its origin and the origin of the order which it exhibits – does not appear until the earlier half of the second millennium B.C. Then it is given in a grandiose composition named *Enuma elish*, 'When above.'[29] *Enuma elish* has a long and complicated history. It is written in Akkadian,[30] seemingly Akkadian of approximately the middle of the second millennium B.C. At that period, then, the composition presumably received the form in which we now have it. Its central figure is Marduk, the god of Babylon, in keeping with the fact that Babylon was at that time the political and cultural centre of the Mesopotamian world. When later on, in the first millennium B.C., Assyria rose to become the dominant power in the Near East, Assyrian scribes apparently replaced Marduk with their own god Assur and made a few changes to make the story fit its new hero. This later version is known to us from copies of the myth found in Assyria.

The substitution of Assur for Marduk as the hero and central figure of the story seems to have been neither the only nor the first such substitution made. Behind our present version with Marduk as the hero undoubtedly lies a still earlier version wherein, not Marduk, but Enlil of Nippur played the central role. This more original form can be deduced from many indications in the myth itself. The most important of these is the fact that Enlil, although he was always at least the second most important Mesopotamian deity, seems to play no part whatever in the myth as we have it, while all the other important gods have appropriate roles. Again, the role which Marduk plays is not in keeping with the character of the god. Marduk was originally an agricultural or perhaps a solar deity, whereas the central role in *Enuma elish* is that of a god of the storm such as Enlil was. Indeed, a central feat ascribed to Marduk in the story – the separating of heaven and earth – is the very feat which other mythological material assigns to Enlil, and with right, for it is the wind which, placed between the sky and the earth, holds them apart like the two sides of an inflated leather bag. It seems, therefore, that Enlil was the original hero of the story and was replaced by Marduk when our earliest known version was composed around the middle of the second millennium B.C. How far the myth itself goes back, we cannot say with certainty. It contains material and reflects ideas which point backward through the third millennium B.C.

A. FUNDAMENTALS OF ORIGIN

We may now turn to the content of the myth. It falls roughly into two sections, one dealing with the origin of the basic features of the universe, the other telling how the present world order was established. There is, however, no rigid separation of these two themes. The actions of the second part of the myth are foreshadowed in, and interlock with, the events told in the first.

The poem begins with a description of the universe as it was in the beginning:

> When a sky above had not (yet even) been mentioned
> (And) the name of firm ground below had not (yet even) been thought of;
> (When) only primeval Apsu, their begetter,
> And Mummu and Ti²amat – she who gave birth to them all –
> Were mingling their waters in one;
> When no bog had formed (and) no island could be found;
> When no god whosoever had appeared,
> Had been named by name, had been determined as to (his) lot,
> Then were gods formed within them.[31]

This description presents the earliest stage of the universe as one of watery chaos. The chaos consisted of three intermingled elements: Apsu, who represents the sweet waters; Ti²amat, who represents the sea; and Mummu, who cannot as yet be identified with certainty but may represent cloud banks and mist. These three types of water were mingled in a large undefined mass. There was not yet even the idea of a sky above or firm ground beneath; all was water; not even a swampy bog had been formed, still less an island; and there were yet no gods.

Then, in the midst of this watery chaos, two gods come into

existence: Lahmu and Lahamu. The text clearly intends us to understand that they were begotten by Apsu, the sweet waters, and born of Ti°amat, the sea. They represent, it would seem, silt which had formed in the waters. From Lahmu and Lahamu derive the next divine pair: Anshar and Kishar, two aspects of 'the horizon'. The myth-maker apparently viewed the horizon as both male and female, as a circle (male) which circumscribed the sky and as a circle (female) which circumscribed the earth.

Anshar and Kishar give birth to Anu, the god of the sky; and Anu engenders Nudimmut. Nudimmut is another name for Ea or Enki, the god of the sweet waters. Here, however, he is apparently to be viewed in his oldest aspect as representing the earth itself; he is *En-ki*, 'lord of the earth'. Anshar is said to have made Anu like himself, for the sky resembles the horizon in so far as it, too, is round. And Anu is said to have made Nudimmut, the earth, in his likeness; for the earth was, in the opinion of the Mesopotamians, shaped like a disc or even like a round bowl:

> Lahmu and Lahamu appeared and they were named;
> Increasing through the ages they grew tall.
> Anshar and Kishar (then) were formed, surpassing them;
> They lived for many days, adding year unto year.
> Their son was Anu, equal to his fathers.
> Anshar made his firstborn, Anu, to his own likeness,
> Anu, to his own likeness also, Nudimmut.
> Nudimmut excelled among the gods, his fathers;
> With ears wide open, wise, mighty in strength,
> Mightier than his father's father Anshar,
> He had no equal among his fellow-gods.

The speculations which here meet us, speculations by which the ancient Mesopotamians thought to penetrate the mystery concealing the origin of the universe, are obviously based upon observation of the way in which new land is actually formed in Mesopotamia. Mesopotamia is an alluvial country. It has been built through thousands of years by silt which has been brought down by the two great rivers, the Euphrates and the Tigris, and has been deposited at their mouths. This process still goes on; and day by day, year by year, the country slowly grows, extending farther out into the Persian Gulf. It is this scene – where the sweet waters of the rivers meet and blend with the salt waters of the sea, while cloud banks hang low over the waters – which has been projected back into the beginning of time. Here still is the primeval watery chaos in which Apsu, the sweet waters, mingles with Ti^{p}amat, the salt waters of the sea; and here the silt – represented by the first of the gods, Lahmu and Lahamu – separates from the water, becomes noticeable, is deposited.

Lahmu and Lahamu gave birth to Anshar and Kishar; that is, the primeval silt, born of the salt and the sweet waters in the original watery chaos, was deposited along its circumference in a gigantic ring: the horizon. From Anshar, the upper side of this ring, and from Kishar, its lower side, grew up through days and years of deposits Anu, heaven, and Nudimmut-Enki, earth. As *Enuma elish* describes this, Anu, the sky, was formed first; and he engendered Nudimmut, the earth.

This presentation breaks the progression by pairs – Lahmu-Lahamu, Anshar-Kishar – after which we expect a third pair An-Ki, 'heaven and earth'; instead, we get Anu followed by Nudimmut. This irregularity suggests that we are here dealing with an alteration of the original story perhaps made by the redactor who introduced Marduk of Babylon as hero of the myth. He may have wanted to stress the male aspect of the earth, Ea-Enki, since the latter figured as father of Marduk in Babylonian theology. Originally, therefore, Anshar-Kishar may have been followed by An-Ki, 'heaven and earth'. This conjecture is supported by a variant of our story preserved in the great ancient Mesopotamian list of gods known as the An-Anum list. Here we find an earlier, more intact version of the speculation: from the horizon, from Anshar and Kishar as a united pair, grew the sky and the earth. Sky and earth are apparently to be viewed as two enormous discs formed from the silt which continued to be deposited along the inside of the ring of the horizon as the latter 'lived many days, added year unto year'. Later on, these discs were forced apart by the wind, who puffed them up into the great bag within which we live, its under side being the earth, its upper side the sky.

In speculating about the origin of the world, the Mesopotamians thus took as their point of departure things they knew and could observe in the geology of their own country. Their earth, Mesopotamia, is formed by silt deposited where fresh water meets salt water; the sky, seemingly formed of solid matter like the earth, must have been deposited in the same manner and must have been raised later to its present lofty position.

B. Fundamentals of World Order

Just as observed facts about the physical origin of his own country form the basis for the Mesopotamian's speculations about the origin of the basic features in the universe, so, it would seem, does a certain amount of knowledge about the origin of his own political organization govern his speculations as to the origin of the organization of the universe. The origin of the world order is seen in a prolonged conflict between two principles, the forces making for activity and the forces making for inactivity. In this conflict the first victory over inactivity is gained by authority alone; the second, the decisive victory, by authority combined with force. The transition mirrors, on the one hand, a historical development from primitive social organization, in which only custom and authority unbacked by force are available to ensure concerted action by the community, to the organization of a real state, in which the ruler commands both authority and force to ensure necessary concerted action. On the other hand, it reflects the normal procedure within the organized state, for here also authority alone is the means brought to bear first, while force, physical compulsion, is only resorted to if authority is not sufficient to produce the conduct desired.

To return to *Enuma elish*: With the birth of the gods from chaos, a new principle – movement, activity – has come into the world. The new beings contrast sharply with the forces of chaos that stand for rest and inactivity. In a typically mythopoeic manner this ideal conflict of activity and inactivity is given concrete form in a pregnant situation: the gods come together to dance.

The divine companions thronged together
and, restlessly surging back and forth, they dis-
      turbed Ti'amat,
disturbed Ti'amat's belly,
dancing within (her depth) where heaven is founded.
Apsu could not subdue their clamour,
and Ti'amat was silent ...
but their actions were abhorrent to her
and their ways not good. ...

The conflict is now manifest. The first power of chaos to come
out openly against the gods and their new ways is Apsu.

Then Apsu, the begetter of the great gods,
called his servant Mummu, saying to him:
'Mummu, my servant, who dost gladden my heart,
come let us go to Ti'amat.'
They went; and seated before Ti'amat,
about the gods their firstborn they took counsel.

Apsu began to speak,
saying to pure Ti'amat:
'Abhorrent have become their ways to me,
I am allowed no rest by day, by night no sleep.
I will abolish, yea, I will destroy their ways,
that peace may reign (again) and we may sleep.'

This news causes consternation among the gods. They run
around aimlessly; then they quiet down and sit in the silence
of despair. Only one, the wise Ea-Enki; is equal to the
situation.

He of supreme intelligence, skilful, ingenious,
Ea, who knows all things, saw through their scheme.
He formed, yea, he set up against it
the configuration of the universe,
and skilfully made his overpowering sacred spell.
Reciting it he cast it on the water (– on Apsu –),
poured slumber over him, so that he soundly slept.

The waters to which Ea here recites his spell, his 'configuration of the universe', are Apsu. Apsu succumbs to the magic
command and falls into a deep slumber. Then Ea takes from
him his crown and drapes himself in Apsu's cloak of fiery rays.

He kills Apsu and establishes his abode above him. Then he locks up Mummu, passes a string through his nose, and sits holding him by the end of this nose-rope.

What all this signifies is perhaps not immediately evident; yet it can be understood. The means which Ea employs to subdue Apsu is a spell, that is, a word of power, an authoritative command. For the Mesopotamians viewed authority as a power inherent in commands, a power which caused a command to be obeyed, caused it to realize itself, to come true. The authority, the power in Ea's command, was great enough to force into being the situation expressed in the command. And the nature of this situation is hinted at when it is called 'the configuration of the universe'; it is the design which now obtains. Ea commanded that things should be as they are, and so they became thus. Apsu, the sweet waters, sank into the sleep of death which now holds the sweet waters immobile underground. Directly above them was established the abode of Ea – earth resting upon Apsu. Ea holds in his hands the nose-rope of captive Mummu, perhaps – if our interpretation of this difficult figure is correct – the cloud banks which float low over the earth. But whatever the details of interpretation may be, it is significant that this first great victory of the gods over the powers of chaos, of the forces of activity over the forces opposing activity, was won through authority and not through physical force. It was gained through the authority implicit in a command, the magic in a spell. It is significant also that it was gained through the power of a single god acting on his own initiative, not by the concerted efforts of the whole community of the gods. The myth moves on a primitive level of social organization where dangers to the community are met by the separate action of one or more powerful individuals, not by co-operation of the community as a whole.

To return to the story: In the dwelling which Ea has thus established on Apsu is born Marduk, the real hero of the myth as we have it; but in more original versions it was undoubtedly Enlil's birth that was told at this juncture. The text describes him:

> Superb of stature, with lightning glance,
> and virile gait, he was a leader born.
> Ea his father, seeing him, rejoiced,
> and brightened and his heart filled with delight.
> He added, yea, he fastened on to him twofold divinity.
> Exceeding tall he was, surpassing in all things.
> Subtle beyond conceit his measure was,
> incomprehensible, terrible to behold.
> Four were his eyes and four his ears;
> fire blazed whenever he moved his lips.

But while Marduk grows up among the gods, new dangers threaten from the forces of chaos. They maliciously chide Ti'amat:

> When they killed Apsu, thy husband,
> thou didst not march at his side but sat quietly.

Finally they succeed in rousing her. Soon the gods hear that all the forces of chaos are making ready to do battle with them:

> Angry, scheming, restless day and night,
> they are bent on fighting, rage and prowl like lions.
> Gathered in council, they plan the attack.
> Mother Hubur – creator of all forms –
> adds irresistible weapons, has borne monster serpents,
> sharp toothed, with fang unsparing;
> has filled their bodies with poison for blood.
> Fierce dragons she has draped with terror,
> crowned with flame and made like gods,
> so that whoever looks upon them shall perish with fear,
> and they, with bodies raised, will not turn back their breast.

At the head of her formidable army Ti'amat has placed her second husband, Kingu. She has given him full authority and entrusted to him the 'tablets of destinies', which symbolize supreme power over the universe. Her forces are ranged in battle order ready to attack the gods.

The first intelligence of what is afoot reaches the always well-informed Ea. At first, a typical primitive reaction, he is completely stunned, and it takes some time before he can pull himself together and begin to act.

Ea heard of these matters,
lapsed into dark silence, wordlessly sat.
Then, having deeply pondered and his inner turmoil quieted,
arose and went to his father Anshar,
went before Anshar, his father who begot him.
All Ti'amat had plotted he recounted.

Anshar also is deeply disturbed and smites his thigh and bites
his lip in his mental anguish. He can think of no better way out
than to send Ea against Ti'amat. He reminds Ea of his victory
over Apsu and Mummu and seems to advise him to use the
same means he used then. But this time Ea's mission is unsuc-
cessful. The word of an individual, even the powerful word of
Ea, is no match for Ti'amat and her host.

Anshar then turns to Anu and bids him go. Anu is armed
with authority even greater than that of Ea, for he is told:

> If she obey not thy command,
> speak unto her our command, that she may subside.

If Ti'amat cannot be overpowered by the authority of any one
god, the command of all gods, having behind it their combined
authority, must be used against her. But that, too, fails; Anu
is unable to face Ti'amat, returns to Anshar, and asks to be
relieved of the task. Unaided authority, even the highest which
the gods command, is not enough. Now the gods face their
hour of gravest peril. Anshar, who has thus far directed the
proceedings, falls silent.

> Anshar grew silent, staring at the ground,
> he shook his head, nodded toward Ea.
> Ranged in assembly, all the Anunnaki
> lips covered, speechless sat.

Then, finally, rising in all his majesty, Anshar proposes that
Ea's son, young Marduk, 'whose strength is mighty', champion his fathers, the gods. Ea is willing to put the proposal to
Marduk, who accepts readily enough but not without a
condition:

> If I am to be your champion,
> vanquish Ti'amat, and save you,
> then assemble and proclaim my lot supreme.
> Sit down together joyfully in Ubshuukkinna;

> let me, like you, by word of mouth determine destiny,
> so that whatever I decide shall not be altered,
> and my spoken command shall not (come) back (to me),
>   shall not be changed.

Marduk is a young god. He has abundant strength, the full prowess of youth, and he looks ahead to the physical contest with complete confidence. But, as a young man, he lacks influence. It is for authority on a par with that of the powerful senior members of the community that he asks. A new and unheard-of union of powers is here envisaged: his demand foreshadows the coming state with its combination of force and authority in the person of the king.

And so the call goes out, and the gods foregather in Ubshu-ukkinna, the court of assembly in Nippur. As they arrive, they meet friends and relatives who have similarly come to participate in the assembly, and there is general embracing. In the sheltered court the gods sit down to a sumptuous meal; wine and strong drink soon put them in a happy and carefree mood, fears and worries vanish, and the meeting is ready to settle down to more serious affairs.

> They smacked their tongues and sat down to the feast;
> They ate and drank,
> Sweet drink dispelled their fears.
> They sang for joy, drinking strong wine.
> Carefree they grew, exceedingly, their hearts elated.
> Of Marduk, (of) their champion, they decreed the destiny.

The 'destiny' mentioned is full authority on a par with that of the highest gods. The assembly first gives Marduk a seat of honour and then proceeds to confer the new powers on him:

> They made a princely dais for him.
> And he sat down, facing his fathers, as a councillor.
> 'Thou art of consequence among the elder gods.
> Thy rank is unsurpassed and thy command is Anu('s).
> Marduk, thou art of consequence among the elder gods;
> Thy rank is unequalled and thy command is Anu('s).
> From this day onward shall thy orders not be altered;
> To elevate and to abase – this be within thy power.
> What thou hast spoken shall come true, thy word shall
>   not prove vain.
> Among the gods none shall encroach upon thy rights.'

What the assembly of the gods here confers upon Marduk is
kingship: the combination of authority with powers of compulsion; a leading voice in the counsels of peace; leadership of
the army in times of war; police powers to penalize evildoers.

> We gave thee kingship, power over all things.
> Take thy seat in the council, may thy word prevail.
> May thy weapon not yield, may it smite thy foes.
> Grant breath of life to lord(s) who put (their) trust
>   in thee.
> But if a god embraces evil, shed his life.

Having conferred authority upon Marduk, the gods want to
know that he really has it, that his command now possesses
that magic quality which makes it come true. So they make a
test:

> They placed a garment in their midst
> And said to Marduk their firstborn:
> 'O Lord, thy lot is truly highest among gods.
> Command annihilation and existence, and may both
>   come true.
> May thy spoken word destroy the garment,
> Then speak again and may it be intact.'
> He spoke – and at his word the garment was destroyed.
> He spoke again, the garment reappeared.
> The gods, his fathers, seeing (the power of) his word,
> Rejoiced, paid homage: 'Marduk is king.'

Then they give him the insignia of kingship – sceptre, throne,
and royal robe(?) – and arm him for the coming conflict. Marduk's weapons are the weapons of a god of storm and thunder
– a circumstance understandable when we remember that the
story was originally the story of the storm-god Enlil. He carries
the rainbow, the arrows of lightning, and a net held by four
winds.

> He made a bow, designed it as his weapon,
> let the arrow ride firmly on the bowstring.
> Grasping his mace in his right hand, he lifted it;
> and fastened bow and quiver at his side.
> He bade lightning precede him,
> and made his body burn with searing flame.

> He made a net to encircle Tiᵓamat,
> bade the four winds hold on, that none of her escape.
> The south wind, north wind, east wind, west wind,
> Gifts from his father Anu, did he place along the edges
> of the net.

In addition, he fashions seven terrible storms, lifts up his mace, which is the flood, mounts his war chariot, 'the irresistible tempest', and rides to battle against Tiᵓamat with his army, the gods milling around him.

At the approach of Marduk, Kingu and the enemy army lose heart and are plunged into utter confusion; only Tiᵓamat stands her ground and challenges the young god to battle. Marduk returns the challenge, and the fight is on. Spreading his mighty net, Marduk envelops Tiᵓamat in its meshes. As she opens her jaws to swallow him, he sends in the winds to hold them open. The winds swell her body, and through her open mouth Marduk shoots an arrow which pierces her heart and kills her. When her followers see Marduk treading on their dead champion, they turn and try to flee; but they are caught in the meshes of his net, and he breaks their weapons and takes them captive. Kingu also is bound, and Marduk takes from him the 'tablets of destinies'.

When complete victory has thus been achieved, Marduk returns to Tiᵓamat's body, crushes her skull with his mace, and cuts her arteries; and the winds carry her blood away. Then he proceeds to cut her body in two and to lift up half of it to form the sky. To make sure that the waters in it will not escape, he sets up locks and appoints guards. He carefully measures the sky which he has thus made; and, as Ea after his victory over Apsu had built his abode on the body of his dead opponent, so now Marduk builds his abode on that part of Tiᵓamat's body which he has made into the sky. By measuring he makes certain that it comes directly opposite Ea's dwelling to form a counterpart of it.

Here we may pause again for a moment to ask what all this means. At the root of the battle between Marduk or Enlil and Tiᵓamat, between wind and water, there probably lies an age-old interpretation of the spring floods. Every spring the waters flood the Mesopotamian plain and the world reverts to a – or rather to 'the' – primeval watery chaos until the winds fight the waters, dry them up, and bring back the dry land. Remnants of this concept may be seen in the detail that the winds carry away Tiᵓamat's blood. But such age-old concepts had early become vehicles for cosmological speculation. We have already mentioned the existence of a view that heaven and earth were two great discs deposited by silt in the watery chaos and forced apart by the wind, so that the present universe is a sort of inflated sack surrounded by waters above and below. This speculation has left clear traces in Sumerian myths and in the An-Anum list, and here in *Enuma elish* we have a variant of it: it is the primeval sea, Tiᵓamat, that is blown up and killed by the winds. Half of her—the present sea—is left down here; the other half is formed into the sky, and locks are affixed so that the water does not escape except once in a while when some of it falls down as rain.

Thus, through the use which it makes of its mythological material, *Enuma elish* accounts in two ways for the creation of the sky. First, the sky comes into being in the person of the god Anu, whose name means sky and who is the god of the sky; then, again, the sky is fashioned by the wind-god out of half of the body of the sea.

In a period, however, when emphasis had already shifted from the visual aspects of the great components of the universe to the powers felt as active in and through them, Anu, as the power behind the sky, would already be felt as sufficiently different from the sky itself to make this inherent contradiction less acute.

Quite as significant as the direct cosmological identification of the actors in these events, however, is the bearing which the events have on the establishing of the cosmic order. Under pressure of an acute crisis, a threatening war, a more or less primitively organized society has developed into a state.

Evaluating this achievement in modern, and admittedly subjective, terms, we might say that the powers of movement and activity, the gods, have won their final and decisive victory over the powers of rest and inertia. To accomplish this, they have had to exert themselves to the utmost, and they have found a method, a form of organization, which permits them to pull their full weight. As the active forces in a society become integrated in the form of the state and thus can overcome the ever threatening tendencies to chaos and inertia, so the active forces in the Mesopotamian universe through that same form, the state, overcome and defeat the powers of chaos, of inactivity and inertia. But, however that may be, this much is certain – that the crisis has imposed upon the gods a state of the type of Primitive Democracy. All major issues are dealt with in a general assembly, where decrees are confirmed, designs are formulated, and judgments are pronounced. To each god is assigned a station, the most important going to the fifty senior gods, among whom are the seven whose opinion is decisive. In addition to this legislative and judiciary assembly, however, there is now an executive, the young king, who is equal in authority to the most influential members of the assembly, is the leader of the army in war, the punisher of evildoers in peacetime, and generally active, with the assent of the assembly, in matters of internal organization.

It is to tasks of internal organization that Marduk turns after his victory. The first was organizing the calendar—ever a matter for the ruler of Mesopotamia. On the sky which he had fashioned he set up constellations of stars to determine, by their rising and setting, the year, the months, and the days. The 'station' of the planet Jupiter was established to make known the 'duties' of the days, when each had to appear:

> To make known their obligations,
> that none might do wrong or be remiss.

He also set on heaven two bands known as 'the ways' of Enlil and Ea. On both sides of the sky, where the sun comes out in the morning and leaves in the evening, Marduk made gates and secured them with strong locks. In the midst of the sky he fixed the zenith, and he made the moon shine forth and gave it its orders.

> He bade the moon come forth; entrusted night to her;
> Made her a creature of the dark, to measure time;
> And every month, unfailingly, adorned her with a crown.

Thereupon Marduk divided the gods and assigned them to Anu, to abide by Anu's instructions. Three hundred he stationed in heaven to do guard duty, and another three hundred were given tasks on earth. Thus the divine forces were organized and assigned to their appropriate tasks throughout the universe.

The gods are truly grateful for Marduk's efforts. To express their gratitude, they take pick in hand for the last time and build him a city and temple with throne daises for each of the gods to use when they meet there for assembly. The first assembly is held on the occasion of the dedication of the temple. As usual, the gods first sit down to a banquet. Thereupon matters of state are discussed and decided, and then, when the current business has been disposed of, Anu rises to confirm Marduk's position as king. He determines the eternal status of Marduk's weapon, the bow; he determines the status of his throne; and, finally, he calls upon the assembled gods to confirm and determine Marduk's own status, his functions in the universe, by recounting his fifty names, each expressing one aspect of his being, each defining one of his functions. With the catalogue of these names the poem comes to an end. The names summarize what Marduk is and what he signifies: the final victory over chaos and the establishing of the ordered, organized universe, the cosmic state of the Mesopotamians.

With *Enuma elish* we have reached a phase of Mesopotamian civilization in which the ancient world view which had formed the subconscious, intuitively accepted framework for all individual speculations begins itself to become a theme of conscious inquiry. Whereas the older myths answered questions concerning origins, order, and evaluation of details, *Enuma elish* answers questions concerning fundamentals. It deals with the origin and the order of the universe as a whole. It deals, however, only with origin and order, not with evaluation. The fundamental question of evaluation concerns the justice of the world order. This question *was* taken up, but not mythologically. The answers given will form the subject of chapter vii, which deals with 'the good life'. Before that, however, we should consider the reflection of the Mesopotamian view of world order in social and political life. We turn to the function of the state.

NOTES

1. Gilgamesh Epic, Old Babylonian version, Yale Tablet IV, 7–8.

2. *CT* XV, 15. 12.

3. Reissner, *SBH* VII, rev. 17–24. The flood serves in this passage as metaphor for the divine verdict.

The English form of the quotations from ancient poetry in these chapters is the work of Mrs. Frankfort, who has been extraordinarily successful in conveying the beauty of the original with a minimum of poetic licence.

4. 'Mythology,' *Encyclopaedia Britannica* (11th ed.), ol. 19, p. 134.

5. *Maqlû*, Tablet VI, 111–19.

6. Verdict on Flint in *Lugal-e*.

7. Cf. the Nidaba hymn, *OECT* I, 36–39.

8. *Maqlû*, Tablet III, 151–52.   9. *Ibid.* VI, 1–8.   10. *KAR* 102.

11. *CT* XXIV, 50, No. 47406 obv. 6 and 8.

12. *Maqlû*, Tablet II, 104–15.   13. *Politics* 1252^b.

14. *RA* XI, 144 obv. 3–5.

15. Thureau-Dangin, *Rit. acc.*, 70 obv. 1–14.

16. Kramer, *AS* XII, 34 and 36, ll. 173–89.

17. *Ibid.*, p. 38, ll. 203–4.   18. *Ibid.*, pp. 38 and 40, ll. 208–18.

19. *KAR* 25. iii. 21–29, and 68 obv. 1–11.   20. *KAR* 375. ii. 1–8.

21. Reissner, *SBH*, pp. 130 ff., ll. 48–55.

22. *CT* XXXVI, Pl. 31, 1–20.

23. Kramer, *Mythology*, nn. 47 and 48.   24. *Ibid.*, nn. 54 and 55.

25. *Ib d.*, n. 59.   26. *Ibid.*, n. 73.

27. Chiera, *SRT*, 4 obv. 17–22.   28. *Ibid.*, 3.

29. Latest translation: Heidel, *The Babylonian Genesis*. See literature there quoted.

30. A Semitic language which had long been spoken side by side with Sumerian in Mesopotamia and which by the end of the third millennium B.C. completely superseded its rival and became the only language spoken in the country.

31. I.e., within Apsu, Mummu, and Ti$^{\circ}$amat.

CHAPTER VI

Mesopotamia: The Function of the State

THE FIRST subject with which we are to deal is 'the function of the state', that is, the particular function which the human state in Mesopotamia was thought to fulfil in the functioning of the universe as a whole. Before we go any further, however, it will be well to consider our modern term 'state', lest it trip us up when we apply it to ancient Mesopotamian concepts. When we speak of a state, we usually imply inner sovereignty and independence of all external control. Moreover, we think of a state as dominating a specific territory, and we see as its chief aim the protection of its members and the furthering of their well-being.

Now in the Mesopotamian view of the world, these attributes do not – indeed, cannot – belong to any human organization. The only truly sovereign state, independent of all external control, is the state which the universe itself constitutes, the state governed by the assembly of the gods. This state, moreover, is the state which dominates the territory of Mesopotamia; the gods own the land, the big estates, in the country. Lastly, since man was created especially for the benefit of the gods, his purpose is to serve the gods. Therefore no human institution can have its primary aim in the welfare of its own human members; it must seek primarily the welfare of the gods.

But if our term 'state' thus rightly applies only to the state which the Mesopotamian universe constituted, what, then, we may ask, are the political units on the human level which we find throughout Mesopotamian history and which historians call city-states and nations? The answer would seem to be that they are secondary power-structures within the true state. The so-called 'city-state' is a private organization and has a primarily economic purpose; it is the manor, the estate, of some great god. The national state also is a secondary power structure, but it has a political function; it may be considered an extension of the executive organs of the world state, a police force.

Having thus defined in general the entities with which we are dealing, we may consider in more detail the function they fulfil in the universe, in the cosmic state.

THE MESOPOTAMIAN CITY-STATE

Throughout the third millennium B.C. Mesopotamia was made up of small political units, the so-called 'city-states'. Each such state consisted of a city with its surrounding territory, cultivated by the people of the city. Sometimes a city-state included more than one city. There might be two or three towns and a number of villages which were dependent on and administered by the chief city. From time to time conquerors arose who succeeded in uniting most of the city-states into a single large national state under their rule; but these national states usually lasted for a relatively short time, after which the country would divide into city-states again.

Central in the city-state was the city, and central in the city was the temple of the city god. The temple of the city god was usually the greatest landowner in the state, and it cultivated its extensive holdings by means of serfs and sharecroppers. Other temples belonging to the city god's spouse, to their divine children, and to deities associated with the chief god similarly had large land holdings, so that it has been estimated that around the middle of the third millennium B.C. most of the lands of a Mesopotamian city-state were temple lands. The larger part of the inhabitants were accordingly earning their livelihood as sharecroppers, serfs, or servants of the gods.

In this situation lie the economic and political realities expressed in the Mesopotamian myths which state that man was created to relieve the gods of toil, to work on the gods' estates. For the Mesopotamian city-state *was* an estate, or rather – like the medieval manor with which we have compared it – it had an estate as basis. That basic estate, the main temple with its lands, was owned and run by the city god, who himself gave all important orders.

To carry out these orders the city god had at his disposal a large staff of divine and human servants. The human servants worked in the house and in the fields and were organized accordingly. The divine servants, minor gods, served as overseers of the work. Each such minor god had his own special province in the running of the estate; and here he infused his divine powers into the labour of his human underlings, so that it prospered and bore fruit.

We are particularly well informed[1] about the organization of the main temple in the city-state of Lagash, which belonged to a god by the name of Ningirsu. This temple may therefore serve as an example.

There are, first, the divine servants of Ningirsu, minor gods who belong to his family and entourage. They fall into two groups: some have their tasks in the manor house, the temple itself; others work on the temple lands, in the fields.

Among the gods who are busy in the manor house we find the son of the owner, the god Igalimma, who is doorkeeper at the Holy of Holies and admits visitors who seek audience with Ningirsu. Another son of Ningirsu, Dunshagana, is the chief butler. He supervises the preparation and serving of food and drink, keeps an eye on the temple breweries, and sees to it that the shepherds deliver lambs and milk products for the god's table. Next come two armourers, who take care of Ningirsu's weapons and follow him as armour-bearers in battle. In more peaceful pursuits Ningirsu has the support of a divine counsellor, who discusses the needs of his city with him. His personal needs are cared for by a body-servant, the god Shakanshabar, who runs errands for Ningirsu, and by his divine chamberlain Urizi, who has charge of the god's dwelling-quarters, sees to it that the god's bed is well and properly made every night, etc. In the stables of the manor we find the coachman, Ensignun, Ningirsu's charioteer, who cares for the god's donkeys and his chariot. Here is also Enlulim, the divine goatherd, who cares for the flocks of the temple and sees to it that there is plenty of milk and butter.

Returning to the dwelling-quarters, we note Ningirsu's musician, who is in charge of the musical instruments and whose task it is to fill the court with joy when he plays. There is also a drummer. He performs chiefly when Ningirsu is disturbed or upset; then the deep beat of the drum will help to soothe the god's heart and to still his tears. Ningirsu has seven daughters by his wife Baba. They act as ladies-in-waiting at his court.

Outside the manor house, in the fields, lie the duties of the god Gishbare, the bailiff of Ningirsu, who is charged with making the fields yield, causing the water to rise in the canals, and filling the temple granaries. Here also is the divine inspector of fisheries, who stocks the ponds with fish, looks after the reed thickets, and sends in his reports to Ningirsu. The wild life on the estate is in the care of a divine gamekeeper or forester, who is to see that the birds lay their eggs in peace and that the young of birds and beasts grow up unmolested.

A divine sheriff, finally, enforces the ordinances in the town, keeping watch on its walls and patrolling it, club in hand.

While these divine overseers bless the tasks performed on Ningirsu's estate, the actual menial labour is done by humans. These human toilers, whether sharecroppers, serfs, or temple servants, shepherds, brewers, or cooks, were organized in groups under human overseers in a hierarchy which culminated in the highest human servant of the god, the *ensi*, manager of the god's estate and manager of his city-state.

We call the *ensi* 'manager' of the god's estate; and his position vis-à-vis the god was actually closely parallel to that of an estate manager, a steward, vis-à-vis the owner. A steward appointed to manage an estate is expected, first of all, to uphold and carry on the established order of that estate; secondly, he is to execute such specific commands as the owner may see fit to give with respect to changes, innovations, or ways to deal with unexpected situations. Quite similarly, the *ensi* was expected to uphold the established order of the god's temple and city in general, and he was expected to consult the god and carry out any specific orders which the god might wish to give.

To the first part of the *ensi*'s task belonged the administration of the temple and its estate. He was in complete charge of all agricultural tasks, of temple forests, and temple fisheries, of the spinneries, looms, mills, breweries, bakeries, kitchens, etc., which formed part of the temple manor. Minute accounts were kept of all these activities by a corps of scribes, and these accounts were submitted to and approved by him. As he managed the temple of the city god, so his wife managed the temple and estate of the divine spouse of the city god, and his children managed the temples of the children of the city god.

In addition to these tasks, the *ensi* was responsible for law and order in the state and was to see to it that everybody was justly treated. Thus we hear about one *ensi* that he 'contracted with the god Ningirsu that he would not deliver up the orphan and the widow to the powerful man'.[2] The *ensi*, therefore, was the highest judicial authority. But he had other duties also: he was commander-in-chief of the army of the city-state, he negotiated for his lord the god with *ensi*'s representing the gods of other city-states, and he made war and peace.

With these last functions we touch on the other aspect of the *ensi*'s task, that of executing the specific commands of the god; for war and peace involved decisions which went beyond the normal order, decisions which could be made only by the god himself. Among other questions which the city-god himself must decide was whether to rebuild the main temple.

To ascertain the will of his master, the *ensi* commanded several approaches. He might receive an order through the occurrence of something unusual and portentous in nature, an omen whose significance the priests could interpret from long catalogues in which such omens and their meanings were listed. He might, however, also seek answer to a definite question by sacrificing an animal to the god and reading the god's message in the shape of the liver of the sacrificial animal. If the answer was not clear at first, he could repeat the process. Still another way of communicating with the god, the most direct one, was through dreams. The *ensi* would go to the temple at night, sacrifice, pray, and lie down to sleep. In dreams the god might then appear to him and give him his orders.

We possess several detailed accounts of how such orders were transmitted from the god to his human steward. An example is an order from the god Ningirsu to his steward Gudea, *ensi* of Lagash.[3] This order concerned the rebuilding of Ningirsu's temple, Eninnu. Gudea first noticed that something was amiss when the river Tigris, which Ningirsu controlled, failed to rise as usual and flood the fields. Gudea immediately betook himself to the temple, and there he had a dream. In the dream he saw a gigantic man with a divine crown, with wings like a great bird, and with a body which ended below in a floodwave. To the right and left of this man lions were lying. The man commanded Gudea to build his temple. Then day broke on the horizon. Next, a woman emerged and proceeded to raze a building plot. In her hand was a stylus of gold and a clay tablet on which constellations of stars were set down; these she studied. Then came a warrior who held a tablet of lapis lazuli upon which he sketched the plan of a house. Before Gudea stood a brick mould and a basket; bird-men unceasingly poured water into a trough; and a male donkey to the right of the god was impatiently pawing the ground.

Though Gudea realized the general purport of this dream, that he was to rebuild Ningirsu's temple, the meanings of the details were not clear to him at all. He therefore decided to consult the goddess Nanshe, who lived in a smaller town in his realm and was especially apt at interpreting dreams. The journey took time, for he stopped at every temple on the way to pray for help and support. Finally he arrived, however, and went straight to the goddess to place his problem before her. She was ready with an answer (how it was conveyed we are not told; all we have is the answer itself): the man with the crown and the wings was Ningirsu commanding Gudea to rebuild his temple Eninnu. The daylight was Gudea's personal god, who would be active all over the world, bringing success to the trade expeditions which Gudea would send out to get building materials for the temple. The goddess who studied the tablet with the stars was determining the particular star under which it would be propitious to rebuild the temple. The plan the god was drawing was that of the temple. Brick mould and basket were the brick mould and basket for the sacred bricks of the temple; the bird-men working incessantly signified that Gudea would permit himself no sleep before he carried out his task; and the impatient donkey pawing the ground symbolized the *ensi* himself, impatient to begin the work.

But the command had not yet been made specific. What kind of temple did Ningirsu want? What should it contain? Nanshe advised Gudea to seek further information from the god. He was to build a new war chariot for Ningirsu, furnish it lavishly, and bring it in to the god to the sound of drums. Then Ningirsu, 'who delights in gifts', would heed Gudea's prayers and tell him exactly how the temple should be built. Gudea followed this advice, and, after spending several nights in the temple without result, he finally saw Ningirsu, who told in detail what units the new temple must contain.

> Gudea awoke, he had been sleeping; he shook himself, it was a dream.
> In acceptance, he bowed his head to the commands of Ningirsu.

Now Gudea could go ahead. He called his people together, told them of the divine command, assigned levies to the building operations, sent out trade expeditions, etc. Now he had his orders, knew what he was to do.

We have here described a divine order to undertake the building of a temple. But in similar manner, by direct divine command, originated all significant undertakings. The god commanded the undertaking of a war, the conclusion of a peace, the introduction of new laws and customs to regulate the community.

The role of the city-state within that larger state which the universe constitutes is thus reasonably clear. It is a private institution with a function which is mainly economic. It belongs to and is headed by a private citizen of the cosmic state, one of the great gods; it is his manor. As a manor, it provides the god with the essentials of life: food, clothing, and shelter. It provides these in such abundance that the god can live the life which befits him, the life of a nobleman surrounded by servants, attendants, and material wealth. Thus he is allowed free and unhindered self-expression.

Now each great god is, as we have seen, the power in and behind some great force of nature – the sky, the storm, or whatever it may be. By upholding a great god, by providing the economic basis which permits that god to enjoy full and free self-expression, the city-state is upholding some great power of the universe and assuring its freedom to function as it should. And this is the function of the human city-state within the cosmos. In this manner it contributes to maintaining and perpetuating the ordered cosmos and its powers.

THE MESOPOTAMIAN NATIONAL STATE

Different in function from the city-state, active on the political rather than on the economic plane, was the national state in Mesopotamia. Both city-state and national state were power-structures which rose ultimately above the purely human level; each had its apex in a great god. But, whereas the lines of the city-state focused on a great god in his capacity as a private citizen of the cosmic state, the lines of the national state focused on a great god in his capacity as an official of the cosmic state. The national state thus became an extension of a governmental organ of the only true and sovereign state.

The ruling body in the cosmic state is, as will be remembered, the assembly of the gods. Here Anu acts as leader of the debate, while Enlil represents the executive powers as sheriff and commander of the armed forces. However, though Enlil typifies the element of force in the world government, he is not its only representative. The assembly may choose any one of its members to maintain internal order and to lead the armed forces, proclaiming him king. The god chosen king then exercises these functions among the gods, while he acts on earth through his human steward, the ruler of his city-state. That human steward accordingly dominates the other rulers in Mesopotamia and through them their city-states. For example, the period around the middle of the second millennium B.C., when the city-states of Inanna, namely, Kish and Agade, successively held sway in Mesopotamia, was the 'period of reign' of Inanna. Later on, when Ur dominated, its god Nanna held office as king among the gods.

So strong, however, were the ties linking Enlil to these executive functions that the kingship was often referred to directly as 'the Enlil functions', and the god who held this office was thought of as acting under Enlil's guidance.

The functions of kingship were twofold: to punish evil-doers and uphold law and order internally and to conduct foreign wars and protect Mesopotamia externally. Two examples may serve to clarify the theory.

When Hammurabi, after thirty years as ruler of the small city-state of Babylon, succeeded in subjugating all of southern Mesopotamia, his success meant – in cosmic terms – that Marduk, the city-god of Babylon, had been chosen by the divine assembly, acting through its leaders Anu and Enlil, to administer the Enlil functions. Correspondingly, Marduk's human steward, Hammurabi, had been entrusted with the administration of these functions on earth. Hammurabi tells about it as follows:

> When lofty Anu, king of the Anunnaki, and Enlil, lord of heaven and earth,
> who determine the destinies of the country, appointed Marduk, the firstborn
> son of Enki, to execute the Enlil functions over the totality of the people, made him great among the Igigi, called Babylon by its exalted name, made it
> surpassing(ly great) in the world, and firmly established for him in its
> midst an enduring kingship whose foundations are (as) firmly grounded as
> (those of) heaven and earth – then did Anu and Enlil call me to afford well-being to the people,
> me, Hammurabi, the obedient, godfearing prince, to cause righteousness to appear in the land,
> to destroy the evil and the wicked, that the strong harm not the weak
> and that I rise like the sun over the black-headed people, lighting up the land.[4]

Marduk, as we see from this passage, is to act as executive for Enlil, Hammurabi for Marduk. Since the passage is taken from the introduction to Hammurabi's law code, it is only natural that those of the Enlil functions which have reference to the maintaining of law and order are especially stressed.

Before the Enlil functions passed to Marduk and Babylon,

they were held by the city of Isin and by its goddess Ninin-sina. We may quote from a text in which the goddess herself tells about her duties; she stresses her function as leader of foreign wars:

> When the heart of the great mountain Enlil has become turbulent,
> when he has knit his brows against a foreign land and determined
>   the fate of a rebellious country,
> then my father Enlil sends me to the rebellious country against
>   which he has knit his brows,
> and I, woman and hero, I, the mighty warrior, I go against it![5]

She continues with a description of the punishment which her armed might inflicts upon the foreign land and tells how she reports back to Enlil in Nippur.

Since the human steward acts for the city-god, even when the city-god has been chosen king and exercises the Enlil functions, the appointment of the human steward also is in such a case no longer a private affair of the city-god's; it needs confirmation from the divine assembly. Accordingly, we hear how, when Nanna, the god of Ur, became king of the gods, he had to travel to Nippur to seek office for his steward, Shulgi. In Nippur, Nanna is received in audience before Enlil, and his proposal is accepted. Says Enlil:

> Let my shepherd, Shulgi, cause pain to rebellious countries;
> let commands of righteousness be in his mouth (?).[6]

He mentions the two outstanding aspects of the office: leadership in war and the upholding of justice. Then Nanna brings back to his human protegé the glad tidings that his candidacy has been accepted.

A more complete and detailed description of such confirmation of an appointment is contained in a petition of the ruler Ishme-Dagan of Isin. He asks first that Enlil give him lordship in north and south and that Anu, at Enlil's suggestion, give him 'all shepherd staves'. Then each of the other great gods is besought to add some feature, to help in a particular way. When thus the appointment and its powers have been fully outlined, the king asks:

May Enki, Ninki, Enul, Ninul, and those of the Anunnaki who
   are fate-determining lords,
(as also) the spirits of Nippur, (and) the genii of Ekur, among
   the great gods
speak concerning the destiny which they have determined, their
   immutable 'Let it be.'[7]

That is, may the assembly of the gods confirm the appointment by their assenting votes.

The fact that the Mesopotamian universe was conceived of
as a state – that the gods who owned and ruled the various
city-states were bound together in a higher unity, the assembly
of the gods, which possessed executive organs for exerting
outward pressure as well as for enforcing law and order internally – had far-reaching consequences for Mesopotamian history and for the ways in which historical events were viewed
and interpreted. It vastly strengthened tendencies toward political unification of the country by sanctioning even the most
violent of means used toward that end. For any conqueror, if
he was successful, was recognized as the agent of Enlil. It
also provided – even at times when national unity was at a low
ebb and the many city-states were, for all practical purposes,
independent units – a background on which international law
could work. We see, already at the dawn of history, that a
boundary dispute between the neighbouring city-states Lagash
and Umma was viewed as a dispute between two divine land-
owners, Ningirsu, the god of Lagash, and Shara, the god of
Umma. As such it could be taken to court and adjudicated by
Enlil in Nippur. Enlil implemented his decision through the
ruler who was then his human representative, Mesilim, king
of Kish. Mesilim measured the disputed territory and marked
the boundary line which Enlil had designated.[8]

In a similar manner other 'kings' throughout Mesopotamian history acted as mediators and judges in disputes between city-states, fulfilling their tasks as Enlil's representatives.
Thus Utuhegal of Uruk, after he had freed and united Shumer,
settled boundary disputes between Lagash and Ur.[9] Again,
Urnammu, the first king of the Third Dynasty of Ur, brought
a similar dispute before the judge of the gods, the sun-god

Utu, and 'in accordance with the righteous verdict of Utu he had the underlying facts cleared up and confirmed (by witnesses)'.[10]

This tendency to view what was, in purely human terms, a naked conflict of force as a legal procedure in the state of the gods, as an execution of a divine verdict, appears in full light in an inscription in which Utuhegal tells how he liberated Shumer from its Gutian oppressors.[11] After an introduction stating the misrule which the Gutians had instituted, Utuhegal tells how Enlil gave a verdict deposing them. Then follows Enlil's commission to Utuhegal, a divine deputy is assigned to him to accompany him and authorize his action as that of a legally empowered agent. And, finally, we hear about his campaign and victory.

The function which the national state performed as extension of the executive organs of the cosmic state was important but not indispensable. There had been a time when the kingship rested in heaven before Anu and had not yet descended to earth, and there were times in history when the gods appointed no human king on earth. Still the universe continued in its course. And, just as the national kingship itself was not indispensable, so was any particular incumbent of this office still less indispensable. From time to time the god and city that exercised the kingship were judged unfit for the function, if only for the reason that the divine assembly desired a change. Then the city 'was smitten with weapons', and the kingship was either conferred on another god and city or held in abeyance.

When such momentous events were shaping the royal city began to feel its grip slipping, its functioning becoming inefficient. All omens and signs became confused, the gods gave no clear answers to man's questions, no orders were transmitted, sinister portents appeared, and with fear and foreboding man awaited the catastrophe.

The gods of the doomed city suffered with it. We know, for instance, the feeling which gripped Ningal, goddess of Ur, in the days when the fall of that city was approaching, when a coming assembly of the gods would decide that the kingship

which Ur had held should pass away from it and the city
should perish in Enlil's terrible storm. The goddess herself
tells about those days:

> When I was grieving for that day of storm,
> that day of storm, destined for me, laid upon me, heavy with tears,
> that day of storm, destined for me, laid upon me, heavy with tears,
> on me, a woman –
> though I was trembling for that day of storm,
> that day of storm, destined for me, laid upon me, heavy with tears,
> that cruel day of storm destined for me –
> I could not flee before that day's fatality.
> And of a sudden I espied no happy days within my reign,
> no happy days within my reign.
> Though I would tremble for that night,
> that night of cruel weeping destined for me,
> I could not flee before that night's fatality.
> Dread of the storm's floodlike destruction weighed on me,
> and of a sudden on my couch at night,
> upon my couch at night no dreams were granted me.
> And of a sudden on my couch oblivion,
> upon my couch oblivion was not granted.
> Because (this) bitter weeping had been destined for my land,
> and I could not, even if I scoured the earth – a cow seeking her calf –
> have brought my people back,
> because (this) bitter sorrow had been destined for my city,
> even if I, birdlike, had stretched my wings,
> and, like a bird, flown to my city,
> yet my city would have been destroyed on its foundation,
> yet Ur would have perished where it lay.
> Because that day of storm had raised its hand,
> and even had I screamed out loud and cried:
> 'Turn back, O day of storm, (turn) to (thy) desert,'
> the breast of that storm would not have been lifted from me.[12]

Though Ningal knows that it is hopeless, that the minds of the
gods are made up, she does her utmost to sway the assembly
when the fateful verdict is given, first imploring the leaders
Anu and Enlil, then, when that has failed, even making a last
attempt in the assembly itself – all to no avail.

> Then verily, to the assembly, where the crowd had not yet risen,
> while the Anunnaki, binding themselves (to uphold the decision),
> were still seated,
> I dragged my feet and I stretched out my arms.

In truth, I shed my tears in front of Anu.
In truth, myself I mourned in front of Enlil:
'May not my city be destroyed?' I said indeed to them.
'May Ur not be destroyed?' I said indeed to them.
'And may its people not be killed?' I said indeed to them.
But Anu never bent towards those words,
and Enlil never with an, 'It is pleasing, let it be,'
did soothe my heart.
(Behold,) they gave instruction that the city be destroyed,
(behold,) they gave instruction that Ur be destroyed,
and as its destiny decreed that its inhabitants be killed.[13]

And so Ur goes down before the onslaught of barbarians. The
gods have decided – as another hymn says of this event:

> To bring on other days, annihilate the plan
> and – while the storms foamed like a flood –
> subvert the ways of Shumer.[14]

We quote these lines because they sum up what was involved
in the national kingship. The national kingship was the guarantee of 'the ways of Shumer' (that is the ways of civilized
Mesopotamia), the orderly, lawful pattern of life. Its function
in the world was to give protection against enemies external
and internal, to ensure the reign of justice and righteousness in
human affairs.

THE STATE AND NATURE

With this discussion of the city-state and the national state we
have outlined the function of the human state in general in the
Mesopotamian universe. The city-state had an economic function. It provided a great god and his entourage with the economic basis which would enable him to live a full life, to realize
his nature unhindered. The national state had a political function. It was an extension of the executive organs of the state of
the universe and enforced on the human level the gods' decisions, ensuring armed protection of their estates, upholding
justice and righteousness as a basis for the intercourse of their
servants, men.

Yet we should not leave our subject, the function of the
state, without calling attention to a curious and interesting
aspect which somehow fails to stand out when the human state

is seen from the viewpoint of the universal state. That aspect is the relation of the human state to nature.

We have mentioned that the city-state furnishes the economic background which permitted the gods to live a full life in unhindered self-expression. This self-expression differed for the different gods; each had his own particular mode of life, his own characteristic observances and rites. This is apparent in the great cult festivals, which sometimes centre in a marriage rite, sometimes in a battle drama, and sometimes in a death and revival drama. These cult festivals were matters of state; frequently the king or the ruler of the city-state performed the chief role in the cult drama. But why should they be matters of state?

We may consider one of these cult festivals in some detail. Around the end of the third millennium the city of Isin, which was then the ruling city in southern Mesopotamia, celebrated yearly the marriage of the goddess Inanna to the god Dumuzi or Tammuz. It is understandable that a marriage should be a typical form of self-expression for the youthful goddess, and – in the view of the universe as a state – it is only logical that her human servants and retainers should officiate at the wedding and take part in the celebration as guests and spectators. Since the goddess is an incarnation of the fertility of nature, and her husband, the shepherd-god Dumuzi, incarnates the creative powers of spring, it is understandable that this annual union of god and goddess signifies and *is* the reawakening of nature in spring. In the marriage of these deities the fertility and the creative powers of nature themselves become manifest. But why, we may ask, should human servants of the gods, the human ruler and – so it seems – a priestess, transcend their human status, take on the identity of the deities Dumuzi and Inanna, and go through their marriage? For this is what took place in the rites. The answer to that question lies back beyond the times when the view of the world as a state took form, back in a remote prehistoric age when the gods were not yet anthropomorphic rulers of states and cities but were still directly the phenomena of nature. In those days man's attitude was not merely one of passive obedience; it called for active intervention, as it does among many primitives today. It is one of the tenets of mythopoeic logic that similarity and identity merge; 'to be like' is as good as 'to be'. Therefore, by being like, by enacting the role of, a force in nature, a god, man could in the cult enter into and clothe himself with the identity of these powers, with the identity of the gods, and through his own actions, when thus identified, cause the powers involved to act as he would have them act. By identifying himself with Dumuzi, the king is Dumuzi; and similarly the priestess is Inanna – our texts clearly state this. Their marriage is the marriage of the creative powers of spring. Thus through a willed act of man is achieved a divine union wherein is the all-pervading, life-giving re-creative potency upon which depends, as our texts tell us, 'the life of all lands' and also the steady flow of days, the renewal of the new moon throughout the new year.[15]

As in this marriage rite, so also with the other types of cult festivals. In the death and revival drama man becomes the god of vegetation, the god of the grass and plants which have disappeared over the dry summer and the cold winter. Having become the god, man lets himself be found and thus causes the return of the god, of the new vegetation that springs up everywhere when spring comes. These rites usually comprise wailing processions lamenting the god who has been lost, a search for the god, finding him, and the triumphant return with him.[16]

This same approach underlies the battle drama. Each new year, when floods threatened to bring back the primeval watery chaos, it was of the essence that the gods should fight again that primeval battle in which the world was first won. And so man took on the identity of a god: in the cult rite the king became Enlil or Marduk or Assur, and as the god he fought the powers of chaos. To the very end of Mesopotamian civilization, a few centuries before our era, the king, every new year in Babylon, took on the identity of Marduk and vanquished Kingu, leader of Ti'amat's host, by burning a lamb in which that deity was incarnate.[17]

In these festivals, which were state festivals, the human state contributed to the control of nature, to the upholding of the orderly cosmos. In the rites man secured the revival of nature

CHAPTER VII

Mesopotamia : The Good Life

THE PRIME VIRTUE: OBEDIENCE

IN A civilization which sees the whole universe as a state, obedience must necessarily stand out as a prime virtue. For a state is built on obedience, on the unquestioned acceptance of authority. It can cause no wonder, therefore, to find that in Mesopotamia the 'good life' was the 'obedient life'. The individual stood at the centre of ever wider circles of authority which delimited his freedom of action. The nearest and smallest of these circles was constituted by authorities in his own family: father and mother, older brother and older sister. We possess a hymn which describes a coming golden age, and we find that age characterized as one of obedience, as

> Days when one man is not insolent to another, when a son reveres his father,
> days when respect is shown in the land, when the lowly honour the great,
> when the younger brother ... respects (?) his older brother,
> when the older child instructs the younger child and he (i.e., the younger) abides by his decisions.[1]

The Mesopotamian is constantly admonished: 'Pay heed to the word of thy mother as to the word of thy god'; 'Revere thy older brother'; 'Pay heed to the word of thy older brother as to the word of thy father'; 'Anger not the heart of thy older sister'.

But obedience to the older members of one's family is merely a beginning. Beyond the family lie other circles, other authorities: the state and society. There is the foreman where one works; there is the bailiff who oversees agricultural works in which one takes part; there is the king. All these can and must claim absolute obedience. The Mesopotamian looked with disapproval and pity, but also with fear, on the crowd which had no leader: 'Soldiers without a king are sheep without their shepherd'.[2]

A crowd with no leader to organize and direct it is lost and bewildered, like a flock of sheep without a shepherd. It is also dangerous, however; it can be destructive, like waters which break the dams that hold them and submerge fields and gardens if the canal inspector is not there to keep the dams in repair: 'Workmen without a foreman are waters without a canal inspector'.[3]

Finally, a leaderless, unorganized crowd is useless and unproductive, like a field which brings forth nothing if it is not ploughed: 'Peasants without a bailiff are a field without a ploughman.'[4]

Hence an orderly world is unthinkable without a superior authority to impose his will. The Mesopotamian feels convinced that authorities are always right: 'The command of the palace, like the command of Anu, cannot be altered. The king's word is right; his utterance, like that of a god, cannot be changed!'[5] And, as there are circles of human authority in family, society, and state, to circumscribe the freedom of the individual, so there are circles of divine authority which may not be trespassed upon. Here again we find more immediate and more remote ties of allegiance. For the ties of the individual to the great gods were – at least in the third millennium – of a somewhat remote character. He served them as a member of his community rather than as an individual; he worked their estates for them, with his neighbours and compatriots he obeyed their laws and decrees, and he took part in their yearly festivals as a spectator. But, just as the serf rarely has intimate personal relations with the lord of the manor, so the individual in Mesopotamia looked upon the great gods as remote forces to whom he could appeal only in some great crisis and then only through intermediaries. Close and personal relations – relations such as he had to the authorities in his family: father, mother, older brother and sister – the individual had only to one deity, to his personal god.

The personal god was usually some minor deity in the pantheon who took a special interest in a man's family or had taken a fancy to the man himself. In a sense, and probably this is the original aspect, the personal god appears as the personification of a man's luck and success. Success is interpreted as an outside power which infuses itself into a man's doings and makes them produce results. It is not man's own ability which brings results, for man is weak and has no power to influence the course of the universe to any appreciable degree. Only a god can do that; therefore, if things come out as man has hoped, or even better, it must needs be that some god has taken an interest in him and his doings and brought him success. He has, to use the Mesopotamian expression for success, 'acquired a god'. This original aspect of the personal god as the power behind a man's success stands out quite clearly in such sayings as

> Without a (personal) god man cannot make his living,
> the young man cannot move his arm heroically in battle,[6]

and in the way the personal god is lined with forethought and planning:

> When thou dost plan ahead, thy god is thine;
> when thou dost not plan ahead, thy god is not thine.[7]

That is to say, only when you plan ahead do you have a chance to succeed; only then is your god with you.

Since the personal god is the power which makes a man's actions succeed, it is quite natural that he or she should also carry the moral responsibility for those actions. When Lugalzaggisi, the ruler of Umma, had attacked and partly destroyed the city of Lagash, the men of Lagash placed the blame unhesitantly on Lugalzaggisi's deity: 'May his personal deity, the goddess Nidaba, bear this crime on her neck!'[8] That is, may the proper divine authorities who rule the universe hold her responsible for what she has aided and abetted.

To this personal god, then, before any other, a man owed worship and obedience. In every house there was a small chapel for the personal god where the owner of the house worshipped and brought his daily offerings.

> A man must truly proclaim the greatness of his god;
> A young man must wholeheartedly obey the command of his god.[9]

REWARDS OF OBEDIENCE

Now, if this monotonous theme of obedience – to family, to rulers, to gods – was the essence of the good, that is, the correct, life in ancient Mesopotamia, what, we may ask, did man stand to gain by leading the good life? The answer is best given in terms of the Mesopotamian world view, in terms of man's position in the cosmic state. Man, you will remember, was created to be the slave of the gods. He is their servant. Now, a diligent and obedient servant can call on his master for protection. A diligent and obedient servant, moreover, can expect to be promoted, to receive favours and rewards from his master. A slothful, disobedient servant, on the other hand, can hope for none of these things. Thus the way of obedience, of service and worship, is the way to achieve protection; and it is also the way to earthly success, to the highest values in Mesopotamian life: health and long life, honoured standing in the community, many sons, wealth.

When we view the Mesopotamian universe from the aspect of what the individual can gain for himself, the personal god becomes a pivotal figure. He is the individual's link with the universe and its forces; he is the Archimedean point from which it may be moved. For the personal god is not remote and awesome like the great gods; he is near and familiar; and he cares. One can talk to him, plead with him, work on his pity – in short, use all the means which a child uses to get his way with his parents. The character of the relationship may be exemplified by a letter from a man to his god, for the Mesopotamians frequently wrote letters to their gods. Perhaps they thought that one could not always be certain to find the god at home when one called, whereas the god would be sure to look at his correspondence. Again, it may often have been because the writer was too ill to come in person and therefore had recourse to a letter. In the case of the letter which we shall quote, it would appear that the writer refrains from coming in person because he is sulking. His feelings are hurt because he thinks his god neglects him. He hints that such neglect is very unwise on the part of the god, for faithful worshippers are hard to get and difficult to replace. But if the god will only comply with his wishes, then he will be there right away and adore him. Finally, he works on the god's pity: the god must consider that there is not only himself but that he has a family and poor little children who also suffer with him. The letter reads:

> To the god my father speak; thus says Apiladad, thy servant:
> 'Why have you neglected me (so)?
> Who is going to give you one who can take my place?
> Write to the god Marduk, who is fond of you,
> that he may break my bondage;
> then I shall see your face and kiss your feet!
> Consider also my family, grown-ups and little ones;
> have mercy on me for their sake, and let your help reach me!' [10]

The bondage of which the letter speaks is some illness. Illness of any kind was seen as an evil demon who had seized the victim and held him captive. Such a case actually goes beyond the powers of the personal god. The personal god can help a man in his undertakings, can give him standing and respect in his community; but he is not strong enough to tear him from the clutches of an evil, lawless demon. However – and this is the most wonderful thing about having connections with those in high places – the personal god has influential friends. He moves in the circles of the great gods, knows them well. So now, when his ward has been seized by an evil demon, it is time to use whatever influence he has to set the cumbersome machinery of divine justice in motion: 'Write to the god Marduk, who is fond of you', says our letter.

Now we who live in a modern state take for granted that the machinery of justice – courts, judges, police – is at the disposal of any man who considers himself wronged. But that is a very modern notion. We need go back only to medieval England to find a state in which it could be very difficult to get the king's court to take up one's case. And the early Mesopotamian state, upon which the cosmic state was patterned, was of far more primitive cast than medieval England. In this primitive state there was as yet no developed executive machinery to carry out the verdict of the court. Execution was left to the winning party; and for that reason a court would not touch a case unless it was certain that the plaintiff had power behind him, a powerful protector who would guarantee that the judgment would be executed. Accordingly, the first step for the personal god was to find such a protector among the great gods. Usually Ea, the god of the sweet waters, was willing to undertake the protectorship. But Ea was so august and remote that the personal god would not approach him directly. He would go to Ea's son, Marduk, and Marduk would then urge his father to act. If Ea agreed to act, he would send his messenger – a human incantation priest – to go with the personal god to the court of the gods, where the messenger would appeal on Ea's behalf that the sun-god (the divine judge) accept this particular case for judgment. This appeal was directed to the rising sun in an impressive ceremony in the temple. After praising the sun as judge, as able to give legal relief against all kinds of demons and to heal the afflicted, the priest continued:

> Sun-god, to relieve them is in thy power;
> thou dost set straight conflicting testimonies as (were they but) one statement.
> I am the messenger of Ea;
> for the relief of the plagued man he has sent me hither,
> (and) the message which Ea gave I have repeated to thee.
> (As for) the man, the son of his god, judge his case, pronounce sentence for him,
> drive off the evil illness from his body.[11]

Through the decision of the sun-god, guaranteed by the mighty Ea, the evil demon was thus constrained to release its hold.

The cases in which the personal god was asked to use his influence to procure divine justice are among those most typical of his usefulness, but naturally he was asked to use it for general well-being and advancement also. He is to say a good word for his ward whenever he can; the ruler Entemena, for example, prays that his personal god be allowed to stand forever before the great god Ningirsu, petitioning for health and long life for Entemena.[12]

If we sum up, then, what our texts tell us about the rewards for the 'good life', we find life to be a pretty arbitrary affair. Through obedience and service man may win the good will of his personal god. The personal god may use his influence with the higher gods to obtain favours for his protégé from them. But even justice is such a favour; it cannot be claimed, but it is obtained through personal connections, personal pressure, through favouritism. Even the most perfect 'good life' held out but a promise, not a certainty, of tangible rewards.

EVALUATION OF FUNDAMENTALS: THE DEMAND FOR A JUST WORLD

While the conception of the cosmic state remained relatively stable throughout the third millennium, the actual human state developed considerably. The central power grew stronger, the machinery of justice became more efficient, punishment followed crime with ever greater regularity. The idea that justice was something to which man had a right began slowly to take form, and in the second millennium – appropriately the millennium of the famous Code of Hammurabi – justice as right rather than justice as favour seems to have become the general conception.

This idea, however, could not but conflict violently with the established view of the world. There emerged fundamental problems, such as the justification of death and the problem of the righteous sufferer. These two problems do not arise with equal clarity, but both have behind them an equally passionate urgency.

A. The Revolt against Death: The Epic of Gilgamesh

The less articulate, less rationalized, of the two was probably the revolt against death. We meet it as a smouldering resentment, a deep-seated feeling of wrong; it is more a feeling than a thought. Yet it can hardly be doubted that this feeling has its basis in the new concept of human rights, in the claim for justice in the universe. Death is an evil – it is as harsh as any punishment, is, indeed, the *supreme* punishment. Why must a man suffer death if he has committed no wrong? In the old, arbitrary world this question had no sting, for both good and evil were arbitrary matters. In the new world of justice as a right it became terribly urgent. We find it treated in the Epic of Gilgamesh, which must have been composed around the beginning of the second millennium. This epic is based on older material, but the older stories have been woven into a new whole, grouped around a new theme, that of death.

In his youthful energy, Gilgamesh, ruler of Uruk in southern Babylonia, drives his people too hard. The people appeal to the gods to create a counterpart to him, that they may compete with each other and the people may find rest. The gods comply and create Enkidu, who becomes Gilgamesh's companion and friend. Together the friends set out on dangerous adventures. They penetrate to 'the cedar forest' in the west, where they slay the terrible monster Huwawa who guards the forest for Enlil. On their return the goddess Inanna falls in love with Gilgamesh, and, when he will have none of her, she sends the awesome 'bull of heaven' against him to kill him. Here again, however, the two heroes conquer. They battle with, and kill, the bull. There seem to be no limits to their strength and power. Even the most terrible opponents go down before their weapons. They can afford to treat a mighty goddess in the most arrogant fashion. Then Enlil decides the Enkidu must die as punishment for slaying Huwawa. So the unconquerable Enkidu falls ill and dies. Until now death has meant little to Gilgamesh. He has accepted the normal standards of a fearless hero and the normal standards of his civilization: death is unavoidable, and it is of no avail to worry about it; if one has to die, let his death be a glorious one, met in combat with a worthy opponent, so that his fame may live. Before the campaign against Huwawa, when Enkidu's courage had failed him momentarily, Gilgamesh upbraided him sternly:

> Who, my friend, was ever so exalted (that he could)
> rise up to heaven and lastingly dwell with Shamash?
> Mere man – his days are numbered,
> whatever he may do, he is but wind.
> You are – already now – afraid of death.
> Where is the fine strength of your courage?
> Let me lead,
> and you (tarrying) can call out to me: 'Close in, fear not!'
> And if I fall, I shall have founded fame.
> 'Gilgamesh fell (they will say) in combat with terrible Huwawa.'

He goes on to relate how in that case Enkidu will be telling Gilgamesh's son about his father's prowess. Here death holds no terror; it is part of the game, and it is mitigated to some extent by fame, for one's name will live in future generations.

But Gilgamesh then knew death only in the abstract. It had never touched him directly in all its stark reality. It does so when Enkidu dies.

> 'My friend, my younger brother – who with me in the
>   foothills
> hunted wild ass, and panther in the plains;
> Enkidu, my friend, my younger brother – who with me
>   in the foothills
> hunted wild ass, and panther in the plains;
> who with me could do all, who climbed the crags,
> seized, killed the bull of heaven;
> flung down Huwawa, dwelling in the cedar forest.
> Now – what sleep is this that seized you?
> You have grown dark and cannot hear me.'
> He did not raise his eyes.
> (Gilgamesh) touched his heart, it was not beating.
> Then he covered his friend, as if he were a bride. ...
> His voice roared out – a lion ...
> a lioness chased from her whelps.
> Again and then again he turned towards his friend,
> tearing his hair and scattering the tufts,
> stripping and flinging down the finery off his body.

The loss which has been visited upon him is too great to bear. He refuses with all his soul to accept it as reality.

> He who with me has shared all hazards –
> the fate of man has overtaken him.
> All day and night have I wept over him
> and would not have him buried –
> my friend might yet rise up at my (loud) cries,
> for seven days and nights –
> until a maggot dropped from his nose.
> Since he is gone, I can no comfort find,
> keep roaming like a hunter in the plains.

The thought of death continues to haunt Gilgamesh. He has but one thought, one aim, to find everlasting life; and so he sets out upon his quest. At the end of the world, beyond the waters of death, lives an ancestor of his who obtained eternal life. He must know the secret. To him will Gilgamesh go. Alone he wanders the long way to the mountains where the sun sets, follows the dark passage through which the sun travels at night, almost despairing of ever seeing the light again, and finally comes out at the shore of a wide sea. Whomsoever he meets on his travels he questions about the way to Utnapishtim and about eternal life. All tell him the quest is hopeless.

> Gilgamesh, whither are you wandering?
> Life, which you look for, you will never find.
> For when the gods created man, they let
> death be his share, and life
> withheld in their own hands.
> Gilgamesh, fill your belly –
> day and night make merry,
> let days be full of joy,
> dance and make music day and night.
> And wear fresh clothes,
> and wash your head and bathe.
> Look at the child that is holding your hand,
> and let your wife delight in your embrace.
> These things alone are the concern of men.

But Gilgamesh cannot give up, cannot resign himself to the common lot. The yearning for everlasting life consumes him and drives him on. On the shore of the sea he meets Utnapishtim's boatman and gains passage over the waters of death. Thus he finally finds Utnapishtim and can ask him how one achieves eternal life; but Utnapishtim cannot help him. The fact that he himself lives for ever is due to unique circumstances that will never be repeated. When the gods in days of old had decided to destroy mankind and, led by Enlil, sent the flood, Utnapishtim and his wife alone were rescued. Utnapishtim had been forewarned; he had built a big boat, and in that he had saved himself, his wife, and pairs of all living things. Later on, Enlil repented the sending of the flood as a rash act and gave Utnapishtim eternal life as a reward for saving life on earth. But such circumstances obviously will not recur.

Yet Gilgamesh may try to fight death. Utnapishtim bids him contend with sleep, a magic sleep which is but another form of death. And Gilgamesh succumbs almost at once. He is about to perish when Utnapishtim's wife, out of pity on him, wakes him just in time. But the quest has failed. Dejected, Gilgamesh takes his departure to return to Uruk. At that moment, Utnapishtim's wife urges her husband to give him a parting gift, and Utnapishtim tells Gilgamesh about a plant which grows on the bottom of the sea and which rejuvenates him who partakes of it. Once more the sagging spirits of Gilgamesh revive. Accompanied by Utnapishtim's boatman, Urshanabi, he finds the right place, dives down, and comes up with the precious plant in his hands. Back they sail towards Uruk, reach the shore of the Persian Gulf, and continue inland on foot. But the day is warm and the journey tiring. When Gilgamesh sees an invitingly cool pool, he flings off his clothes and goes in for a swim. The plant he leaves on the bank. And while it is lying there a snake smells it, comes out of its hole, and snatches it away.

Therefore – because they ate of that plant – snakes do not die. When they become old, they slough off their old bodies and are reborn in youthful vigour. Mankind, cheated of Gilgamesh's plant, cannot thus return eternally to youth; and Gilgamesh, full of bitterness, contemplates the ironic end of his quest.

> Then Gilgamesh sat down and wept,
> tears streaming down his cheeks.
>
> . . . .
>
> 'For whose sake, Urshanabi, have I strained my muscles?
> For whose sake has my heart's blood been spent?
> I brought no blessing on myself –
> I did the serpent underground good service.'

The Epic of Gilgamesh does not come to an harmonious end; the emotions which rage in it are not assuaged; nor is there, as in tragedy, any sense of catharsis, any fundamental acceptance of the inevitable. It is a jeering, unhappy, unsatisfying ending. An inner turmoil is left to rage on, a vital question finds no answer.

B. THE RIGHTEOUS SUFFERER: 'LUDLUL BEL NEMEQI'[12]

More articulate, more reasoned, and therefore less forceful in its expression is the rebellion against the general unjustness of the world. But – as we have already mentioned (p. 223) – it, too, has its basis in the swing from 'justice as favour' to 'justice as right' which precipitated the protest against death.

As the human state grew more centralized and tightly organized, its policing grew more effective. Robbers and bandits, who had been an ever present threat, now became less of a menace, a less powerful element in daily life. This decrease of the power of human robbers and bandits seems to have influenced the evaluation of the cosmic robbers and bandits, the evil demons. They loomed less large in the cosmic state. It has been pointed out by von Soden that there was a subtle change in the concept of the personal god around the beginning of the second millennium. Before that time he had been thought to be powerless against demons who attacked his ward and had had to appeal to some great god for help. With the advent of the second millennium, however, the demons had lost power, so that the personal god was fully capable of protecting his human ward against them. If now they succeeded in an attack, it was because the personal god had turned away in anger and had left his ward to shift for himself. Offences which would anger a personal god came to include, moreover, almost all serious lapses from ethical and moral standards.

With this change, minute as it may seem, the whole outlook on the world actually shifted. Man no longer permitted his world to be essentially arbitrary; he demanded that it have a firm moral basis. Evil and illness, attacks by demons, are no longer considered mere happenings, accidents : the gods, by allowing them to happen, are ultimately responsible, for only when an offence has been committed should the personal god be angered and turn away. Thus in human moral and ethical values man had found a yardstick with which he presumptuously proceeded to measure the gods and their deeds. A conflict was immediately apparent. Divine will and human ethics proved incommensurable. The stinging problem of the righteous sufferer emerged.

We have several Mesopotamian treatments of this problem. Here, however, we shall deal only with the one best known, the composition called *Ludlul bel nemeqi*, 'I will praise the lord of wisdom'. It is a counterpart of, though much inferior to, the

Book of Job. The hero of the poem knows himself to have been righteous, to have lived the good life, but doubts about the value of living assail him:

> I only heeded prayer and supplication,
> my very thought was supplication, sacrifice habitual to me.
> The days when gods were worshipped were my heart's delight,
> those when I followed (the procession) of the goddess were
>   my gain and profit.
> Adoration of the king was joy to me,
> music for him a source of pleasure.
> And I instructed my estate to observe the ritual of the gods,
> I taught my people to revere the names of the goddess.
> Illustrious royal deeds I likened to (the deeds) of gods,
> and I taught soldiers to revere the palace.
> Would that I knew these things are pleasing to a god.

For in spite of his righteousness, evils of the most serious kind have befallen him:

> *Alu*-disease covers my body like a garment;
> sleep in a net enmeshes me;
> my eyes stare but see not,
> my ears are open, but hear not,
> weakness has seized my body.

He laments that

> The lash laid upon me holds terror;
> I have been goaded, piercing is the sting.
> All day a persecutor chases me,
> at night he gives me no respite at all.

His god has abandoned him:

> No god came to my aid, or grasped my hand,
> my goddess did not pity me or succour me.

Everyone has already given him up for dead and acts accordingly:

> The grave was open still when they rifled my treasures,
> while I was not yet dead, already they stopped mourning.

All his enemies are jubilant:

> My evil-wisher heard of it and his face brightened,
> to her who wished me evil they brought happy tidings
> and her liver felt good.

And there the problem is, neatly posed; a man who has been

righteous throughout may yet be dealt with by the powers who govern existence as though he were the blackest offender. For his pious deeds he has received the wages of the ungodly; he has been treated like one

> Who has not bowed his face, is not seen to prostrate himself,
> from whose mouth prayers and supplication are barred.

The reality of the problem cannot be disputed. The case of the righteous sufferer may be rare in such extreme form, yet none could be blind to its general validity. Righteousness, the good life, is no guarantee of health and happiness. Often, indeed, the unrighteous life seems a better way to success.

Is there an answer? Our text gives two: one to the mind, which struggles with an intellectual problem; one to the heart, whose emotions have been stirred by contemplation of the wrongs done to this particular righteous sufferer. The answer to the mind is a denial that human standards of values can be applied to the gods. Man is too small, too limited in outlook, to pass judgment on things that are divine. He has no right to set up his human values against the values which the gods hold.

> What seems praiseworthy to one's self, is but contemptible be-
> fore the god(s),
> What to one's heart seems bad, is good before one's god.
> Who may comprehend the mind of gods in heaven's depth?
> The thoughts of a god are like deep waters, who could fathom
> them?
> How could mankind, beclouded, comprehend the ways of gods?

Human judgment cannot be true judgment, for man is a creature of the moment; he can take no long-range view, his mood changes from moment to moment, he cannot attain to the deeper understanding which motivates the timeless and eternal gods.

> Who came to life yesterday, died today.
> In but a moment man is cast into gloom, suddenly crushed.
> One moment he will sing for joy,
> and in an instant he will wail – a mourner.
> Between morning and nightfall men's mood may change:
> when they are hungry they become like corpses,
> when they are full they will rival their god,
> when things go well they will prate of rising up to heaven
> and when in trouble, rant about descending into Hades.

What, therefore, is man's judgment that he should presume to set it up against that of a god?

But, though this stern *non licet* may satisfy the mind, may show that its question is not permissible, it will hardly satisfy the heart. Deep emotions have been stirred, a sense of bitter wrong has been evoked. And so to the heart our poem holds out as answer the duty to hope and to trust. The righteous sufferer did not remain in his sufferings. When all hope seemingly had fled, then came his deliverance; in his darkest hour the gods had mercy on him and turned to him full of goodness and light. Marduk restored him to health and dignity, purified him, and all was happiness again. Thus our poem is an encouragement to trust and hope. The ways of the gods may seem inexplicable to man, but that is because man lacks the deeper understanding which actuates the gods. And though man may be plunged in the deepest despair, the gods do not abandon him; he shall and must trust to their mercy and goodness.

C. The Negation of All Values: A Dialogue of Pessimism[14]

It is a well-known fact that, as a civilization grows old, its basic values are in danger of losing their hold upon the individuals who participate in it. Scepticism, doubt, and indifference begin to undermine the spiritual structure which comprises the civilization. Such scepticism toward all values, utter negation of the possibility of a 'good life', begins to make its appearance in Mesopotamian civilization in the first millennium B.C. This scepticism has found expression in a long dialogue between a master and his slave; it is known as the 'Dialogue of Pessimism'.

The pattern of the dialogue is extremely simple. The master announces to the slave that he intends to do a particular thing, and the slave encourages him by enumerating all the pleasant aspects of what the master proposes. But by then the master has already tired of his idea and states that he will not do the thing in question. This, too, is praised by the slave, who enumerates all the darker sides of the proposed activity. In this manner all the typical activities of a Mesopotamian nobleman are weighed and found wanting. Nothing is inherently good, nothing is worth while, whether it be seeking favours at court, the pleasures of the table, razzias against nomads in the desert, the excitement of a rebel's life, the beginning of a lawsuit, or what not. We shall quote a few of the stanzas, first about love:

> 'Servant, agree with me!' 'Yes, my lord, yes!'
> 'I will love a woman!' 'So love, my lord, so love!
> The man who loves a woman forgets want and misery!'.
> 'No, slave, I will not love a woman!'
> 'Love not, my lord, love not!
> Woman is a snare, a trap, a pitfall;
> woman is a sharpened iron sword
> which will cut a young man's neck!'

About piety:

> 'Slave, agree with me!' 'Yes, my lord, yes!'
> 'Straightway order me water for my hands,
> and bring it hither. I will make a libation to my god!'
> 'Do, my lord, do! (As for) the man who makes a libation
> to his god, his heart is at ease;
> he makes loan upon loan!'
> 'No, slave, I will not make a libation to my god!'
> 'Make it not, my lord, make it not!
> Teach the god to run after thee like a dog
> when he demands, be it "my service," be it "thou hast
> not asked," be it anything else, from thee.'

In other words, 'be uppish with the god'; let him feel that he depends upon you for service, for prayer, and for many other things, so that he will run after you, begging you to worship him.

No better than piety fares charity:

> 'Slave, agree with me!' 'Yes, my lord, yes!'
> 'I say, I will give alms to my land!'
> 'So do, my lord, so do!
> (As for) the man who gives alms to his land,
> his alms have been put on the palms of the god
> Marduk himself.'

That is, it is as though Marduk himself received them and will reciprocate to the giver.

> 'No, slave, I will not give alms to my land!'
> 'Do it not, my lord, do it not!
> Mount thou upon the ruined mounds of ancient
>   cities and walk around;
> behold the skulls of those of earlier and later times.
> Who is the evildoer, who is the benefactor?'

It is all one whether man does good or evil; none will remember it in times to come. We know not who was good, who evil among the ancients; they lie forgotten in their forgotten cities.

And so the argument sums up: there is nothing which is truly good; all is vanity.

> 'Slave, agree with me!' 'Yes, my lord, yes!'
> 'Now then, what is good?
> To break my neck and thy neck,
> to fall into the river – that is good!'

With the world all vanity, only death seems attractive. The slave answers stoically with an ancient saying which expresses resignation:

> 'Who is tall enough to reach up to heaven?
> Who is broad enough that he might encompass the earth?'

If it is vain to seek for an absolute good, we might as well resign and give up; we cannot do the impossible. But once more the master changes his mind:

> 'No, slave, I will kill only thee and let thee precede me!'
> 'And would my lord want to live (even) three days after me?'

asks the slave. If there is no profit in life, if nothing is good, if all is vanity, what benefit can the master possibly see in prolonging life? How can he suffer it for even three more days?

And with this denial of all values, denial that a 'good life' existed, we end our survey of Mesopotamian speculative thought. Mesopotamian civilization with the values it embodied was about to lose its hold on man. It had run its course and was ready to give way before new and different, more vigorous, patterns of thought.

NOTES

1. *STVC*, 66 and 67; *TRS*, 15, 11th KI-RU-GÚ.
2. *RA* XVII, p. 123, rev. ii., 14'–15'.
3. *Ibid.*, 16'–17'.
4. *Ibid.*, 18'–19'.
5. *Ibid.*, p. 132; K4160, 1–3.
6. *STVC* I, i, 15–18.
7. *RA* XVII, p. 122, iii and iv, 5–8.
8. Urukagina, Clay Tablet.
9. *STVC* I, i, 1–4.
10. *YOS*, 2, 141.
11. *Bît Rimki* Tablet III.
12. Entemena, Brick B.
13. Langdon, *Babylonian Wisdom*, pp. 35–66.
14. *Ibid.*, pp. 67–81.

SUGGESTED READINGS

DHORME, ÉDOUARD. *Les Religions de Babylonie et d'Assyrie*. Paris, 1945.

HEHN, JOHANNES. *Die biblische und die babylonische Gottesidee*. Leipzig, 1913.

HEIDEL, ALEXANDER. *The Babylonian Genesis*. Chicago, 1942.

———. *The Gilgamesh Epic and Old Testament Parallels*. Chicago, 1946.

JACOBSEN, THORKILD. 'Sumerian Mythology: A Review Article,' *Journal of Near Eastern Studies*, V (1946), 128–52.

KRAMER, SAMUEL N. *Sumerian Mythology: A Study of Spiritual and Literary Achievement in the Third Millennium B.C.* Philadelphia, 1944.

LANGDON, STEPHEN. *Babylonian Wisdom* ... London, 1923.

PALLIS, SVEND AA. *The Babylonian Akîtu Festival*. Copenhagen, 1926.

VON SODEN, WOLFRAM. 'Religion und Sittlichkeit nach den Anschauungen der Babylonier,' *Zeitschrift der Deutschen Morgenländischen Gesellschaft*, Vol. LXXXIX (1935).

CONCLUSION

H. and H. A. Frankfort

CHAPTER VIII

The Emancipation of Thought from Myth

WHEN WE read in Psalm xix that 'the heavens declare the glory of God; and the firmament sheweth his handiwork', we hear a voice which mocks the beliefs of Egyptians and Babylonians. The heavens, which were to the psalmist but a witness of God's greatness, were to the Mesopotamians the very majesty of god-head, the highest ruler, Anu. To the Egyptians the heavens signified the mystery of the divine mother through whom man was reborn. In Egypt and Mesopotamia the divine was com-prehended as immanent: the gods were in nature. The Egyp-tians saw in the sun all that a man may know of the Creator; the Mesopotamians viewed the sun as the god Shamash, the guarantor of justice. But to the psalmist the sun was God's devoted servant who 'is as a bridegroom coming out of his chamber, and rejoiceth as a strong man to run a race'. The God of the psalmists and the prophets was not in nature. He trans-cended nature – and transcended, likewise, the realm of mytho-poeic thought. It would seem that the Hebrews, no less than the Greeks, broke with the mode of speculation which had prevailed up to their time.

*

The mainspring of the acts, thoughts, and feelings of early man was the conviction that the divine was immanent in nature, and nature intimately connected with society. Dr. Wilson emphasized this fact by calling the Egyptians monophysites. Dr. Jacobsen indicated that his approach to Mesopotamian thought could not do full justice to it; but the myths and beliefs which he discussed reflect it at every turn. And in our first chapter we found that the assumption of an essential correla-tion between nature and man provided us with a basis for the understanding of mythopoeic thought. Its logic, its peculiar structure, was seen to derive from an unceasing awareness of a live relationship between man and the phenomenal world.

In the significant moments of his life, early man was confronted not by an inanimate, impersonal nature – not by an 'It' – but by a 'Thou'. We have seen that such a relationship involved not only man's intellect but the whole of his being – his feeling and his will, no less than his thought. Hence early man would have rejected the detachment of a purely intellectual attitude towards nature, had he been able to conceive it, as inadequate to his experience.

As long as the peoples of the ancient Near East preserved their cultural integrity – from the middle of the fourth to the middle of the first millennium B.C. – they remained conscious of their close bond with nature. And that awareness remained vivid notwithstanding the conditions of city life. The efflorescence of civilization in Egypt and Mesopotamia brought with it the need for a division of labour and a diversification of life possible only when people congregate in sufficient numbers for some to be freed from preoccupation with earning a livelihood. But the ancient cities were small by our standards, and their inhabitants were not cut off from the land. On the contrary, most of them derived their sustenance from the surrounding fields; all of them worshipped gods personifying natural powers; and all of them participated in rites which marked the turning-points in the farmer's year. In the great metropolis of Babylon the outstanding annual event was the New Year's Festival celebrating the renewal of the generative force of nature. In all Mesopotamian cities the business of everyday life was interrupted several times in the course of each month when the moon completed one of its phases or other natural events called for appropriate action on the part of the community. In Egypt, too, the husbandman's preoccupations found expression in festivals at Thebes, Memphis, and other Egyptian cities where celebrations marked the rise of the Nile, the end of the inundation, or the completion of the harvest. Thus urban life in no way diminished man's awareness of his essential involvement in nature.

When we accentuate the basic conception of ancient Near Eastern thought, as we have just done, we are necessarily obscuring its richness and diversity. Within the scope of mythopoeic thought a great variety of attitudes and outlooks are possible; and contrast as well as variety become apparent when we compare the speculative myths of Egypt and Mesopotamia. It is true that the same natural phenomena were often personified in these two countries and that the same images were often used to describe them. Yet the mood of the myths and the significance of the images are most unlike.

In both countries, for instance, the existing world was believed to have emerged from the waters of chaos. In Egypt this primeval ocean was male – the god Nūn. In other words, it was conceived as a fertilizing agent, and as such it was a permanent factor in the created universe recognized in the subsoil water and in the annual flood of the Nile. In Mesopotamia the fertilizing power in water was personified as the god Enki or Ea. But he was entirely unrelated to the primordial ocean. This ocean was a female, Tiᵒamat, the mother who brought forth gods and monsters in such profusion that her unbounded fruitfulness endangered the very existence of the universe. She was killed in combat by Marduk, who formed the world from her body. Thus water was significant to both Babylonians and Egyptians as the source and also as the sustainer of life. Yet these conceptions were very differently expressed by the two peoples.

A similar contrast appears in relation to earth. Mesopotamia worshipped a beneficial Great Mother whose fertility was seen in the produce of the earth and who gained additional religious importance by a variety of associations. The earth was viewed as the counterpart (and hence the spouse) of Heaven, Anu; or of the waters, Enki; or even of Enlil, the kingly storm-god. In Egypt, on the other hand, the earth was a male – Geb or Ptah or Osiris: the ubiquitous mother-goddess was not connected with the soil. Her image was either cast in the primitive and ancient guise of the cow or projected on the sky which, as Nūt, gave birth to the sun and stars each day at dawn and dusk. Moreover, the dead entered her body to be reborn as immortals. The sustained Egyptian preoccupation with death and the hereafter, however, found no equivalent in Mesopotamia. On the contrary, death was understood there as an almost complete destruction of personality; and man's chief desires were for a worthy life and freedom from disease, with a good reputation and descendants to survive him; and the sky was not a goddess bending over her children but the most unapproachable of male gods.

The differences which we have enumerated do not merely represent a meaningless variety of images; they betray a thorough contrast between the Egyptian and Mesopotamian views as to the nature of the universe in which man lives. Throughout the Mesopotamian texts we hear overtones of anxiety which seem to express a haunting fear that the unaccountable and turbulent powers may at any time bring disaster to human society. But in Egypt the gods were powerful without being violent. Nature presented itself as an established order in which changes were either superficial and insignificant or an unfolding in time of what had been preordained from the beginning. Moreover, Egyptian kingship guaranteed stability to society. For, as Dr. Wilson explained, one of the gods occupied the throne. Pharaoh was divine, the son and image of the Creator. Thus Pharaoh insured an harmonious integration of nature and society at all times. But in Mesopotamia the assembly of the gods assigned a mere mortal to rule men, and the divine favour might at any time be withdrawn from him. Man was at the mercy of decisions he could neither influence nor gauge. Hence the king and his counsellors watched for portents on earth and in the sky which might reveal a changing constellation of divine grace, so that catastrophe might be foreseen and possibly averted. In Egypt neither astrology nor prophecy ever developed to any great extent.

The contrast between the temper of the two countries was concisely expressed in their creation myths. In Egypt creation was viewed as the brilliant act of an omnipotent Creator disposing of submissive elements. Of the lasting order which he created, society formed an unchanging part. In Mesopotamia the Creator had been chosen by a divine assembly helpless before the threat of the powers of chaos. Their champion, Marduk, had followed up his victory over these antagonists by the creation of the universe. This took place almost as an afterthought, and man was especially designed as a servant of the gods. There was no permanence in the human sphere. The gods assembled on every New Year's Day to 'establish (such) destinies' for mankind as they pleased.

The differences between the Egyptian and Mesopotamian manners of viewing the world are very far-reaching. Yet the two peoples agreed in the fundamental assumptions that the individual is part of society, that society is embedded in nature, and that nature is but the manifestation of the divine. This doctrine was, in fact, universally accepted by the peoples of the ancient world with the single exception of the Hebrews.

*

The Hebrews arrived late upon the scene and settled in a country pervaded by influences from the two superior adjacent cultures. One would expect the newcomers to have assimilated alien modes of thought, since these were supported by such vast prestige. Untold immigrants from deserts and mountains had done so in the past; and many individual Hebrews did, in fact, conform to the ways of the Gentiles. But assimilation was not characteristic for Hebrew thought. On the contrary, it held out with a peculiar stubbornness and insolence against the wisdom of Israel's neighbours. It is possible to detect the reflection of Egyptian and Mesopotamian beliefs in many episodes of the Old Testament; but the overwhelming impression left by that document is one, not of derivation, but of originality.

The dominant tenet of Hebrew thought is the absolute transcendence of God. Yahweh is not in nature. Neither earth nor sun nor heaven is divine; even the most potent natural phenomena are but reflections of God's greatness. It is not even possible properly to name God:

And Moses said unto God, Behold, when I come unto the children of Israel and shall say unto them, The God of your fathers hath sent me unto you; and they shall say to me: What is his name? what shall I say unto them?
And God said unto Moses: I AM THAT I AM: and he said, Thus shalt thou say unto the children of Israel, I AM hath sent me unto you (Exod. iii, 13–14).

The God of the Hebrews is pure being, unqualified, ineffable. He is *holy*. That means that he is *sui generis*. It does not mean that he is taboo or that he is power. It means that all values are ultimately attributes of God alone. Hence, all concrete phenomena are devaluated. It may be true that in Hebrew thought man and nature are not necessarily corrupt; but both are necessarily *valueless* before God. As Eliphaz said to Job (and we use the Chicago translation):

> Can a mortal be righteous before God
> Or a man be pure before his Maker?
> Even in his servants he does not trust,
> And his angels he charges with error.
> How much less them that dwell in houses of clay,
> Whose foundation is in the dust ... (Job iv, 17–19*a*).

A similar meaning lies in the words of Deutero-Isaiah (lxiv, 6*a*): 'We are all as an unclean thing, and all our righteousnesses are as filthy rags'. Even man's righteousness, his highest virtue, is devaluated by the comparison with the absolute.

In the field of material culture such a conception of God leads to iconoclasm; and it needs an effort of the imagination to realize the shattering boldness of a contempt for imagery at the time, and in the particular historical setting, of the Hebrews. Everywhere religious fervour not only inspired verse and rite but also sought plastic and pictorial expression. The Hebrews, however, denied the relevancy of the 'graven image'; the boundless could not be given form, the unqualified could but be offended by a representation, whatever the skill and the devotion that went into its making. Every finite reality shrivelled to nothingness before the absolute value which was God.

The abysmal difference between the Hebrew and the normal Near Eastern viewpoints can best be illustrated by the manner in which an identical theme, the instability of the social order, is treated. We have a number of Egyptian texts which deal with the period of social upheaval which followed the great era of the pyramid builders. The disturbance of the established order was viewed with horror. Neferrohu said:

I show thee the land in lamentation and distress. The man with a weak arm (now) has (a strong) arm. ... I show thee how the undermost is turned to uppermost. ... The poor man will acquire riches.[1]

The most famous of the sages, Ipuwer, is even more explicit. For instance, he condemns as a disastrous parody of order the fact that

> gold and lapis lazuli are hung about the necks of slave girls. But noble ladies walk through the land and mistresses of houses say: 'Would that we had something to eat. ... Behold they that possessed beds now lie upon the ground. He that slept with dirt upon him now stuffeth for himself a cushion.'

The upshot is unmitigated misery for all: 'Nay, but great and small say: I wish I were dead'.[2]

In the Old Testament we meet the same theme – the reversal of established social conditions. When Hannah, after years of barrenness, had prayed for a son, and Samuel was born, she praised God:

> There is none holy as the Lord: for there is none beside thee: neither is there any rock like our God. ... The bows of the mighty men are broken, and they that stumbled are girded with strength. They that were full have hired out themselves for bread; and they that were hungry ceased. ...The Lord maketh poor and maketh rich: he bringeth low, and lifteth up. He raiseth up the poor out of the dust, and lifteth up the beggar from the dunghill, to set them among princes, and to make them inherit the throne of glory: for the pillars of the earth are the Lord's and he hath set the world upon them (I Sam. ii, 2–8).

Notice that the last verses state explicitly that God created the existing social order; but, quite characteristically, this order did not derive any sacredness, any value, from its divine origin. The sacredness and value remain attributes of God alone, and the violent changes of fortune observed in social life are but signs of God's omnipotence. Nowhere else do we meet this fanatical devaluation of the phenomena of nature and the achievements of man: art, virtue, social order – in view of the unique significance of the divine. It has been rightly pointed out that the monotheism of the Hebrews is a correlate of their insistence on the unconditioned nature of God.[3] Only a God who transcends every phenomenon, who is not conditioned by any mode of manifestation – only an unqualified God can be the one and only ground of *all* existence.

This conception of God represents so high a degree of

abstraction that, in reaching it, the Hebrews seem to have left the realm of mythopoeic thought. The impression that they did so is strengthened when we observe that the Old Testament is remarkably poor in mythology of the type we have encountered in Egypt and Mesopotamia. But this impression requires correction. The processes of mythopoeic thought are decisive for many sections of the Old Testament. For instance, the magnificent verses from the Book of Proverbs (viii, 22-31) describe the Wisdom of God, personified and substantialized in the same manner in which the corresponding concept of *ma^cat* is treated by the Egyptians. Even the great conception of an only and transcendent God was not entirely free from myth, for it was not the fruit of detached speculation but of a passionate and dynamic experience. Hebrew thought did not entirely overcome mythopoeic thought. It created, in fact, a new myth – the myth of the Will of God.

Although the great 'Thou' which confronted the Hebrews transcended nature, it stood in a specific relationship to the people. For when they were freed from bondage and roamed in 'a desert land ... the waste howling wilderness ... the Lord alone did lead (them) and there was no strange god with (them)' (Deut. xxxii, 10-12). And God had said:

> But thou, Israel, art my servant, Jacob whom I have chosen, the seed of Abraham my friend. Thou whom I have taken from the ends of the earth, and called thee from the chief men thereof, and said unto thee, Thou art my servant; I have chosen thee, and not cast thee away (Isa. xli, 8-9).

Thus God's will was felt to be focused on one particular and concrete group of human beings; it was asserted to have manifested itself at one decisive moment in their history and ceaselessly and relentlessly to have urged, rewarded, or chastised the people of its choice. For in Sinai, God had said, 'Ye shall be unto me a kingdom of priests and an holy nation' (Exod. xix, 6).

It is a poignant myth, this Hebrew myth of a chosen people, of a divine promise made, of a terrifying moral burden imposed – a prelude to the later myth of the Kingdom of God, that more remote and more spiritual 'promised land'. For in the myth of the chosen people the ineffable majesty of God and the worthlessness of man are correlated in a dramatic situation that is to unfold in time and is moving toward a future where the distant yet related parallels of human and divine existence are to meet in infinity.

Not cosmic phenomena, but history itself, had here become pregnant with meaning; history had become a revelation of the dynamic will of God. The human being was not merely the servant of the god as he was in Mesopotamia; nor was he placed, as in Egypt, at a pre-ordained station in a static universe which did not need to be – and, in fact, could not be – questioned. Man, according to Hebrew thought, was the interpreter and the servant of God; he was even honoured with the task of bringing about the realization of God's will. Thus man was condemned to unending efforts which were doomed to fail because of his inadequacy. In the Old Testament we find man possessed of a new freedom and of a new burden of responsibility. We also find there a new and utter lack of *eudaimonia*, of harmony – whether with the world of reason or with the world of perception.

All this may help to explain the strange poignancy of single individuals in the Old Testament. Nowhere in the literature of Egypt or Babylonia do we meet the loneliness of the biblical figures, astonishingly real in their mixture of ugliness and beauty, pride and contrition, achievement and failure. There is the tragic figure of Saul, the problematical David; there are countless others. We find single men in terrible isolation facing a transcendent God: Abraham trudging to the place of sacrifice with his son, Jacob in his struggle, and Moses and the prophets. In Egypt and Mesopotamia man was dominated, but also supported, by the great rhythm of nature. If in his dark moments he felt himself caught and held in the net of unfathomable decisions, his involvement in nature had, on the whole, a soothing character. He was gently carried along on the perennial cosmic tides of the seasons. The depth and intimacy of man's relationship with nature found expression in the ancient symbol of the mother-goddess. But Hebrew thought ignored this image entirely. It only recognized the stern Father, of whom it was said: 'he led him (Jacob, the people)

about, he instructed him, he kept him as the apple of his eye',
(Deut. xxxii, 10*b*).

The bond between Yahweh and his chosen people had been
finally established during the Exodus. The Hebrews considered
the forty years in the desert the decisive phase in their development. And we, too, may understand the originality and the
coherence of their speculations if we relate them to their experience in the desert.

The reader will remember that preceding chapters took
great care to describe the Egyptian and Mesopotamian land-
scapes. In doing so, the authors did not succumb to an unwar-
ranted naturalism; they did not claim that cultural phenomena
could be derived from physiographical causes. They merely
suggested that a relation between land and culture may exist,
a suggestion we can accept the more readily since we have seen
that the surrounding world confronted early man as a 'Thou'.
We may ask, then, what was the natural setting which determined the Hebrew's experience of the world around him. Now,
the Hebrews, whatever their ancestry and historical antecedents, were tribal nomads. And since they were nomads in the
Near East, they must have lived, not in boundless steppes, but
between the desert and the sown, between the most fertile of
lands and the total negation of life, which, in this remarkable
corner of the earth, lie cheek by jowl. They must, therefore,
have known through experience both the reward and the cost
of existence in either.

The Hebrews craved to settle for good in the fertile plains.
But characteristically they dreamed of lands overflowing with
milk and honey, not lands of super-abundant crops like those
the Egyptians imagined for their hereafter. It seems that the
desert as a metaphysical experience loomed very large for the
Hebrews and coloured all their valuations. It is, perhaps, the
tension between two valuations – between a desire and a contempt for what is desired – that may explain some of the para-
doxes of ancient Hebrew beliefs.

The organized states of the ancient Near East were agricultural; but the values of an agricultural community are the
opposites of those of the nomadic tribe, especially of the

extreme type of nomads of the desert. The settled peasant's reverence for impersonal authority, and the bondage, the constraint which the organized state imposes, mean an intolerable lack of personal freedom for the tribesman. The farmer's everlasting preoccupation with phenomena of growth and his total dependence on these phenomena appear to the nomad a form of slavery. Moreover, to him the desert is clean, but the scene of life, which is also the scene of decay, is sordid.

On the other hand, nomadic freedom can be bought only at a price; for whoever rejects the complexities and mutual dependencies of agricultural society not only gains freedom but also loses the bond with the phenomenal world; in fact, he gains his freedom at the cost of significant form. For, wherever we find reverence for the phenomena of life and growth, we find preoccupation with the immanence of the divine and with the *form* of its manifestation. But in the stark solitude of the desert, where nothing changes, nothing moves (except man at his own free will), where features in the landscape are only pointers, landmarks, without significance in themselves – there we may expect the image of God to transcend concrete phenomena altogether. Man confronting God will not contemplate him but will hear his voice and command, as Moses did, and the prophets, and Mohammed.

When we compared the lands of origin of Egyptians, and Mesopotamians, we were concerned, not with the relation between group psychology and habitat, but with profound differences in pristine religious experience. The peculiar experience which we have just described seems characteristic for all the most significant figures of the Old Testament. It is important to realize this, not because it enables us to understand them better as individuals, but because we then recognize what coloured and integrated their thought. They propounded, not speculative theory, but revolutionary and dynamic teaching. The doctrine of a single, unconditioned, transcendent God rejected time-honoured values, proclaimed new ones, and postulated a metaphysical significance for history and for man's actions. With infinite *moral* courage the Hebrews worshipped an absolute God and accepted as the correlate of their faith the sacrifice of an harmonious existence. In transcending the Near Eastern myths of immanent godhead, they created, as we have seen, the new myth of the will of God. It remained for the Greeks, with their peculiar *intellectual* courage, to discover a form of speculative thought in which myth was entirely overcome.

*

In the sixth century B.C. the Greeks, in their great cities on the coast of Asia Minor, were in touch with all the leading centres of the civilized world: Egypt and Phoenicia; Lydia, Persia, and Babylon. There can be no doubt that this contact played some part in the meteoric development of Greek culture. But it is impossible to estimate the Greek indebtedness to the ancient Near East. As is usual when cultural contact is truly fruitful, simple derivations are rare. What the Greeks borrowed, they transmuted.

In the Greek mystery religions we meet well-known oriental themes. Demeter was the sorrowing mother-goddess searching for her child; Dionysus died a violent death but was resurrected. In some of the rites the participants experienced an immediate relationship with the divine in nature; and in this respect there is similarity with the ancient Near East. But it would be hard to find antecedents for the individual salvation vouchsafed to the initiates. A possible parallel would be the Osiris cult; but, as far as we know, the Egyptian did not undergo an initiation or share the god's fate during his lifetime. In any case, the Greek mysteries show several features which were without precedent. These generally amount to a diminished distance between men and gods. The initiate of the Orphic mysteries, for instance, not only hoped to be liberated from the 'wheel of births' but actually emerged as a god from his union with the mother-goddess, 'queen of the dead'. The Orphic myths contain speculations about the nature of man which are characteristically Greek in their tenor. It was said that the Titans had devoured Dionysus-Zagreus and were therefore destroyed by the lightning of Zeus, who made man from their ashes. Man, in so far as he consists of the substance of the Titans, is evil and ephemeral; but since the Titans had partaken of a god's body, man contains a divine and immortal spark. Such dualism and the recognition of an immortal part in man are unknown in the ancient Near East outside Persia.

It is not only in the mystery religions that the Greeks placed man closer to the gods than the Egyptians or Babylonians had ever done. Greek literature names many women who had gods for lovers and bore them children, and it has been pointed out that the typical sinner in Greece was the man who had attempted to do violence to a goddess.[4] Moreover, the Olympian gods, though they were manifest in nature, had not made the universe and could not dispose of man as their creature with the same unquestioned right of ownership which the ancient Near Eastern gods exercised. In fact, the Greek claimed a common ancestry with the gods and, consequently, suffered the more acutely because of his own disabilities. Pindar's Sixth Nemean Ode, for instance, starts as follows:

Of one race, one only, are men and gods. Both of one mother's womb we draw our breath; but far asunder is all our power divided, and fences us apart; here there is nothingness, and there, in strength of bronze, a seat unshaken, eternal, abides the heaven. (After Cornford.)

The spirit of such poetry differs profoundly from that of the ancient Near East, even though, at this time, Greece still shared many beliefs with the Orient. The common mother of gods and men to whom Pindar refers is Gaea, the earth; and the earth, as Ninhursaga, was often regarded as the Great Mother in Mesopotamia. Homer still knew of the primeval waters: 'Okeanos from whom the gods are sprung'.[5] Yet more important than such echoes of Near Eastern beliefs is the similarity between the Greek and the oriental methods of interpreting nature: an ordered view of the universe was obtained by bringing its elements in a genealogical relationship with one another. In Greece this procedure found monumental expression in Hesiod's Theogony, written probably about 700 B.C. Hesiod starts his account with Chaos and proclaims Sky and Earth the parents of gods and men. He introduces numerous personifications which recall Egyptian *ma°at* or the 'Wisdom of God' in the Book of Proverbs. '... Next he (Zeus) wedded bright Themis who bare the Horai, even Eunomia (Good Government) and Dike (Justice) and blooming Eirene (Peace) who care for the works of mortal man', (ll. 901-3).[6]

Associations and 'participations' typical of mythopoeic thought appear often. A particularly clear example is: 'And Night bare hateful Doom; and black Fate and Death and Sleep she bare, and she bare the tribe of dreams; all these did dark Night bear, albeit mated unto none', (ll. 211 ff.). The natural process of procreation thus supplied Hesiod with a scheme which allowed him to connect the phenomena and to arrange them in a comprehensible system. The Babylonian Epic of Creation and the An-Anum list use the same device; and we meet it in Egypt when Atum is said to have begotten Shū and Tefnūt (Air and Moisture), who, in their turn, brought forth Geb and Nūt (Earth and Sky).

And yet Hesiod is without oriental precedent in one respect: the gods and the universe were described by him as a matter of private interest. Such freedom was unheard of in the Near East, except among the Hebrews, where Amos, for instance, was a herdsman. In Egypt and Mesopotamia religious subjects were treated by members of the established hierarchy. But Hesiod was a Boeotian farmer called by the Muses, 'which time he tended his flocks under holy Helicon'. He says: '(The Muses) breathed in me a voice divine that I might celebrate the things that shall be and the things that were aforetime. They bade me sing the race of the Blessed Ones that are forever' (ll. 29 ff.). Thus a Greek layman recognized his vocation and became a singer who took the gods and nature as his theme, although he continued to use the traditional forms of epic poetry.

The same freedom, the same unconcern as regards special function and hierarchy, is characteristic for the Ionian philosophers who lived a century or more after Hesiod. Thales seems to have been an engineer and statesman; Anaximander, a map-maker. Cicero stated: 'Almost all those whom the Greeks called the Seven Sages, you will see to have been engaged in public life', (*De Rep.* i. 7). These men, then, in contrast to the priests of the Near East, were not charged by their communities to concern themselves with spiritual matters.

They were moved by their own desire for an understanding of nature; and they did not hesitate to publish their findings, although they were not professional seers. Their curiosity was as lively as it was unhampered by dogma. Like Hesiod, the Ionian philosophers gave their attention to the problem of origins; but for them it assumed an entirely new character. The origin, the ἀρχή, which they sought was not understood in the terms of myth. They did not describe an ancestral divinity or a progenitor. They did not even look for an 'origin' in the sense of an initial condition which was superseded by subsequent states of being. The Ionians asked for an immanent and *lasting* ground of existence. 'Αρχή means 'origin', not as 'beginning', but as 'sustaining principle' or 'first cause'.

This change of viewpoint is breath-taking. It transfers the problems of man in nature from the realm of faith and poetic intuition to the intellectual sphere. A critical appraisal of each theory, and hence a continuous inquiry into the nature of reality, became possible. A cosmogonic myth is beyond discussion. It describes a sequence of sacred events, which one can either accept or reject. But no cosmogony can become part of a progressive and cumulative increase of knowledge. As we said in our first chapter, myth claims recognition by the faithful, not justification before the critical. But a sustaining principle or first cause must be comprehensible, even if it was first discovered in a flash of insight. It does not pose the alternative of acceptance or rejection. It may be analysed, modified, or corrected. In short, it is subject to intellectual judgment.

Yet the doctrines of the early Greek philosophers are not couched in the language of detached and systematic reflection. Their sayings sound rather like inspired oracles. And no wonder, for these men proceeded, with preposterous boldness, on an entirely unproved assumption. They held that the universe is an intelligible whole. In other words, they presumed that a single order underlies the chaos of our perceptions and, furthermore, that we are able to comprehend that order.

The speculative courage of the Ionians is often overlooked. Their teachings were, in fact, predestined to be misunderstood by modern – or rather, nineteenth-century – scholars. When

Thales proclaims water to be the first cause, or Anaximenes air; when Anaximander speaks of the 'Boundless', and Heraclitus of fire; when, moreover, Democritus' theory of atoms can be considered the outcome of these earlier speculations; then we need not be astonished that commentators in a positivistic age unwittingly read familiar connotations into the quasi-materialist doctrines of the Ionians and regarded these earliest philosophers as the first scientists. No bias could more insidiously disfigure the greatness of the Ionian achievement. The materialist interpretation of their teachings takes for granted what was to be discovered only as a result of the labours of these ancient thinkers – the distinction between the objective and the subjective. And only on the basis of this distinction is scientific thought possible.

In actual fact the Ionians moved in a curious borderland. They forefelt the possibility of establishing an intelligible coherence in the phenomenal world; yet they were still under the spell of an undissolved relationship between man and nature. And so we remain somewhat uncertain of the exact connotations of the Ionian sayings which have been preserved. Thales, for instance, said that water was the ἀρχή, the first principle or cause of all things; but he also said: 'All things are full of gods. The magnet is alive for it has the power of moving iron'.[7] Anaximenes said: 'Just as our soul, being air, holds us together, so do breath and air encompass the whole world.'

It is clear that Anaximenes did not consider air merely as a physical substance, although he did consider it, among other things, a substance whose properties changed when it was either condensed or rarefied. But at the same time air was mysteriously connected with the maintenance of life itself: it was an agent of vitality. Anaximenes recognized in air something variable enough to make it seem possible to interpret the most diverse phenomena as its manifestations. Thales had preferred water, but he, too, did not consider his first cause merely as a neutral, colourless liquid. We must remember that seeds and bulbs and the eggs of insects lie lifeless in the rich soil of Eastern Mediterranean lands until the rains come – remember, also, the preponderant role of watery substances in the processes of conception and birth in the animal kingdom. It is possible that the ancient oriental view of water as a fertilizing agent had retained its validity for Thales. It is equally possible that he endorsed the oriental conception of a primeval ocean from which all life came forth. Homer, as we have seen, called Okeanos the origin of gods and men. Thales' pupil, Anaximander, stated explicitly: 'the living creatures came forth from the moist element'. There are many other symbolic meanings which we can impute to Thales' theory; for, after all, the sea exercises its magic even today. Thus it has been supposed (by Joel) that Thales regarded the sea as the epitome of change, as many poets since have done.

Now to claim, on any or all of these analogies, that water is the first cause of all things is to argue in the manner of mythopoeic thought. But observe that Thales speaks of *water*, not of a water-god; Anaximenes refers to *air*, not to a god of air or storms. Here lies the astonishing novelty o their approach. Even though 'all things are full of gods', these men attempt to understand the coherence of the *things*. When Anaximenes explains that air is the first cause, 'just as our soul, being air, holds us together', he continues to specify how air can function as such a sustaining principle: 'It (air) differs in different substances in virtue of its rarefaction and condensation'. Or, even more specifically:

When it (air) is dilated so as to be rarer it becomes fire; while winds, on the other hand, are condensed air. Cloud is formed from air by felting; and this, still further condensed, becomes water. Water, condensed still more, turns to earth; and when condensed as much as it can be, to stones.

There is nowhere a precedent for this type of argument. It shows a twofold originality. In the first place, early Greek philosophy (in Cornford's words) 'ignored with astonishing boldness the prescriptive sanctities of religious representation'.[8] Its second characteristic is a passionate consistency. Once a theory is adopted, it is followed up to its ultimate conclusion irrespective of conflicts with observed facts or probabilities. Both of these characteristics indicate an implicit recognition of the autonomy of thought; they also emphasize the intermediate position of early Greek philosophy. The absence of personification, of gods, sets it apart from mythopoeic thought. Its disregard for the data of experience in its pursuit of consistency distinguishes it from later thought. Its hypotheses were not induced from systematic observations but were much more in the nature of inspired conjectures or divinations by which it was attempted to reach a vantage point where the phenomena would reveal their hidden coherence. It was the unshakable conviction of the Ionians, Pythagoreans, and early Eleatics that such a vantage point existed; and they searched for the road towards it, not in the manner of scientists, but in that of conquistadors.

Anaximander, a pupil of Thales, made an important new advance. He realized that the sustaining principle of all determinate phenomena could not be itself determinate. The ground of all existence had to be essentially different from the elements of actuality; it had to be $\acute{\epsilon}\tau\epsilon\rho\alpha$ $\varphi'\sigma\iota\varsigma$ – of another nature– while yet containing all contrasts and specific qualities. Anaximander called the $\alpha\varrho\chi\acute{\eta}$ the $\mathring{\alpha}\pi\epsilon\iota\varrho\text{ov}$, the 'Infinite' or 'Boundless'. It is reported by Theophrastos that Anaximander 'said that the material cause and first element of things was the Infinite. ... He says it is neither water nor any other of the so-called elements but a substance different from them which is infinite, from which arise all the heavens and the worlds within them.'[9] Notice that Anaximander submits to the substantializing tendency of mythopoeic thought by calling the $\mathring{\alpha}\pi\epsilon\iota\varrho\text{ov}$ a substance – or, in the following quotation, a body: 'He did not ascribe the origin of things to any alteration in matter, but said that the oppositions in the substratum, which was a boundless body, were separated out'.

The opposites which Anaximander found in actuality were the traditional ones: warm and cold, moist and dry. When he stated that these opposites 'separated out' from the 'Boundless', he did not refer (as we would expect) to a mechanistic process. He put it as follows: 'And into that from which things take their rise they pass away once more, as is meet; for they make reparation and satisfaction to one another for their injustice according to the ordering of time.' In the winter, cold commits an injustice to heat, etc. Again we meet the marvellous blend of imaginative, emotional, and intellectual vigour which was characteristic of the sixth and fifth centuries B.C. in Greece. Even that most abstract of notions, the Boundless itself, is described by Anaximander as 'eternal and ageless' – ἀθάνατος καὶ ἀγρήως – words which serve as a stock phrase in Homer to characterize the gods. Yet Anaximander, like Thales and Anaximenes, describes the universe in purely secular terms. We happen to know a good deal of his cosmography. Let us quote, as characteristic samples, his statement that 'the earth swings free, held in its place by nothing. It stays where it is because of its equal distance from everything'. The heavenly bodies are described as 'wheels of fire': 'And there are breath-ing-holes, certain pipe-like passages, at which the heavenly bodies show themselves'. Thunder and lightning are blasts of the winds – a theory broadly parodied in Aristophanes' *Clouds* – and, as to living beings, we find this curious anticipation of phylogenetics: 'Living creatures arose from the moist element as it was evaporated by the sun. Man was like another animal, namely, a fish in the beginning.' Again, Anaximander presents a curious hybrid of empirical and mythopoeic thought. But in his recognition that the ground of all determinate existence could not itself be determinate, in his claim that not water nor air nor any other 'element' but only the 'Boundless' from which all opposites 'separated out', could be the ἀρχή, he showed a power of abstraction beyond anything known before his day.

With Heraclitus of Ephesus philosophy found its *locus standi*. 'Wisdom is one thing. It is to know the *thought* by which all things are steered through all things'.[10] Here, for the first time, attention is centred, not on the thing known, but on the knowing of it. Thought, γνώμη (which may also be translated 'judgment', or 'understanding'), controls the phenomena as it constitutes the thinker. The problem of understanding nature is moved once more to a new plane. In the ancient Near East it had remained within the sphere of myth. The Milesian school of philosophers had moved it to the realm of the intellect in that they claimed the universe to be an *intelligible* whole. The manifold was to be understood as deriving from a sustaining principle or first cause, but this was to be looked for in the

phenomena. The question of how we can know what is outside us was not raised. Heraclitus asserted that the universe
was intelligible because it was ruled by 'thought' or 'judgment',
and that the same principle, therefore, governed both existence
and knowledge. He was conscious that this wisdom surpassed
even the loftiest conception of Greek mythopoeic thought:
'The wise is one only. It is unwilling and willing to be called
by the name of Zeus.'[11]

Heraclitus calls this wisdom *Logos*, a term so heavily laden
with associations as to be an embarrassment whether we translate it or not. 'Reason' is perhaps the least objectionable rendering. 'It is wise to hearken, not to me, but to the Logos and
to confess that all things are one.'[12] All things are one. Things
that are distinct from one another, or qualities that are each
other's opposites, have no permanent existence. They are but
transitory stages in a perpetual flux. No static description of
the universe is true. 'Being' is but 'becoming'. The cosmos is
but the dynamics of existence. The opposites which Anaximander saw 'separating out' from the 'Boundless' are for
Heraclitus united by a tension which causes each of them ultimately to change into its opposite. 'Men do not know how
what is at variance agrees with itself. It is an attunement
(ἁρμονίη) of opposite tensions, like that of the bow and the
lyre.'[13]

But if the universe changes continually according to the tensions between opposites, it is senseless to ask for its origin in
the manner of myth. There is no beginning and no end; there
is only existence. Heraclitus states magnificently: 'This world
(κόσμος) which is the same for all, no one of the gods or men
has made; but it was ever, is now, and ever shall be an ever-
living fire, with measures of it kindling, and measures going
out.'[14] Fire is the symbol for a universe in flux between ten-
sional opposites. As Burnet says: 'The quantity of fire in
a flame burning steadily appears to remain the same, the flame
seems to be what we call a "thing". And yet the substance of it
is continually changing. It is always passing away in smoke,
and its place is always taken by fresh matter from the fuel that
feeds it.'[15]

Heraclitus takes pains to stress that it is only the total process that is lasting and, hence, significant: 'The way up and the way down is one and the same,'[16] or 'it rests by changing',[17] or, more metaphorically, 'fire is want *and* surfeit',[18] or one 'cannot step twice in the same river, for fresh waters are forever flowing in upon you'.[19]

No momentary phase in this perpetual change is more important than any other; all opposites are transitory: 'Fire lives the death of air and air lives the death of fire; water lives the death of earth, earth that of water.'[20] This fragment might startle us, for here fire appears as one of the 'elements' on a par with earth, air, and water; and we would seem to be back on the level of Thales and Anaximenes. Heraclitus is using fire here as one of the traditional four elements in order to insist on the impermanence of the distinction among them. In another fragment the emergence and resorbtion of all determinate things in the one lasting flux of change is expressed as follows: 'All things are an exchange for fire and fire for all things, even as wares for gold and gold for wares.'[21] Here the symbolical significance of fire is obvious.

In the writing of Heraclitus, to a larger degree than ever before, the images do not impose their burden of concreteness but are entirely subservient to the achievement of clarity and precision. Even for Thales and Anaximenes, water and air are no mere constituents of the material world; they also possess a symbolical connotation, if only as agents of vitality. But for Heraclitus fire is purely a symbol of reality in flux; he calls wisdom 'to know the thought by which all things are steered through all things'.

Heraclitus gives the sharpest and profoundest expression to the Ionian postulate that the universe is an intelligible whole. It is intelligible, since *thought* steers all things. It is a whole, since it is a perpetual flux of change. Yet in this form the doctrine retains one contradiction. Mere change and flux cannot be intelligible, for they achieve not cosmos but chaos. Heraclitus solved this difficulty by recognizing in the flux of change an inherent dominant measure. We remember that the world was 'an ever-living fire, with measures of it kindling and measures going out'. The continuous transition of everything into its opposite was regulated by this measure. It was, as we have also seen, 'an attunement of opposite tensions, like that of the bow and of the lyre'. For this reason Heraclitus rejected the doctrine of Anaximander according to which the opposites had to make reparation to one another for their injustice. He held that it was in the nature of things that they should be continually replaced by their opposites:

We must know that war is common to all and strife is justice and that all things come into being and pass away (?) through strife.[22]

War is the father of all and the king of all, and some he has made gods and some men, some bond and some free.[23]

Homer was wrong in saying 'Would that strife might perish from among gods and men.' He did not see that he was praying for the destruction of the universe, for, if his prayer were heard, all things would pass away.[24]

Heraclitus did not mean to equate existence with a blind conflict of opposing force, but he called war the dynamics of existence which necessarily involved 'the hidden attunement (which) is better than the open'.[25] This attunement is of the essence of existence; it is valid in the same manner in which we claim the laws of nature to be valid: 'The sun will not overstep his measures; if he does the Erinyes, the handmaids of justice, will find him out.'[26] This reference to the sun indicates, perhaps, that the regularity of the movements of the heavenly bodies suggested to Heraclitus that all change was subject to a 'hidden attunement'. If this surmise were correct, it would link him appropriately with both mythopoeic and Platonic thought.

The philosophy of Heraclitus shows both parallels and contrasts to that of his older contemporary Pythagoras. According to Pythagoras, also, a hidden measure dominated all the phenomena. But, while Heraclitus was satisfied with proclaiming its existence, the Pythagoreans were anxious to determine it quantitatively. They believed a knowledge of essentials to be a knowledge of numbers, and they attempted to discover the immanent proportionality of the existing world. The starting-point for their enterprise was a remarkable discovery by Pythagoras. Measuring the lengths on the string of the lyre between the places where the four principal notes of the Greek scale were sounded, he found that they had the proportion 6:8:12. This harmonic proportion contains the octave (12:6), the fifth (12:8), and the fourth (8:6). If we attempt to regard the discovery naïvely, we shall admit that it is astonishing. It correlates musical harmonies, which belong to the world of the spirit no less than to that of sensual perception, with the precise abstractions of numerical ratios. It seemed legitimate for the Pythagoreans to expect that similar correlations would be discovered; and, with the truly Greek passion for following up a thought to its ultimate consequences, they maintained that certain arithmetical proportions explained every facet of actuality. Heraclitus said contemptuously: 'The learning of many things teacheth not understanding, else it would have taught Hesiod and Pythagoras.'[27]

Moreover, the Pythagoreans were far from sharing Heraclitus' views. While he had said proudly, 'I have sought for myself',[28] the Pythagoreans endorsed much traditional lore. While Heraclitus stated that all being was but a becoming, the Pythagoreans accepted the reality of the opposites and shared the common preference for the light, static, and unified aspects of existence, assigning the dark, the changing, and the manifold to the side of evil. Their dualism, their belief in the transmigration of souls, and their hope of liberation from the 'wheel of births' connected the Pythagorean doctrine with Orphism. In fact, the teachings of Pythagoras belong preponderantly to the sphere of mythopoeic thought. This can be explained if we remember his orientation. Pythagoras was not concerned with knowledge for its own sake; he did not share the detached curiosity of the Ionians. He taught a way of life. The Pythagorean society was a religious fraternity striving for the sanctification of its members. In this, too, it resembled the Orphic societies; but its god was Apollo, not Dionysus; its method comprehension, not rapture. For the Pythagoreans, knowledge was part of the art of living; and living was seeking for salvation. We saw in the first chapter that man, when thus involved with the whole of his being, cannot achieve intellectual detachment. Therefore, Pythagorean thought is steeped in myth. Yet it was a member of the Pythagorean society, who after his apostasy, destroyed the last hold of myth on thought. This man was Parmenides, the founder of the Eleatic School.

Parmenides once more interpreted the Ionian postulate that the world forms an intelligible whole. But, as Burnet puts it, 'he showed once and for all that if you take the One seriously you are bound to deny everything else'.[29] Parmenides saw that not only each theory of origin, but even each theory of change or movement, made the concept of being problematical. Absolute being cannot be conceived as coming into existence out of a state of non-existence.

How, then, can what *is* be going to be in the future? Or how could it come into being? If it came into being, it is not; nor is it, if it is going to be in the future. Thus is becoming extinguished and passing away not to be heard of.[30]

Parmenides' conclusion that this is so is a purely logical one, and hence we may say that the autonomy of thought was definitely established by him. We have seen that Heraclitus went far in this direction, claiming the congruity of truth and existence when he said: 'Wisdom is one thing. It is to know the thought by which all things are steered through all things.'

When Parmenides restated this thesis, he eliminated the last vestige of mythical concreteness and imagery which had survived in the 'steered' of Heraclitus' saying and also in his symbol of fire. Parmenides said: 'The thing that can be thought, and that for the sake of which the thought exists, is the same; for you cannot find thought without something that is, as to which it is uttered.'[31] But since Parmenides considered 'becoming extinguished and passing away not to be heard of', he assumed an entirely new position. The Milesians had attempted to correlate *being* (as the static ground of existence) and *becoming* (observed in the phenomena). Heraclitus had declared *being* a perpetual *becoming* and had correlated the two concepts with his 'hidden attunement'. Now Parmenides declared the two to be mutually exclusive, and only *being* to be real.

Come now, I will tell thee – and do thou hearken to my saying and carry it away – the only two ways of search that can be thought of. The first, namely, that *It is*, and that it is impossible for it not to be, is the way of conviction,[32] for truth is its companion. The other, namely, that *It is not*, and that it must needs not be – that, I tell thee, is a path that none can learn of at all. For thou canst not know what is not -- that is impossible – nor utter it; for it is the same thing that can be thought and that can be.[33]

And again:

One path only is left for us to speak of, namely, that *It is*. In this path are very many tokens that what is is uncreated and indestructible; for it is complete, immovable and without end. Nor was it ever, nor will it be; for now *it is*, all at once, a continuous one. For what origin for it wilt thou look for? In what way and from what source could it have drawn its increase? ... I shall not let thee say nor think that it came from what is not; for it can neither be thought nor uttered that anything is not.[34]

Here, in what Parmenides calls 'the unshaken heart of well-rounded truth', we meet a philosophical *absolute* that reminds us of the religious absolute of the Old Testament. In the strictly idealistic position of Parmenides the autonomy of thought is vindicated, and every concrescence of myth is stripped off. Yet Parmenides is strongly connected with his predecessors in one respect. In his denial of the reality of movement, change, and distinctiveness, he reached a conclusion which, like theirs, was oddly at variance with the data of experience. He was aware of this and appealed to reason in defiance of the testimony of the senses: 'But do thou restrain thy thought from this way of inquiry, nor let habit by its much experience force thee to cast upon this way a wandering eye or sounding ear or tongue; but judge by reason[35] the much disputed proof uttered by me.'[36]

This same attitude was, implicitly or explicitly, adopted by all Greek thinkers of the sixth and fifth centuries B.C. For neither their basic assumption – that the world is an intelligible whole – nor their further explanation – that it unfolds in opposites – nor any of their other theses can be proved by logic or by experiment or by observation. With conviction they propounded theories which resulted from intuitive insight and which were elaborated by deductive reasoning. Each system was based upon an assumption held to be true and made to bear a structure erected without further reference to empirical data. Consistency was valued more highly than probability. This fact in itself shows that throughout early Greek philosophy *reason* is acknowledged as the highest arbiter, even though the Logos is not mentioned before Heraclitus and Parmenides. It is this tacit or outspoken appeal to reason, no less than the independence from 'the prescriptive sanctities of religion', which places early Greek philosophy in the sharpest contrast with the thought of the ancient Near East.

As we have said before, the cosmologies of mythopoeic thought are basically revelations received in a confrontation with a cosmic 'Thou'. And one cannot argue about a revelation; it transcends reason. But in the systems of the Greeks the human mind recognizes its own. It may take back what it created or change or develop it. This is true even of the Milesian philosophies, although they have not entirely shed the concrescence of myth. It is patently true of the doctrine of Heraclitus, which established the sovereignty of thought, rejected Anaximander and Pythagoras, and proclaimed an absolute *becoming*. It is equally true of the teaching of Parmenides, who confounded Heraclitus and proclaimed an absolute *being*.

One question remains to be answered. If mythopoeic thought took shape in an undissolved relationship between man and nature, what became of that relationship when thought was emancipated? We may answer this question with a quotation to balance the one with which we began this chapter. We saw that in Psalm xix nature appears bereaved of divinity before an absolute God: 'The heavens declare the glory of God and the firmament sheweth his handiwork.' And we read in Plato's *Timaeus*, in Jowett's translation (47c):

... had we never seen the stars, and the sun, and the heaven, none of the words which we have spoken about the universe would ever have been uttered. But now the sight of day and night, and the months and the revolutions of the years, have created number, and have given us a conception of time; and the power of enquiring about the nature of the universe; and from this source we have derived philosophy, than which no greater good ever was or will be given by the gods to mortal man.

NOTES

1. Blackman's translation of Erman, *Literature of the Egyptians*, p. 115.
2. After Blackman, *ibid.*, pp. 94 ff.
3. Johannes Hehn, *Die biblische und die babylonische Gottes dee* (1913), p. 284.
4. F. M. Cornford, *From Religion to Philosophy* (London, 1912), 119–20.
5. *Iliad* xiv. 201, 241.
6. This and the following quotations are taken from A. W. Mair, *Hesiod, the Poems and Fragments* (Oxford: Clarendon Press, 1908).
7. This and the following quotations are taken from J. Burnet, *Early Greek Philosophy* (4th ed.; London, 1930).
8. *Cambridge Ancient History*, IV, 532.   9. Burnet, *op. cit.*, p. 52.
10. Burnet, Frag. 19.
11. Burnet, Frag. 65. This statement gains in pregnancy if we remember that Heraclitus was a contemporary of Aeschylus.
12. Burnet, Frag. 1. Burnet translates 'my word.'
13. Burnet, Frag. 45.   14. Burnet, Frag. 20.   15. *Op. cit.*, p. 145.
16. Burnet, Frag. 69.   17. Burnet, Frag. 83.   18. Burnet, Frag. 24.
19. Burnet, Frags. 41–42. 20. Burnet, Frag. 25.   21. Burnet, Frag. 22.
22. Burnet, Frag. 62.   23. Burnet, Frag. 44.   24. Burnet, Frag. 43.
25. Burnet, Frag. 47.   26. Burnet, Frag. 29.   27. Burnet, Frag. 16.
28. Burnet, Frag. 80.   29. *Op. cit.*, p. 179.
30. *Ibid.*, p. 175, ll. 19–22.   31. *Ibid.*, p. 176, ll. 34–36.
32. Burnet (*ibid.*, p. 173) translates 'belief'.
33. *Ibid.*, p. 173; Frags. 4 and 5.   34. *Ibid.*, p. 174; Frag. 8, ll. 1–9.
35. Burnet (*ibid.*, p. 173 n.) defends a translation of *logos* by 'argument'.
36. *Ibid.*, ll. 33–36.

SUGGESTED READINGS

BURNET, JOHN. *Early Greek Philosophy.* London, 1930.
CASSIRER, ERNST. 'Die Philosophie der Griechen von den Anfängen bis Platon', in MAX DESSOIR, *Handbuch der Philosophie*, I, 7–140. Berlin, 1925.
CORNFORD, F. M. *From Religion to Philosophy.* London, 1912.
JOËL, KARL. *Geschichte der antiken Philosophie*, Vol. I. Tübingen 1921.
MYERS, J. L. 'The Background of Greek Science,' *University of California Chronicle*, Vol. XIV, No. 4.

INDEX

*A selection of other Pelicans
is given on the
next pages*

WHAT HAPPENED IN HISTORY

GORDON CHILDE

A108

'Professor V. Gordon Childe is one of the foremost pre-historians. He has travelled widely and has done much work of great importance to the specialist; he has, as it were, personally added many bricks to the edifice of pre-historic knowledge. But he has also long realized that prehistory and early history form a continuum, and that, by standing back and contemplating the whole, many general conclusions can be arrived at with regard to the rise and fall of civilizations . . .

'For this reason a special welcome must be accorded to Professor Childe's fascinating little book now under re-view. In it he discusses the changes in material well-being and mental outlook which have taken place throughout the ages up to the break-up of the Roman Empire. He gives us a brief survey of what he describes as Palaeolithic and Mesolithic savagery, of Neolithic barbarism, of the rise of the Metal Age cultures, and so on until a climax was reached as a result of the Old World unity made possible by the exploits of Alexander the Great. Finally, there is a stimulating chapter with the author's views about the decline and fall of the ancient world . . .

'This more than worth-while book contains many facts – the background material for the study; but it is primarily intended to stimulate thought and to help the reader to understand the general story of human development and, may be, to draw lessons which will help when our own civilization, now in danger of collapse, is once again in process of reconstruction.' – M. C. Burkitt, in *Nature*.

A SHORT HISTORY OF THE WORLD

H. G. WELLS

A5

This is meant, as the author says in his Preface, to be read straightforwardly almost as a novel is read. It gives in the most general way an account of our present knowledge of history, shorn of elaborations and complications. From it the reader should be able to get that general view of history which is so necessary a framework for the study of a particular period or the history of a particular country. Its special end is to meet the needs of the busy general reader, too driven to study the maps and time charts of that *Outline* in detail, who wishes to refresh and repair his faded or fragmentary conceptions of the great adventure of mankind. It is not an abstract or condensation of that former work. Within its aim the *Outline* admits of no further condensation. This is a much more generalized History, planned and written afresh. This edition gives the book in its completed form as revised by the author on the eve of his death in 1946. There are twenty sketch-maps by the famous cartographer J. F. Horrabin.

THE ETRUSCANS

M. PALLOTTINO

A310

Before the Romans could establish their empire they had first to conquer and unify the other cities and peoples in Italy. The most powerful and highly civilized of these other peoples were the Etruscans. In this study Professor Pallottino discusses the origins, culture, religion, and language of this ancient and little known civilization which flourished so brilliantly 2,500 years ago, and whose history has been neglected for so long.

This translation by J. A. Cremona of the Third Italian Edition contains maps and diagrams and an inset of thirty-two plates, showing some of the wonderful objects that have survived the neglect of succeeding generations.

'This is an admirable introduction to the study of a subject little known to the general reader.' – *The Times Literary Supplement*

'*The Etruscans* is a good introduction to the subject because he can communicate his own interest in it with his learning. . . . Professor Pallottino's chapters on the Etruscan language are exceptionally good and clear.' – *Manchester Guardian Weekly*

LEONARDO DA VINCI

KENNETH CLARK

A430

Sir Kenneth Clark made his name as a scholar of Leonardo da Vinci by a Critical Catalogue of Leonardo's drawings at Windsor Castle, published in 1935, which was recognized as establishing the subject on a firmer chronological basis. Four years later he produced this short book on Leonardo as an artist, which has been generally regarded as the clearest and sanest introduction to this great and controversial subject. This is the first book on Leonardo written after critics had reached general agreement as to which works were really by his own hand. It is also the first study of Leonardo to take advantage of our wider range of aesthetic experience and our fuller knowledge of psychology. Sir Kenneth writes 'that all great art should be reinterpreted for each generation', but although his interpretation of Leonardo is twenty years old, it remains valid today. He has written a fresh introduction which goes rather deeper than his previous conclusions, and for this edition has made extensive revisions to the text.

'Your true critic must be doubly armed, with knowledge and intuition. Sir Kenneth Clark, armed with both to a remarkable degree, has written a book on Leonardo's development as an artist which (I do not exaggerate) will set a new standard in art criticism in England.' – *Sunday Times*

'It is so intelligent, so modest, so beautifully written and so wise.' – Harold Nicolson

LANDSCAPE INTO ART

KENNETH CLARK

A369

Sir Kenneth Clark has shown the belief that art is a part of our general consciousness and gives a special value to all our experiences. In this book, which is based on his first course of lectures as Slade Professor at Oxford, he is concerned with man's relation to nature as reflected in the history of landscape painting. In the first part he considers the acceptance of descriptive symbols, the curiosity about facts, the creation of fantasy to relieve his fears, and a belief in a Golden Age of order. The great landscape painters of the nineteenth century, Constable and Corot, Turner and Van Gogh, Cézanne and Seurat, are treated in detail. Finally he considers the future of landscape painting at a time when the more vital artists have turned away from nature.

'The importance of this book to art criticism and to the history of art can scarcely be exaggerated. Ruskin and others have written notable pages on the art of landscape painting, but no such complete work on it as a separate branch of art has appeared in English.' – *Cambridge Review*

LASCAUX:
PAINTINGS AND ENGRAVINGS

ANNETTE LAMING

A419

The painted cave of Lascaux, near Montignac in the Dordogne, was discovered by chance in 1941. Its paintings and engravings are now world-famous, and each year it is visited by thousands of people from many lands who are attracted by the appeal of its magnificent prehistoric works of art, which are in a remarkable state of preservation. The quality, design, and technique of a number of these are unique in the archaeological record. This book gives a clear and precise description of the cave and its masterpieces, and offers a new explanation of the motives which inspired the hunter artist. A study of the ritual and purpose of hunting magic provides a picture of the way of life and the religion of Quaternary man, and in the light of the most recent research and with the aid of numerous photographs and drawings, it also presents for the general reader a valuable appreciation of the aesthetic quality of the paintings and engravings.

CHILDREN AND THE LAW

F. T. GILES

A436

Our attitude as a community to our young people is often most clearly shown in our laws with regard to them. Are we too parental – too indulgent – too lax – perhaps too indifferent?

It can scarcely be said we are indifferent, because the laws about children are now so considerable that if fully set out they would fill several volumes. This development, however, is of comparatively recent growth, most of it being less than a hundred years old and much of it having been enacted during the present century.

Children may now be legally adopted. Those whose misfortune it is to be bereft of their natural protectors are no longer left to their own devices but become the responsibility of the County Councils. Disputes between parents and guardians can be settled by the courts – most of them quickly and inexpensively by the local magistrates. The criminal law affords them protection from cruelty and despoliation, while special tribunals have been set up to deal with juvenile delinquents.

The laws which have been devised to deal with all these contingencies are described, with an estimate of their practical usefulness and a consideration of plans and proposals for increasing their efficacy.

IRAN

R. GHIRSHMAN

A239

Midway between Mesopotamia and India, the meeting-ground of Semitic and Aryan influence, the cradle of a great religion which, in either of its modified forms of Mithraism or Manichaeism, might easily have become that of the Western world of today, Iran – Persia – has for three millennia been a meeting-place of peoples and a battle-ground of civilizations.

Its prehistory, now being uncovered by the efforts of Western and of Russian scholars, has not hitherto been exhaustively and competently dealt with between the covers of a single volume in a way that will appeal to the general reader. Professor Ghirshman, who has spent many years in field research in Persia, here outlines its story from the earliest times until the great wars in which over centuries the Persian Empire tried its strength with Greece and Rome, leaving the issue undecided until its unique Iranian civilization was reshaped and transformed by the Islamic conquest. With 48 pages of plates and many line illustrations.

MAN ON HIS NATURE

SIR CHARLES SHERRINGTON

A322

This book, which was originally given as the Gifford Lectures, 1937–38, is a free, fearless, and invigorating expression of a biologist's philosophy. Sir Charles Sherrington contrasts a modern biologist's attitude towards the origins of life with that essentially held by a physician-philosopher of the sixteenth century. He shows that there is no longer any logical division of matter into living and non-living, and that 'growth' is likely to be expressible in terms identical with those used in atomic physics: chemical action, upon which growth depends, being but a name for a complex of inter-atomic electrical changes.

The principle of life, it may turn out, is no more than a useful human convention. But what of the Mind? Mind knows itself and knows the world. Chemistry and physics, explaining so much, cannot undertake to explain Mind itself. It can intensify knowledge of Nature, but it cannot be shown that Mind has hitherto directed the operations of Nature. In that sense Mind and Nature are different. Mind, by finding that 'blind' electrical-chemical forces are the instruments by which all matter exists, points to itself as something unique in nature. And this the author accepts as a heartening challenge: if blind forces can do so much to wonder at, what cannot directed forces achieve?

THE ORIGIN OF THE EARTH

W. M. SMART

A339

This mortal-man's-eye view of the universe is given by an astronomer. It began in talks to groups of soldiers during the last war, and although it has grown a great deal since then it still addresses itself to those who are not astronomers. It refers to the latest knowledge about the cosmic and the atomic aspects of creation; it distinguishes between scientific knowledge and intuitive knowledge, and makes clear the author's authoritative grasp of the one, and his inability to dismiss the other. It propounds no personal philosophical speculations; it is modest as well as learned.

'In plain, straightforward uncoloured English, its sober lucidity makes it as convincing as it is informative. Not least of its merits is its scientific caution: throughout it explains the evidence on which conclusions are drawn, and distinguishes reasonably acceptable theory from speculation and guesswork . . . It is in exemplary contrast to one or two quasi-scientific romances that have recently appeared. It is popular in the best sense, and is wholly to be welcomed.' – *Literary Guide*